GENERAL
BAPTIST HISTORY,

BY
D. B. MONTGOMERY.

GENERAL
Baptist History.

EDITED AND PUBLISHED BY

D. B. MONTGOMERY,

OF THE

GENERAL BAPTIST CHURCH

OF

OWENSVILLE, IND.

EVANSVILLE.
Courier Company, Book and Job Printers.
1882.

PREFACE.

The following historical lines styled "General Baptists in England and Europe," are a part only of a series of lectures on Church History delivered in the Clayville Church of General Baptists in the Summer of 1876, in reply to a series of centennial sermons by the United Baptists, a short time previous.

These lectures were so hastily gotten up, only a few days being allowed in their preparation, that they necessarily contain inaccuracies and imperfections in grammar, diction, etc.

It was the intention to carefully re-write and re-arrange the whole of them and include with them enough additional matter, so as to give a sufficiently full and replete history of all Baptist denominations, particularly liberal Baptists.

This was undertaken at the request of the General Association of the General Baptists of America in the Fall of 1876.

A sufficient historical library was procured for this purpose, the notes all taken and the work out-lined; but in the midst of this work I was taken with hemorrage of the lungs, which forbade that I should persist further in the prosecution of this work, hence it was abandoned for the time being.

I am glad to say that an abler pen than mine has undertaken this duty and as a result of his labors in this direction, we have this little volume of Baptist history.

It, as a whole is somewhat disjointed and evidently contains imperfections, but dear reader, whoever you may be or whether you read its pages in search of Baptist truths, or simply as a critic, or as a confiding General Baptist, you are kindly asked to remember that it is the first effort of the author, REV. D. B. MONTGOMERY.

Indeed that part of the work written by him is in fact the first history of the liberal or open Communion Baptists, located in the South and West of the American States.

It is a pioneer work with but little data from which to write a history of these Baptists, therefore we lay tribute upon the liberality and indulgence of the reader.

It was against my judgment, that that part of it written by myself, should go to press in its present style as a lecture to a public audience, but the author ruled differently and I have consented.

It will but blaze the path for a new addition, or open up the way for an entirely new work which will be given to the reading public at no distant future.

Fraternally,

JEFF. HOLEMAN.

INDEX.

A

	PAGES
Ana-Baptists	14—15
Atonement General	30
Authors consulted	109—10
An offending Brother	254
An Academy	261
An Association in Arkansas	362—64
A Denominational Paper	393—98

B

Baptists Early Divided	11
Baptists, General and Particular	11
Brownist	15—22
Baptists, General and Particular in England	22—3
Badtism	28—9
Baptists Return to England	55—7
Baptism of Infants opposed	75
Baptists for Soul Liberty	78
Baptists all of the General persuasion previous to 1633	101—7
Baptists, Free Communion, decendants from the old General Baptists	122—30
Baptists, Free-Will, Treatise of Faith	226—7
Biographies of the Living	247—48
Baptists Union	272—3
Bethany Association	362

C

Communion 11
Confession of 1611 .... 48—55
Confession of 1660 .... 78—82
Communion .... 89—97
Communion 114
Communion .... 121—2
Confession of Faith of General Baptists in the
  West .... 211—13
Communion .... 215—16
College .... 225—6
College Name .... 226—7
Cavanah George P .... 236—47
Christian Conference .... 250—51
Correspondence .... 258—60
Convention of Liberal Baptists .... 267—72
Correspondence, large .... 267—8
Cumberland Association weak 308
Cumberland Association .... 316—17
Central Illinois Association .... 348—9

D

Division in the Church .... 9—10
Different Names 10
Dissenters .... 24—5
Dissenters favored 82
Dunn Berry T 203
Division of Liberty Association .... 228—9
Deacons Duties 230
Death of three Ministers 272

E

Ensle J. G .... 276—9
Educational Interest .... 404—8

F

Fuller Thomas .... 206—9
Family Worship 235
Fidelity to the Church .... 251—2
Free-Will Baptists in Tennessee 274
Flat Creek Association .... 359—61

VI

G

General Baptist Books	58—62
General Baptist Books	65—6
General Baptist Books	74
General Baptist Growth	75
General Baptist Statistics in England in 1689	82
General Baptists decline	83
General Baptists, New Connection	84—88
General Baptist Church 26 years older than the Particular Baptistr	98—100
General Baptists in the United States	109—10
General Baptists in Maryland, South and North Carolina and Virginia	130—47
General Baptists in North Carolina by Elder Hearn	148—78
General Baptists in the West	179
General Baptist History	230, 400—1
General Association	253
General Baptist Banner	262
General Baptists number five Associations	161—2
General Association	278—02

H

Holeman's Lecture	9
Hume Elder Joel, life	192—98
Help Wanted, Kentucky	254
Hancock Esma	290—
Holeman Jacob	291—2
Henry I. H	301—5
Hymn Books	398—400
Holeman's History	402—3
Home Missions	403—4

I

Iglehart J. H	309

K

Knight's Account of Early Baptist Churches in America	115—20

L

Laying on ef Hands	88—9
Laying on of Hands	113
Lane Jesse, sr	200—2
Liberty Association Organized	209—11

Liberty Association moves South, East and West... 234—5
Letter of Dismission. 235
Little Bethel Associatian of United Baptists........ 306
Liberty Association, Missouri..................... 346—8
Little Vine Association..................... .. ...371—72

M

Minutes transcribed............................. 252
Members dismissed............ 260
Members received............................... 261
Missions................... .. .. 274—5
McAndrew Geo. W............................289—90
Ministers of Union Association................ ....310—13
Millikan Wm................................... 338
Missouri Association.... .. ..352—56
Mt. Union Association.............. ....368—70
Mt. Glivet Association.................... ....359—61

N

New Liberty Association........ ....372—77

O

Ohio Association .... 336—9

P

Persecution.... .... 66—74
Parker Alvah .... 204—6
Polk A. H...................................... 225
Polk A. H., Missionary........................... 263—5

R

Reavis Wm.. .... 231—4
Rhodes Solomon.... .... 345—6
Reavis' life of Benoni Stinson..................... 401—2

S

Succession .... 12—13
Smith examined Scriptures..................... .. 26—7
Smith written against.. .... 31—2
Smith defends his Principles... .... 34—5
Smith and his Church vindicated............. .....37—42
Succession in Baptism................. .... 46—8
Statues of Gold................................. 62—5
Succession Principles 107

VIII

Summing up .... 107—8
Stinson Benoni moves to Indiana; a Delegate to
 Wabash District Association; joins Liberty
 Church; Organized Liberty Association and
 adopted the name General Baptists; Debates
 with strong Men ....180—92
Stinson Benoni, death..... 199
Speer Elder Jacob...............................218—23
Strain Elder T. M.... ....248—50
Sabbath Schools............................... 253
Stinson John B.... 255
State of the Country............................ 265
School at Oakland.............................. 266
Superanuated fund ....279—80
Speer Elder Jacob, retired...................... 280
Statistics.. .. .. 282—4
Stinson and Polk in Kentucky.. 306
Statistics of Union Association..................314—15
Southern Illinois Association.....................317—35
Social Band Association...... ....364—67

U

Union Association................................ 285
United Association..............................339—44
Union Grove Association........................350—52

CHAPTER I.

GENERAL BAPTISTS IN ENGLAND AND EUROPE.

BY JEFF. HOLEMAM, M. D.

The vicissitudes or changes, and the countless persecutions through which the peculiar denomination of people termed Baptists have passed, and the false reproaches heaped upon them, only need to be hinted at in order to refresh the memory of those familiar with ecclesiastical history.

Parties and sects were unknown in the earliest history of the Christian church. All parties who encouraged a division of the church stand rebuked by the Holy Scriptures. In the earliest history of the

Christian church its members were known only by the name of Christians—followers of Christ.

But in later periods divisions sprung up in the church, which were prompted by ambitious leaders and differences upon doctrinal points. The various circumstances gave birth to many sects or denominations. Some assumed the name of their leaders; others, again, were named from some peculiar feature of doctrine they earnestly advocated. Bloody persecution and war was the legitimate result of these divisions. Those of the true faith, who seem to have been in the minority, were largely persecuted by the majority, who had departed from the teaching of the Apostles. By the force of existing circumstances the true followers of Christ and the Apostles, in the vicissitudes through which the church was forced to travel by persecution and war, assumed different names at various times and in different places. Hence, the name of Christians, first; then (171) Montanists; then (251) Novationists; then, in the fourth century, the Danatists; then (653) the Paulicians and then the Waldenses; and finally, in 1543, the Mennonites. These people, by the revolution of time and surrounding influences, seem to have undergone a change of faith and practice in their respective bodies. Many points of doctrine occupied by these people in the beginning of their denominational life, among which was the mode of baptism and the question of communion, were abandoned by them in later days. When the ancient mode of baptism by immersion was revived in England, which seems to have fallen into disuse, for some time, at least, as it was practiced upon the adult and the responsible, those who revived the ancient mode were called Baptists. The Christian world, about this time, was divided upon the question of election and foreordination. One class, with John Calvin as their leader, held that only the elect could be saved; while another, with James Arminius at its head, held that it was possible for all men to be saved.

Upon this question the Baptists were early divided. Those who believed in a general atonement were called General Baptists, while those who believed in a particular atonement were called Particular Baptists. These two denominations of Baptists in England are still known by these names. Both practice baptism by immersion upon the believer.

The General Baptist church was organized in 1611 —the Particular Baptist church in 1633. At the organization of these denominations close communion was the prevailing rule among the various denominations. Open communion was the natural outgrowth of the General Baptists, as now practiced by all their churches, both in England and America. The Particular Baptists in England have grown very liberal upon this question, and many—perhaps a majority—of their churches practice open communion.

We will now, without further notice of the above sects or dissenters, proceed to briefly trace the history of the General Baptist denominations in Europe.

"The true origin of that sect which acquired the denomination of Ana-Baptists * * * is hidden in the depths of antiquity, and is, of consequence, difficult to be ascertained."

The Baptists give this as a proof of their succession from these Ana-Baptists. They tell us that Baptists and Ana-Baptists are synonymous terms, and that as a denomination, or rather as the true church of God, that they are exclusively entitled to the name "Baptist," while other kinds of Baptists, in order to distinguish themselves from this great body of Baptists, must employ some of the prefixes, such as General, Separate, etc.

Now, if these Close or United Baptists, if they have a succession extending back, it is through the Particular Baptists, of England, who originated in 1633, from the church of Independents, under the pastoral care of Henry Jacobs, which grew, in a short time, into seven churches, and met in the City of London, in 1643, and there formed a confession of faith, and in a preface to the same, declared it was "A confession of faith of seven congregations or churches of Christ, in London, which are commonly, but unjustly called Ana-Baptists." See Crosby's History of Baptists, vol. 1, appendix page 7; also page 89; Baptist Succession, by D. B. Ray, page 188. From this declaration of these Particular Baptists in the preface of this, their first confession of faith, which I have just read, you see for yourselves these Baptists most positively asserted that they were not Ana-Baptists. I am very much inclined to leave it with them, rather than these men of the succession order. We have thus far spoken of the Ana-Baptists and Mennonites as one people. In this we have followed most writers, as we did not wish to go into details. "The Mennonites," says Mr. Benedict, "in the Old World, for ages past, have, as a general thing, administered baptism by pouring, and laying on of hands; and the same that is true of them in the Old World is true in this country, both of the old and the new connection." See Milner's Religious Denominations of the World, page 162. I mention this fact as a proof against the idea that all of these Ana-Baptists and Mennonites were genuine Baptists and will now for further proof of my position, read from Mr. Benedict's History of Baptists, page 930, which is as follows: "Baptists and Ana-Baptists, from time immemorial, have been, by most writers, regarded as synonymous and convertible terms.

This, though generally true, is not necessarily so. Pedo-Baptists, as well as Baptists, may come under this head. If they re-baptize their subjects, for whatever cause, whether infants or adults, whether by dipping or by other modes, they become *de facto*, Ana-Baptists, according to the true and proper meaning of the word. The Ana-Baptists in Germany were, no doubt, generally baptistically inclined, and a good portion of them were of the genuine Baptist order; but the term "Ana-Baptist," there, as in England, in the time of the Commonwealth, was very loosely applied to a promiscous multitude who differed widely from each other. All, however, dissented from the established religion, and were the advocates for freedom, civil and religious. Infant baptisim they generally condemn. Some of them, however, continued in the practice after the name "Ana-Baptist" was applied to them; and as to the mode of baptism, it is certain that the Ana-Baptists were not all dippers, as the following quotations will show: "The first recorded instance of re-baptism took place at Zwickan, near Zurich, in 1525, and then says the person in whose house the ceremony was performed, they were all baptized with a dipper. Another re-baptism took place in Grebel's house. Hubmeyer, on the occasion of re-baptising in his church at Waldshut, directed water to be brought in a milk pail and baptized about three hundred."

While they were generally Baptists, and universally re-baptized all coming from one sect to another; yet many of them were Pedo-Baptists, and baptized by pouring and sprinkling.

They were divided into innumerable sects, and had every shade of religious belief, and almost each party among them, like our United Baptist friends, claimed that they (for certain reasons which they claimed were supported by the Holy Bible) were the only true church of God. So you see, if our United friends came through these people by succession, as their legitimate successors, their communion and baptism (according to their definition) cannot be pure.

We will now speak of the Baptists, both General and Particular—their rise and progress, and in order to give you an idea of their true origin, we will necessarily have to give a short history of the Brownists and Independents, with whose history the origin of Baptists is interwoven.

BROWNISTS.

The English Baptists, both General and Particular, were the legitimate descendents or successors of these Brownists, who originated in the reformation under

Robt. Brown, who established their first church in 1581, in Norwich, England. See Mosheim's Ecclesiastical History, vol. 111, page 181.

Milner's Denominations of the World, pages 185 207 says:

"Robt. Brown became prominent among those who, in 1677, resisted the attempts of Queen Elizabeth, of England, to suppress, by forcible measures, the doctrines and assemblies of the Puritans. He contended that each church or society of Christians, meeting in a single place, was a body corporate, possessing full power within itself, to admit or exclude members, to choose and ordain officers, and also depose them without being in any respect responsible to synods, councils, or any other ecclesiastical authority. He denied the supremacy of the Queen in religious and ecclesiastical matters, he refused to admit that the established Church of England was a Scriptural church, and asserted that the Scriptures were the only authoritative guide in matters of faith and discipline." Milner's Denominations of the World, page 184.

"The freedom and self-government of the local church were developed and reduced to practice by Robt. Brown, in 1596."

Those who adopted his views were at first called "Brownists."

Orchard's History of Baptists, vol. 2, page 232, says: "In 1583, a numerous congregation of Dutch Ana-Baptists was known to exist at Norwich. From among these persons Robert Brown selected a few to begin a new interest of Independents." He wielded a great influence. Milner's Denominations of the World, page 185, says: "In 1602, a second society of Independents or Congregationalists was formed in the north of England, of whom John Robinson was the pastor. Mr. Clifton became co-pastor with John Robinson in this church."

"John Smith, a beneficed clergyman at Gainsborough, and who is said to have been M. A., spent nine months in investigating the controversies on ceremonies. Being convinced of their unscriptural character, he withdrew from the establishment."

Orchard's History of Baptists, vol. 2, page 237, "On leaving that church he became a minister among the Brownists, who esteemed him so highly that Bishop Hall called him their oracle in general." Cramp's History of Baptists, page 286.

Crosby's History of Baptists, vol. 1, page 265, "John Smith, of whom mention is made in the foregoing history, was a divine of the Church of England, and did, in the former part of the reign of King James I., embrace the opinions of the Baptists." (Brownists.) See Benedict's History of Baptists, page 327. Taylor's History of General Baptists, page 66. Wood's History of General Baptists, page 103.

These Brownists, called, by some, Separatists or Nonconformists, became very popular and numerous, and were looked upon by the Queen of England and the established church with great jealousy and fear. Crosby's History of Baptists, page 79, says: "But to close the reign of Queen Elizabeth, having by her proclamation commanded all Ana-Baptists and other heretics to depart the land, whether they were natives or foreigners, under the penalty of imprisonment or loss of life, all that were of this opinion were obliged either to conceal their principles or fly into some other country, where they might enjoy the liberty of their religion; upon which many of the dissenters went over to Holland; among whom were not a few Baptists, as well as English and Dutch, so that there was now no great number of dissenters that dared openly to appear."

Wood's History of General Baptists, page 101, says: "The number of Baptists still increasing, a proclamation was issued in 1600 by which all Ana-Baptists and other heretics were ordered to leave the kingdom." "All these dissenters or non-conformists were called Puritans. For those who refused to conform to the Church of England were counted among the

Puritans." Crosby's History of Baptists, vol. 1, page 82.

In speaking of the results of the opinions of these Brownists, Milner's Denominations of the World, page 185, says: "As might have been naturally expected in such an age and among such a community as England was, the announcement of such opinions soon led to persecutions. Brown was hooted in the streets, pelted with stones, and became the victim of general obloquy. Nevertheless, he persisted in his course * * * until at last the condition of the Puritans became intolerable. They resolved to escape, and fled into Holland." Here, Robt. Brown, in the City of Amsterdam, established, or rather re-established his church, called Brownists. But he subsequently turned traitor, left his church, returned to England and rejoined the established Church of England. See Benedict's history. The emigration of these so-called Puritans became very general into Holland; so much so that John Smith, John Robinson and Cliftons retired thither.

Orchard, vol. 2, page 237, says: "The harrassing conduct of the high court compelled Mr. Smith, with Mr. Robinson and Mr. Clifton, to remove into Holland. These good men united with a (English) church at Amsterdam, with Robert Brown, and of which Johnson was pastor and Ainsworth teacher."

Taylor's History of General Baptists, page 66, says: "But being grievously harrassed by the high commissioned court, and seeing no prospect of redress from the new monarch, Mr. Smith and his church, and Messrs Robinson and Clifton, who were co-pastors of a neighboring church, with their congregation determined to leave the kingdom and seek liberty of conscience in a foreign country. They arrived in Holland in 1606, and all joined Ainsworth's society, which received such an addition with peculiar satisfaction." (See Cramp's History of Baptists, page 286; Benedict's History of Baptists, page 328; Crosby's History of Baptists, page 91; Wood's History of General Baptists, page 103; Night's History of General Baptists, page 24.)

This church, thus formed, soon became a great ecclesiastical power, and some historians claim that it stood for at least a hundred years, notwithstanding dissension shortly sprung up among them, as we shall shortly see in our investigation. A majority of those who went into this church organization were Calvinistic Pedo-Baptists, while no doubt the most of the others were, in faith, what the General Baptists, both in Europe and America, are to-day.

Crosby's History of Baptists, vol. 1, page 91, says of John Smith: "But when his search after truth and resolution to reform religion according to the primitive constitution and practice, had led him to entertain some principles different from his brethren, particularly that of baptizing believers only, they set themselves to violently oppose him; they cast him out of the church, representing him as one that had proclaimed open war against God's everlasting covenant, and that would murder the souls of babes and sucklings by depriving them of the visible seal of salvation. They published several books wherein they endeavored to expose him and his principles to the world."

The principal causes which led Mr. Smith and his followers to separate themselves from this church of Brownists are mostly given by Mr. Orchard, in vol. 2, page 237: "Mr. Smith knew that Brown and his associates denied the Church of England to be a true church of Christ, and that her ministers' ordinations were not valid; yet these same people allowed the baptism of the Church of England. This course of proceeding, by Brown and his community, in distinguishing acts done by persons unscripturally situated, led Mr. Smith to express his surprise and to inquire into the origin of these rites, which terminated in Mr. Smith's renouncing infant baptism. On being thus decided for believers' immersion, Mr. Smith, with his brethren who were of the same opinion in religion with him, settled in Ley, Holland." Thus

Mr. Smith and his followers became true Baptists, in the true sense of the term, believing that faith and repentance must precede baptism.

ENGLISH BAPTISTS—GENERAL AND PARTICULAR.

We will now take up the history of the Baptists of England. Unfortunately, they are divided into different denominations—General and Particular—"which differ," says Mr. Benedict, "from each other mainly in their doctrinal sentiments; the Generals being Arminians, and the others Calvinists. In their discipline, their association, their terms of communion and indeed, in all matters, they are alike. See Crosby, vol. 1, page 173.

"There have been two parties of the English Baptists in England, ever since the beginning of the reformation; those that have followed the Calvinistical scheme or doctrines, and from the principal point therein, personal election, have been termed *Particular Baptists;* and those that have professed the Arminian or remonstrant tenets; and have, also, from the chief of those doctrines, *universal redemption*, been called "General Baptists." Again, says Crosby:

"The English Baptists, though they are unhappily disunited and distinguished by the title of Generals and Particulars, yet it is the only point I know of wherein they differ from the primitive churches."

All true Baptists, certainly, regret the division among us.

Not only in England are the Baptists divided on the question of "Election and Reprobation," but wherever they exist we find them differing on this question. In America, we shall find them divided into two principal families, and differing, not only on the question of election, but also, unhappily, on the " Communion " question.

Wishing to follow the English Baptists in their rise and progress, in order to give the chronological history, we will necessarily have to give, first, the history of the

GENERAL BAPTISTS.

The history of this denomination will, no doubt, be more interesting to the larger part of our readers than the previous part of our subject. It, indeed, should be of thrilling interest to all General Baptists. We have already seen, when investigating the history of the Brownists, that John Smith, who organized the General Baptist Church in Amsterdam, Holland, after leaving the established church of England, figured very prominently among these Brownists. Says Mr. Cramp, page 268 :

"John Smith had been a clergyman of the Church of England, and held the living of Gainsborough,

Lincolnshire. On leaving that chuich he became a minister among the Brownists, who esteemed him so highly that Bishop Hall calls him their "oracle in general." After a toilsome and perilous service of about fifteen years, during which time he and his friends suffered much from Elizabeth's tyrany, it was deemed necessary to abandon the field in order to preserve life and liberty." In the year 1605, he joined a party of emigrants to settle in Amsterdam. All dissenters were commanded by Elizabeth to "depart the land." Says Mr. Crosby, vol. 1, page 79 :

" Queen Elizabeth, having by her proclamation commanded all Ana-Baptists and other heretics to depart the land, whether they were natives or foreigners, under the penalty of imprisonment or loss of goods. All that were of this opinion were obliged to conceal their principles or fly into some other country, where they might enjoy the liberty of their religion. Upon which many of the dissenters went over to Holland. Among, whom, there were not a few Baptists, as well as English and Dutch, so that there was now no great number of any denomination that dared openly appear." We have already seen that previous to the departure of these dissenters, the Brownists were numerous in England.

"The laws were executed with great severity on the Brownists. Their books were prohibited by

Queen Elizabeth, their persons imprisioned, and some hanged. They were so much persecuted that they at last resolved to quit the country. Accordingly many retired and settled at Amsterdam where they formed a church and chose Johnson their pastor, and after him, Ainsworth. Their church flourished near a hundred years." Milner's Regular Denomination, page 205.

Says Taylor's History of General Baptists, vol. 1, page 65:

"Here they flourished sometime in peace, and were joined by many of their countrymen, who left England to preserve a good concience."

This church was joined by Smith, as we shall now see, by some of the most renowned divines of that age.

Says Night's History of General Baptists, page 24:

"But being grievously persecuted and harrassed by the court, and seeing no prospect of redress, he (Smith) and his church, Messrs. Robinson and Clifton, co-pastors of a neighboring church, (Brownists) with their congregation, determined to leave the Kingdom and seek liberty of conscience in a foreign country. They arrived in Holland in 1606, and all joined Mr. Ainsworth's society, who received such an addition with peculiar satisfaction." See Orchard's History of Baptists, vol. 2, page 137.

Cramp's History of the Baptists, page 286, says:

"He had left the Church of England, for the Brownists, and now more mature reflection led him to take another step."

Taylor's History of the General Baptists, vol. 1, pages 67-8, says:

"Mr. Smith being now at leisure to consult the scriptures, and in a country where he might pursue his inquiries and divulge the result without danger, proceeded with redoubled zeal in the search of truth. He soon found reason to dispose of the practice of his associates in various points relating to the worship and discipline of a church of Christ, and avowed his disbelief of the doctrine of personal election and reprobation."

This statement is corroborated by Crosby, vol. 1, page 267. After speaking of the persecutions of these people, (General Baptists) he, with Mr. Smith, says:

"But it is to be observed, that at the same time they accuse him after this manner, they are forced to acknowledge that he was more refined than the common sorts of Ana-Baptists, and that he did not go with that heretical sect. Nay, more, that he had

such a dislike and aversion to their gross errors, that his conscience would not permit him to be re-baptised by any of them. * * * *
The English refugees were such as in his opinion, had no true baptism, having only been sprinkled in their infancy; and the foreign Ana-Baptists were such as denied Christ having taken flesh of the Virgin Mary the lawfulness of magistracy and the like, which he and his followers looked upon as very great errors. So that neither the one nor the other could be thought by him to be proper administration of baptism."

Says Orchard's History of Baptists, vol. 1, page 374:

"His Armenian views might have prevented his uniting with the Mennonites." But we think in this he was mistaken, and that we have already seen the reason why Smith and his converts did not unite with the Ana-Baptists and Mennonites, from Messrs. Taylor and Crosby.

The founders of the General Baptist denomination repudiated all the limitarian views of the Calvinists, and held, on the contrary, that the compassionate love of God embraced not only those who should be ultimately saved, but extended to all mankind, that when Jesus suffered the just for the unjust, He died not for a chosen number only—not for those only who should be saved, but for all the world and every dweller in it; and that those who shall perish for for rejecting the gospel, shall not perish because there was no provision made for their salvation, but solely because they refused to accept salvation as God's free gift in Jesus. "That the Divine election is not to faith, but through faith." And the only proper mode of baptism was by immersion." That he only who "endures to the end shall be saved." These are some of the vital truths which were held by the founders of the General Baptists and the importance of which, in their judgment, justified them in laboring apart from the various denominations we have named. They were, therefore, reduced to the painful alternative either of renouncing what they believed to be important truths of Christianity, or of gathering churches in which they should be free to proclaim and to teach all these truths." " And dare we censure them for the course they pursued in adding another sect to the number which, unhappily, already existed?" We have already seen that Mr. Smith's opinions prevailed greatly, especially that of denying infant baptism; and he soon had proselytes enough to form a distinct church of that persuasion, even among the English exiles." Crosby, vol. 1, page 94.

In the organization of this church they adopted the only expedient under such circumstances.

IN ENGLAND AND EUROPE.   29

"It is most probable that those who were convinced of believer's baptism, first formed themselves into a church, and then appointed two of their number (perhaps Mr. Smith and Mr. Helwisse) to baptize the rest." Taylor's History of the General Baptists, page 71.

"This appears to have been the first Baptist church composed of Englishmen, after the reformation. It was formed about 1607 or 1608, about twenty years prior to the church under the care of Spilsbury." This was called a General Baptist church. It was constituted on the basis of religious liberty. It possessed the simplicity of a "New Testament" church, a society of equals, voluntarily associated to promote the glory of the Great Head of the church, by attending to His ordinances and worship, and to advance the good of mankind by supporting and extending his kingdom among men. See Taylor's History of the General Baptists, vol. 1, page 75.

"Many suppose we are called General Baptists because we receive Pedo-Baptists to commune with us in the supper of our Lord, but this is a mistake." It is true, that the General Baptists, both in Europe and America, including the Free Wills, are free communion, but this did not give origin to the name General Baptist. They rejected infant baptism as unscriptural, and required repentance and faith upon the part of the subject previous to baptism," and did not admit of the term, "mode of baptism." Hence, in their opinion "Baptism could only be administered to the believing adult—by being buried, with Christ, in Baptism." They therefore rejected the term "Ana-Baptism," and the Ana-Baptists. They did not, like many of those who were properly called "Ana-Baptists," baptize all who come into their communion, who have previously received "believer's baptism," but baptize such only as have not received believer's baptism. They, also, like the first Particular Baptists, denied any affiliation with the Ana-Baptists. The term "General" was employed to denote that the founders of our denomination dissented from the views which were entertained by the Calvinists respecting election, atonement, effectual calling, and other kindred topics, and that Jesus Christ, by his death, procured salvation for universal man. Hence, we were called, and very appropriately, "General Baptists." Notwithstanding their repeated denials that they were not Ana-Baptists, they were generally called by that name, and sometimes by the name of "Anti-Pedo-Baptists." And in tracing their history, we find these terms used by most historians.

Says Crosby, vol. 1, pages, 90-91, in speaking o the churches which the dissenters set up in Holland under Robinson, Ainsworth, Johnson and John Smith:

"The latter of which went under the name of Ana-Baptists; so that to do justice to the history, we must now follow them into those parts, but I shall confine myself to the English only." Mr. Smith was accused by the other Puritans and Dissenters, and Calvinistic Pedo-Baptists, like many of our United Baptists now accuse us of setting up a new baptism, but he ably defended this reviving of immersion, and indeed, this expedient was afterward very ably defended by many of the founders of the United Baptist church—"Particular Baptist church, as being Scriptural." Says Crosby: "they wrote several books wherein they endeavored to expose him and his principles to the world." "Thomas Wall calls him the beginner of baptism by dipping, and the captain of this and other errors, &c." Crosby, vol 1, page 95.

As we have before stated, Ainsworth, Johnson, Clifton, Robinson and Jessop all took up the pen against Smith and his church, and their "Ana-Baptistic errors." One of the books written against him, "A Discovery of the Errors of the English Ana-Baptists," was presented to King James, and says Crosby, vol. 1, page 92, "It is easy to guess with what design that was done." It was to suppress, if possible, their opinion against the idea of succession of baptism in order to valid baptism; for they thought if this could be done Pedo-Baptism would be perpetuated in the churches, and immersion would cease. As an example of their hatred and opposition to Smith and the reviving of immersion by him and his followers, Thomas Wall says: "If you can find no better administrator, your ministry will be found to come out of the bottomless pit, as Rome's ministry did. Crosby, vol. 1, page 97: "In like manner did they now argue against the reviving of the practice of immersion." And again, on page 104: "Some make it such an error, and so far from any rule or example for a man to baptize others, who is himself unbaptized, and so think thereby to shut up the ordinances of God in such a strain that none can come by it, but through the authority of the Popedom of Rome." This was the language of Mr. Spilsbury, pastor of the first Particular Baptist church. It certainly had its influence. I will repeat, therefore, some more of his language: "I fear men put more than is of a right due to it—that so prefer it above the church and all other ordinances besides; for they can assume and erect a church, take in and cast out members, elect and ordain officers, and administer the Supper, and all anew without looking after succession any further than the Scriptures. But as for baptism, they must have that successively from the Apostles, though it comes through the hands of Pope Joan. What is the cause of this, that men can do all from the word but only baptism?" This was the key note for those times, and should be well heeded by those who make so much to do about a legal administrator of baptism and "proper succession of baptism."

But to return to Mr. Smith and his opinions. We have already seen that these dissenters who oppressed the General Baptists, held to succession of ordination to be necessary in order to its validity.

Says Orchard, vol. 2, page 237: "Mr. Smith knew that Brown and his associates denied the Church of England to be a true church of Christ, and that her ministers' ordinations were not valid; yet these same people allowed the baptism of the Church of England."

So when they accused Smith of setting up anew the ordinance of baptism, he responds to these accusations, while in Holland, in a work entitled, "The Character of the Beast." Says he (Orchard, vol. 2, page 248): "The Ana-Baptists, as you call them, do not set up a new covenant and gospel, though they set up anew the apostolic baptism, which anti-Christ had overthrown; and whereas, you say they have no warrant to baptize themselves, I say, as much as you have to set up a new church; yea, fully as much." His arguments were strong and told on his enemies, and his influence grew rapidly.

Says Crosby, vol. 1, page 98: "Mr. Smith is justifying to the Brownists his authority to begin a new form of baptizing, from the same principle by which they justified their beginning new churches. * * * There is as good warrant for a man churching himself; for two men singly are no church jointly. They are a church so two men may put baptism on themselves." As I before stated, his opinion and others, supported as they are from the Bible, gained for them many disciples. Says Crosby, vol. 1, page 95: "Mr. Smith and his disciples do, as it were, swallow up all the separation besides." Also, Taylor's History of General Baptists, vol 1, page 71: "Mr. Smith appears to have labored with diligence and success. His followers increased so rapidly as to alarm the Pedo-Baptists."

We will now proceed with the history of this church of General Baptists, and will necessarily have to state occasionally to answer the charges made against them by those who assert that Smith and his followers were unauthorized in reviving immersion, and that they were by this reason unbaptized.

These good people, after being persecuted, misrepresented and traduced to the world as Atheists, by their enemies, who were extravagant in their charges against them—"To vindicate themselves from these aspersions," says Taylor's History of General Baptists, vol. 1, page 86, "the Baptists published in 1611, a confession of faith, accompanied with an appendix giving some account of Mr. Smith's last illness and death. It was called "The Confession of Faith," published in certain conclusions by the remainder of Mr. Smith's company, and was supposed to have been chiefly drawn up by Mr. Smith himself." See also Crosby's History of Baptists, vol. 1, page 271.

This, doubtless, was the confession adopted by these people at the organization of their church, and the one by which they were governed in their church and in their deliberations, not, however, as a creed that proposed to fix the opinions and liberty of the members, but as a declaration of principles over which they themselves had had absolute control or supremacy. It can be found in full in Crosby's History of Baptists, vol. 2, appendix page 1. It resemembles very much the confession adopted by the General Baptists in the United States.

I will hereafter speak of some of its doctrinal features. The most of the objections made against this church and its members by our United Baptist brethren, who plead for succession, are to be found in Ray's Succession, pp. 78 to 84, inclusive.

I will now notice some of these statements and will take the privilege of condensing them still more, so as to be as brief as possible:

1st. It is said that John Smith was never an English Baptist in his life. Just precisely what is here meant by "English Baptists" I am unable to tell, but in the language of Crosby, vol. 1, page 92, when speaking of the object of the Dissenters in presenting to King James a work entitled "A Discovery of the English Ana-Baptists," "It is easy to guess with what design that was done."

Now, we have already seen from Crosby, vol. 1, page 173, that the English Baptists were divided into "General and Particular." Then, if the church which he organized at Amsterdam, was a General Baptist church, as he himself was a member of it, he necessarily must have been an English Baptist. With our United Baptist friends the question of its being a Baptist church depends upon the succession of baptism. I will hereafter notice this theory.

Orchard, vol. 2, page 238, says: "Mr. Smith becoming the only teacher or pastor, was the first instance of our churches conforming to the regular establishment." Mr. Orchard was a member of the Particular Baptist church, and pledged for succession, but still he claimed him as a Baptist and his church as a Baptist church—an English Baptist church. Mr. Crosby's History, vol. 1, page 265, recognizes this fact, and places Smith at the head of the list which he gives of Baptist ministers. He says: "I shall now give a brief account of some of the Baptist ministers who lived in the times to which the preceding history refers, whereby it will appear that men of the greatest learning and piety have neither been ashamed nor afraid in the worst of times to stand up in vindication of a principle truly apostolical, though ever so much despised and hated." Then he gives a short history of the life and success of Mr. John Smith as a Baptist. Many other proofs of a historical character could be produced to prove that Smith was an English Baptist.

2d. It is said that Smith's baptism was not a valid baptism. I suppose this statement is made independent of historical facts, and altogether from their peculiar views of the necessity of an uninterrupted succession of baptism, in order to its legal or valid dispensation upon the believing subject.

As this lecture is mostly of a historical character, I shall here refrain from any quotations from the Scriptures, but will bring United or Particular Baptist historians to my assistance in proof of the incorrectness of this statement of theirs. Crosby's History of Baptists, vol. 1, page 105, says: "It cannot reasonably be objected that he that baptizeth should necessarily be a baptized person. For although ordinarily it will be so, yet it is not necessary to the ordinance; for not the personal baptism of him that administers, but the due commission he hath for baptizing, is alone considered to make him a true minister of baptism. And here that expression holds not—one can not give what he hath not; as a man can not teach me that wants knowledge himself; because no man gives his own baptism, but conveys, as a public person, that which is given by Christ." When the first United or Particular Baptist church was formed in 1633, from which, according to the history of Ray's Succession, and other works, the American (United) Baptists descended, they sent one Richard Blount over to the Netherlands to procure baptism from the Mennonites, who were descended from the Waldensian churches. They had been told by the Pedo-Baptists, who, from the same theory of succession in regard to ordinations had sent "ministers into the Netherlands for ordination," that these Waldensian churches were still to be found in the Netherlands. After they had procured this baptism, Mr. Spilsbury, their first minister, with a full knowledge of all this, and no doubt to counteract this tendency of the members, said: "I fear men put more than is of a right due to it, (baptism) that so prefer it above the church and all other ordinances besides; for they can assume and erect a church, take in and cast out members, elect and ordain officers, administer the Lord's Supper, and all anew without any looking after succession any further than the Scriptures. But as for baptism, they must have that successively from the Apostles, though it comes through the hands of Pope Joan. What is the cause of this, that men can do all from the world but only baptism?" Crosby, vol. 1, page 104.

In vol. 3 we find that Crosby says that the greatest number and the most judicious of the English Baptists received their baptism just as John Smith received his—"that after a general corruption of baptism, and unbaptized persons might warrantably baptize and re-begin a reformation."

So you see, my friends, if the baptism of Mr. Smith was not valid, Baptists, according to these historians of the United or Particular Baptists, are generally without baptism. I will notice this succession of baptism again, while tracing the history of the Particular Baptists of England.

3d. It is said that Smith did not belong to an English Baptist church or a legitimate Baptist church at all.

We have already seen that if he belonged to a General Baptist church, it was an English Baptist church;

but it all turns upon the validity of the organization to which he belongs. We have seen the manner in which this church was organized. Says Benedict, page 450, on this manner of the organization of churches; "Any company of Christians may commence a church in gospel order, by their own mutual agreement, without any reference to any other body; and this church has all the power to appoint any one of their number, whether minister or layman, to commence anew the administration of gospel institutions."

Mr. Benedict was a noted divine and historian among the United Baptists. If he is correct, as this is the principle upon which Smith's church was organized, it certainly follows that this was a legitimate Baptist church, and as Smith was a member thereof, he, beyond a doubt, was himself a Baptist.

4th. It is said that Smith and a part of his church, upon the account of a difficulty in his church, were turned out; repudiated their baptism and church organization, confessed their errors, sought admission into one of the Pedo-Baptist Mennonite churches and were received therein

These statements are taken from Evans' History of Early English Baptists, who appears to be fair, candid and honest, but they are not regarded as correct by most historians.

Some of our United Baptist friends who plead for succession are very remarkable for discovering divisions among General Baptist churches, and the repudiation of the baptism received in these churches as in the "John Smith affair," and the "Roger Williams affair"—their baptism was too "informal." John Smith certainly died a member of the church which he established, was faithful to its principles to the last. His church, as an expression of their gratefulness to him for his counsel to them, and their deep regard for his earnest piety, published, after his death, in 1611, their confession of faith, which he had drawn up while living, and appended to it, a short history of the last sickness and death of Mr. Smith. See Taylor's History of the General Baptists, vol. 1, page 86,

"At his (Smith's) death," says Cramp's History of Baptists, page 287, "which took place in 1611, Mr. Thomas Helwisse was appointed in his place."

This, certainly, is sufficient evidence that Smith was a Baptist until death. I refer, however, for further proof, to a correspondence between Rev. John Cotton, a Congregational minister of America and Roger Williams, in which Cotton says:

"Sad and woeful is the memory of Mr. Smith's strong consolations on his death-bed, which is set as a seal to his gross and damnable Armanianism and enthusiasm, delivered to the confession of faith, prefixed to the story of his life and death." This you will find in Wood's History of the General Baptists, page 150. Cotton was an enemy to John Smith's Armanian and Baptistic views.

5th. It is said that Helwisse, with a remnant of Smith's church, returned to England in 1611 or 1612 and that this was the second division of his church. We have just seen, after the death of Smith, Helwisse was appointed in his place, over the church Smith had organized.

Says Cramp's History of Baptists, page 287: "Shortly after this publication of the confession, Mr. Helwisse, accompanied by most of the church, returned to England."

The difference in those statements is, Ray's Succession says: "A few of the remnants of Mr. Smith's company," and Cramp says: "Most of the members of Smith's church."

I will now refer you to Crosby's History of Baptists, vol. 1, page 268:

"The time of his death does not appear, but by a book written by Mr. Robinson, in 1614, it appears that he was then dead, and that a great part of his congregation were returned into England with the aforesaid persons," (Helwisse and Morton.) There was no more division in this church than would ordinarily occur in removing from one locality to another. It is quite natural that all who were natives of Holland and members of this church would remain.

6th. It is said that Helwisse's labors, after he had formed a church of General Baptists in London, were not attended with very great success.

Mr. Helwisse did not form a church after he arrived in London, but brought his church, which Smith left to his care at his death, with him, and there had their regular church meetings as regular "as the evil of the times world permit."

Mr. Crosby, in vol. 1, page 271, fully explains this. He says:

"About the same time, also, Mr. Helwisse began to reflect upon his own conduct, and that of the other English dssenters, in leaving their own country and friends, and flying into a strange land to escape persecution. Whether this did not proceed from fear and cowardice, and whether they ought not return, that they might bear testimony for the truth in their own land, where it was in danger of being wholly extinguished; and that they might also encourage and comfort their brethren who were there, suffering persecution, for Christ's sake. The conclusion of this, was, that he and his church quickly left Amsterdam and removed to London, where they continued their church state, and assemblies for worship as publicly as the evil of the times would permit."

Having now seen that Helwisse did not organize a new church on arriving in London, but acted as pastor of the original church organized by Smith.

I will now proceed to show you, notwithstanding the statement that he did not meet with "very great success," that his success *was* very great. For a proof of my assertion I refer you to Crosby, vol. 1, page 275, which is as follows:

"How long Mr. Helwisse lived, and continued the elder of this church of Baptists at London I cannot find. The books wrote against them at this time show that they went on with great courage and resolution; and notwithstanding the severities used against them by the civil power, increased very much in their numbers.

One author, to prove their doctrines plain and easy to be understood, particularly that of baptism, says: "Witness the multitude of these diciples."

"And when the famous Dod and Cleaver united their forces to censure their supposed errors, they apologized for their attempt, alleging that the people of this persuasion took great pains to propogate their doctrine, and that divers of persons, of good note and piety, had been prevailed upon by them, as has been before observed."

For the same proof, see Crosby, pages 95, 133, 139 and 141 of the same volumn; also Orchard's of Baptists, vol. 2, page 253; Taylor's History of the General Baptists, pages 93, 94 and 95; Benedict's History of Baptists, page 331.

Besides the denial of infant Baptism, they also denied the doctrine of election, reprobation and final perseverance; and that their sentiments, both respecting baptism and predestination gained a multitude of disciples; in other words, the General Baptists increased rapidly in numbers," says Wood's History of General Baptists, pages 108 and 109. Enough then upon this statement.

7th. After endeavoring to prove the want of validity for the "informal baptism" of the John Smith affair, in using the language of Crosby, vol. 1, pages 99 and 100, which says:

"If he were guilty of what they charge him with, 'tis no blemish on the English Baptists, who neither approved of any such method, nor did they receive their baptism from him." They evidently fail to present the object of Crosby in making this statement. Thomas Wall had charged John Smith with having baptized himself, and that he afterwards baptized Mr. John Spillsbury, the first minister of the first Particular Baptist church, and that he (Spillsbury) transmitted this same baptism to the English Baptists by succession of baptism.

This Crosby was endeavoring to show was false, and that the English Baptists did not receive their baptism by succession from any minister, either General or Particular, from John Smith or John Spillsbury. That while most, or all of John Spillsbury's church had received baptism from a church in the Netherlands through Mr. Richard Blount, the greatest number and the more judicious English Baptists had received their baptism just as John Smith had received his— had received it through an unbaptized person. The English Baptists held to the principle and acted accordingly, that any company of Christians may commence a church in Gospel order, by their own mutual agreement, without any reference to any other body, and that this church has all power to appoint any one of their number, whether minister or layman to commence anew the administration of Gospel institutions. See Benedict's History of Baptists, page 450.

No, my Christian friends, the English Baptists, as a mass, did not receive their baptism from John Smith, John Spillsbury, Richard Blount, or any one other Baptist, by succession of Baptism. Neither did the entire General Baptists receive their baptism by transmission from John Smith of his church of

General Baptists, notwithstanding their baptism was valid baptism. A majority of the English Baptists, both General and Particular, discarding the old and exploded doctrine of an uninterrupted Apostolic succession and succession of baptism, in order to its validity, affirmed that "any company of Christians may commence a church in gospel order, without any reference to any other body," etc., (as we have already seen) that "it is lawful for an unbaptised person to baptize, and his baptism is valid;" that "it is not the personal baptism of him that administers, but the commission he hath, is alone considerable, to make him a true minister of baptism;" that "no man gives his own baptism, but conveys, as a public person, that which was given us by Christ."

In speaking of the right to begin the administration of gospel institutions which includes baptism upon the principles just named.

Mr. Benedict's History of Baptists, page 450, says:

"This is the Baptist doctrine of Apostolical succession which they prefer to receive from good men, rather than through the poluted channels of the papal power."

Hence, if the English Baptists acted upon this principle or basis, in establishing the early Baptist churches, they could not have received their baptism by succession, from John Smith, John Spillsbury, Richard Blount, or any other one man. Then if Smith had baptized himself, which Crosby says: "It is not likely he did," as he could not give the same by succession to any of the English Baptists—it could not have been any blemish on them. The English Baptists rejected this charge against Smith and fully recognized his right to baptize, as well as his baptism by Helwisse.

Now, as Ivimey and Crosby, who were members of Particular Baptist churches, and were unprejudiced and faithful historians, they, as English Baptists, are as well qualified to tell their origin as any others. We will let them speak. We will hereafter see, from Crosby, particularly, that while most, or all of the members of the first Particular Baptist church, which came out of the Independent Pedo-Baptist church, that the greatest number and the more judicious of the English Baptists received their baptism just as John Smith and his church, the Baptists in Leicestershire. The Tunkers, or German Baptists, and Roger Williams and his church, did, "by an unbaptized person baptizing, and so beginning a reformation."

THE GENERAL BAPTIST CONFESSION OF 1611.

This church of General Baptists, organized by Smith and Helwisse in 1606 or 1607, was composed of members who were warm advocates of religious liberty, as we shall now find by an examination of their confession of faith, which, as we have seen, was written by Smith before his death and (most likely) on the organization of this church, and published in 1611 The Rev. R. D. Peay, a United Baptist minister, in a sermon preached to his own congregation, August 15, 1875, in Henderson, Ky., in speaking of "Religious Liberty," says of this confession of faith: "The earliest modern declaration on this subject that we find published, is the 'Baptist Confession of Faith,' published in 1611, many years before Baltimore, and two years before Jeremiah Taylor was born. This declaration says: 'We believe that the magistrate is not to meddle with religion or matters of conscience, nor compel men to this or that form of religion, because Christ is the King and Law. Giver of the church and conscience.'"

This quotation of Mr. Peay's can be found in Crosby's History of General Baptists, vol. 1. appendix page 71, article 85. This confession referred to by Mr. Peay is not the genuine confession of Smith and church, but the confession reported by Mr. John Robinson (as being theirs) of whom we have spoken, who was the former associate of Smith, but afterwards an enemy of Smith and the General Baptists. He was a Calvinistic Pedo-Baptist, and father of the

Independents (Congregationalists). His purpose was to misrepresent the sentiments of the General Baptists to their civil oppressors. For an explanation, see Crosby's History of Baptists, vol. 1, pp. 268-271. He says: "Mr. Robinson, the pastor of an English congregation of Brownists at Leyden, published three years after his remarks upon it (the confession of 1611), and has therein collected those passages which were thought the most obscure or erroneous in it." The true language of this confession on religious liberty (which only differs in the manner of expression, but is the same in spirit,) may be found in Crosby's History of Baptists, vol. 2, appendix page 8, article 24. They were not only warm advocates for religious liberty before the civil law, but they were decided advocates for liberty at the Lord's table.

As we will now see by their confession, Crosby's History of Baptists, vol. 2, appendix page 6, article 15, says: "The Lord's Supper is the outward manifestation of the spiritual communion between Christ and the faithful, mutually to declare his death until he come."

Again, Art. 19 declares, "That every church ought, according to the example of Christ's disciples and primitive churches, upon every first day of the week, being the Lord's Day, to assemble together, pray, prophesy, praise God, and break bread, and perform all other parts of spiritual communion for the worship of God, their own mutual edification and the preservation of true religion and piety in the church. And they ought not to labor in their callings according to the equity of the moral law, which Christ came not to abolish but to fulfill."

Mr. Orchard, who was a close communionist, and attributed liberty at the Lord's table to looseness, after asserting (probably from reading Wiston's Memoirs), that this church of General Baptists received to their communion Socinians and Arians, in vol. 2, page 262, says of them: "Nor do they reject any from their communion who profess themselves Christians and receive the Holy Scriptures as the source of truth and the rule of faith."

Yes, my Christian friends, all Christians who receive the Scriptures as their rule of faith and are soundly converted, are qualified to sit down together at the same table to the "Lord's Supper, and mutually declare his death until he come."

The same confession from which Mr. Peay quotes, which he styles a "Baptist Confession of Faith"— Crosby's History of Baptists, vol. 1, appendix page 70, article 82—says: "That there is no succession in that outward church, but that all the succession is from heaven, and the new creature only hath the thing signified and substance; whereof the outward church and ordinances are shadows."

You remember, in the beginning of my lectures, when I was merely giving the basis of the lecture that was to follow, I asserted that, as a matter of right, myself or any other person, as a lay member of the church, could administer the Lord's Supper or baptism, and that such dispensation of the ordinances would be valid. While it was recognized among the early General Baptists as orderly that ordained ministers should dispense the ordinances, yet they conceded the lay members had a perfect right, in the absence of such ministers, to administer all the ordinances of the church. For proof of this I refer you to Crosby's History of Baptists, vol. 2, appendix page 5, article 11; "That though in respect to Christ the church be one, yet it consisteth of divers particular congregations, even so many as there shall be in the world; every one of which congregations, though there are but two or three, have Christ given them, with all the means of their salvation, are the body of Christ and a whole church; and therefore may, and ought, when they come together, to pray, prophesy, break bread and admininister in all the holy ordinances; although as yet they have no officers, or that their officers should be in prison, or sick, or by any other means hindered from the church."

This position of this General Baptist church that it was simply orderly for only ordained ministers to administer the ordinances was one step in the direction of the Church of England, and other ecclesiastical powers. On this subject Mr. Orchard's History of Baptists, vol. 2, page 238, remarks:

"We observe all our early churches on the continent, allowed no distinct order of men as clergy; all the men members were brethren, and each one could teach who possessed any talent. This was also maintained among the Brownists." Neal 1, page 304, says: "These early churches all had a plurality of elders, as may be traced to a later period.

Mr. Smith becoming the only teacher, or pastor, was the first instance of our churches conforming to the regular establishment, by a sanctified separation of one brother from the rest of the flock."

Though it is a slight diversion, I will here refer you, for further proof of my position, to Benedict's History of Baptists, page 308. In speaking of the Lollards, who were the ancestors, in principle, to the subsequent Baptist churches, he says:

"They formed separate and distinct societies agreeable to the scriptures. In these churches all were equal; each could preach, baptize and break bread. They were united in opinion as one man, and were called "Bible men," since they allowed no office not enjoined in the Word of God." In this confession, upon the possibility of apostasy, in Crosby's

History of Baptists, vol. 2, appendix, page 3, article 7, they say:

"Men may fall away from the grace of God, and from the truth which they have received and acknowledged, after they have tasted of the heavenly gift, and made partakers of the Holy Ghost, and have tasted of the good word of God, and of the powers of the world to come, and after they have escaped from the filthiness of the world, may be entangled again therein and overcome. That a righteous man may forsake his righteousness and perish. And, therefore let no man presume to think that because he hath or once had grace, therefore he shall always have grace, but let all men have assurance that if they continue unto the end they shall be saved. Let no man then, presume; but let all work out their salvation with fear and trembling." The other articles in this confession generally agree with the General Baptist confession of faith, published in the General Baptist Herald.

I will, perhaps compare some of the articles of this confession and others of the General Baptists, adopted subsequently with some of the articles of the different confessions of the Particular Baptists at the conclusion of the examination of the history of the English Baptists.

Having now reviewed this confession of faith of

the General Baptists at Amsterdam, Holland, which continued for many years the confession of this church under the care of Helwisse in London, and other General Baptist churchs, we will now speak of the return of the church from Amsterdam to London England.

Says Cramp's History of Baptists, page 289: "So they went back to their native shores and established themselves in London, meeting for worship in strict privacy. They had encountered a great risk in returning at such a time. The fires of persecution had been lighted again, and men were burned to ashes for heresy."

Though they were sorely persecuted on all hands by both ecclesiastical and civil powers, many converts were made to their faith, and other General Baptists were organized, which met for worship in caves, cellars, garrets and forests, and in fact anywhere to evade the wrath of bloody persecutors.

Says Taylor's History of General Baptists, vol. 1, page 87: "Non-Conformists, who continued in exile, were highly displeased with this decided conduct. They ascribed it to natural confidence rather than spiritual courage, and represented it as openly defying the government and courting persecution. To remove these objections, the Baptists took occasion, in a book which they published in the following year, to explain the motives of their proceedings." This book was called "Fleeing on Account of Persecution," and is quite an interesting work to all Baptists. It pleads for liberty.

Says Benedict's History of Baptists, page 330: "The principal arguments in favor of their returning course were—

"1st. That fleeing from persecution hath been the overthrow of religion in this island, the best, ablest and greater part being gone, and leaving behind them some few who, by the other departures, have had their afflictions and their contempts increased, hath been the cause of many falling back and of their adversaries rejoicing.

"2d. Great help and encouragement would it be to God's people, in affliction, imprisonment and the like, to have their brethren's presence to administer to their souls and bodies, and for which cause Christ will say, 'I was in prison and ye visited me; in distress and ye comforted me.' 'Religious Peace, or a Plea for Liberty of Conscience.''

Says Cramp's History of Baptists, page 271: "Though the Baptists were debarred the use of the pulpit, the press did them good service. Two extracts published by them soon after the events just recorded, were honorable alike to their good sense and pious feelings. The first appeared in 1614. It was entitled 'Religious Peace, or a Plea for Liberty of Conscience,' and is the earliest published work on the subject in the English language. Of the author, Leonard Busher, Woods' History of General Baptists, page 105, says: 'The author was a citizen of London, and had been in exile; from some of his remarks he appears to have been a General Baptist, but it is not ascertained whether he was a member of Mr. Smith's church."

In this treatise, which was addressed to the King and Parliament, the author earnestly pleads for pardon, and certain reasons against prosecutions, for the Baptists in particular and dissenters in general. He says: "Christ's kingdom is not of this world; therefore it may not be purchased or defended with the weapons of this world, but by the Sword and Spirit." "It is not only unmerciful, but unnatural and abominable—yea, monstrous—for one Christian to vex and destroy another, for difference on questions of religion."

"It is not the gallows, nor prisons, nor burning, nor banishing, that can defend the faith. Indeed, the King and the State may defend religious peace by their sword and civil power, but not the faith, otherwise than by the sword and spirit of God." See Cramp's History of Baptists, pp. 292–3.

PERSECUTION FOR RELIGION JUDGED AND CONDEMNED.

Says Taylor's History of General Baptists, vol. 1, page 89: "This open avowal of their sentiments, and steady continuance at the post of duty as they esteemed it, exposed the General Baptists to great suffering. 'It was not uncommon,' to use their own words, 'to lie many years in filthy prisons, in hunger, cold and idleness; divided from wife, family and calling; left in continual miseries and temptations, so that death itself would be, to many, less punishment. Many of them were exposed to want, lost their estates, and were confined in noisome dungeons till death released them.' These severities induced them to appeal to their rulers and fellow subjects. In 1615 they published a pamphlet entitled 'Persecution for Religion Judged and Condemned, in a discourse between a Christian and anti-Christian, proving, by the law of God and King James, many declarations that no man ought to be persecuted for his religion so he testifies his allegiance by the oath appointed by the law'."

Of this work, Crosby's History of Baptists, vol. 1, pp. 272-3, says: "In the year 1615, Mr. Helwisse and his church in London, published a treatise entitled 'Persecution for Religion Judged and Condemned.' 'Tis true there is no author's name to it, but at the end of the epistle dedicatory, instead of names it is subscribed thus: 'By Christ's unworthy witnesses, his Majesty's faithful subjects, commonly, but most falsely called Ana-Baptists." But it appears to be theirs, because towards the end of the book, to clear themselves from those gross errors held by some Ana-Baptists, and to prove their orthodoxy on the point of Christ's incarnation, the lawfulness of magistracy, &c., they refer the reader to their confession of faith before mentioned, printed four years before this, and called it *their* Confession." "They assert that every man has a right to judge for himself in matters of religion, and that to persecute any on that account is illegal and Anti-Christian." So you see that these General Baptists, in their treatise, deny that they are Ana-Baptists. See Orchard's History of Baptists, vol. 2, pp. 252–3; Wood's History of the General Baptists, pp. 106–7.

This treatise gives abundant evidence of emancipation from ritualistic prejudices, together with great vigor of thought and boldness of speech. General and United Baptists would do well to read the argument contained in it.

This tract contains the following: Cramp's History of Baptists, page 206.

"Christian is asked: 'Who, then, shall baptize

after Anti-Christ's exaltation?' That is, how shall baptism be recovered where it has been lost through the long prevalence of Anti-Christian rule?" The answer is thus given:

"We, and others affirm, that any disciple of Christ, in what part of the world soever, coming to the Lord's way, he by the Word and Spirit of God, preaching unto others and converting—he may and ought also to baptize them."

This confirms my position in regard to a legal administrator of baptism.

Continues Cramp's History on this subject:

"These extracts will serve to show that our Baptist forefathers were distiguished for mental vigor and independence. They had shot ahead of their religious contemporaries, too many of whom, instead of sympathizing with them, caricatured their principles, and excited popular fury against their persons."

Some of my United Baptist friends may object to what I have just read from Cramp's History of Baptists, and contend that the principle that an unbaptized person can legally administer baptism, was only advocated by the General Baptists. But we shall hereafter see that "the greater number of the English Baptists, and the more judicious," maintained this principle. Indeed, if there were any other Baptists at this time (1615) than General Baptists, they endorsed it.

Crosby's History of Baptists, vol. 1, page 124, says:

"It appears to be written, or at least approved of, by the whole body of Baptists, who then remained in England."

Says Taylor's History of the General Baptists, vol. 1, pages 90-91:

"That this book was published by the General Baptists, is clear, from their reference to their confession of faith; but it appears to have been sanctioned by all the Baptists in England."

This could not have been sanctioned by the Particular Baptists at the date of its first publication, as they did not exist as a distinct denomination, until 1633, but was approved by them after organization. Hence, if this treatise expressed the true sentiments and practices of the Baptists of those times, they totally rejected the error of churchism and priestly rule, but recognized every disciple or believer an annointed priest of God, and fully authorized by the Holy Scriptures to preach, to convert men and then baptize them. While they believed in local churches and organized them when practical, it was a distinctive doctrine with them, that the churches so organized were for the benefit of the individual Christian, and not as an ecclesiastical power to rule or oppress him in any respect whatever. These people understood true Christian liberty, and asserted that it was centered in personal duties and individual rights, and without these the local churches could not have thus wanted vigor and life.

THE STATUES OF GOLD.

Says Wood's History of the General Baptists, page 110:

"The assertion and maintenance of great principles in the time of ignorance and persecution, confer a title to the gratitude of posterity. Those persons who propogated the principles of religious liberty at the commencement of the period under review, are regarded by Independents and Baptists as being worthy of all honor. So great is their claim in the estimation of Messrs. Bogne and Bennett, that in their history of dissenters they observe: 'Were Britain to erect a statute of gold to the memory of the first patrons of this sentiment, she would but imperfectly discharge the debt to those who have been the source of her wealth, her strength and her glory. But while these gentlemen form a correct estimate of the services rendered, they are in error as to the parties entitled to the award. 'It is the distinguished glory of the independents,' they state, 'to have first recommended a principle so noble as religious liberty to the esteem of the world.' But the first independent church was not founded until the year 1616, the year after the pamphlet entitled 'Persecution for Religion, Judged and Condemned,' was published by the General Baptists—a work, Mr. Ivimny declares, 'well-deserving immortality, * * a monument more valuable and durable than even one of pure gold. The same author candidly acknowledges the honor claimed for the Indepentents. I do not hesitate to say belongs to a General Baptist church in London, who, when all the world wandered after the beast, proclaimed at the expense of liberty, and even of life, the noble sentiment which was afterwards re-echoed by the excellent Roger Williams, and embodied in the institutions of Rhode Island. May we not claim, then,

THE STATUE OF GOLD

TO THE MEMORY OF

THE GENERAL BAPTISTS OF 1615,

IN THE PROSPECT OF IMPRISONMENT AND

DEATH,

NOBLY STOOD FORTH

AS THE DISSENTERS AND DEFENDERS OF

RELIGIOUS LIBERTY WHEN THE

WORLD WANDERED AFTER

THE BEAST.

So, my friends, you see by this the glory that was achieved by this noble church of General Baptists at London was won through blood, death, imprisonment, fines and poverty. While many historians were loath to award to the General Baptists the honor which was due them, Messrs. Crosby and Ivmny do not hesitate to proclaim them as earnest and able defenders of religious liberty, and as the genuine authors of those excellent treaties on true "Soul Liberty," that appeared in the beginning of the reign of James 1st.

I will now call your attention to what was known by the early Baptists as "The Dutch Book on Baptism, or a Plain and Well-grounded treaties on Baptism."

Says Crosby's History of Baptists, vol. 1, page 128, of this book:

"In the year 1610, there came forth a book vindicating the principles of the Baptists. This was translated from the Dutch, and is thought to be the first that was published in English against the baptizing of infants."

Says Taylor's History of General Baptists, vol. 1, page 91, of this book: "It was a translation from the Dutch, and probably the work of Mr. Helwisse or some of his friends, who had lately returned from Holland." And again, on the same page, in a note, he says Crosby reckons this the first book published in English against infant baptism; but he had not seen Smith's "Character of the Beast," a work written by Mr. Smith in defense of "Only Believer's Baptism," or "Concerning True Christian Baptism."

The work above referred to as the production of Helwisse or of some of his friends, contains eight propositions. Crosby's History of Baptists, vol. 1, page 128:

1st. "That Christ commanded his apostles and servants of the Holy Ghost, first of all to preach the gospel and make disciples, and afterward to baptize those that were instructed in the faith, "in calling upon and confessing the name of God."

"2d. That the apostles and servants of the Holy Ghost, have, according to the commandments of the Lord Jesus Christ, first of all taught, and then afterterwards those that were instructed in the mysteries of the kingdom of God were baptized, upon the confessing of their faith."

The other six propositions are similar to these, and confine baptism to the believing penitent.

Says Taylor's History of the General Baptists, vol. 1, page 91: "It is probable, indeed, that all of the opposers of infant baptism at that time were General Baptists, as the Particulars are not mentioned till several years after this period." (See Benedict's History of Baptists, page 331.)

This quotation disproves the idea that is prevalent among the people, that, because of our fraternal greetings with the Pedo-Baptists, we, as a denomination, both in Europe and America, are not decided advocates of only believer's baptism; and corrects the impresssion that, because of our communion with Pedo-Baptists, we have been called General Baptists. But this has been fully done while on the origin of our denomination.

But to return to our subject proper. See Taylor's History of the General Baptists, vol. 1, page 91: "The Baptists still groaned under persecution, which produced its constant effect; their numbers increased in their affliction, yet they thought themselves called upon to take every lawful method to obtain relief, and in 1620 presented an humble supplication to King James I. and the Parliament, for redress. In this they acknowledge it to be their duty to pray for kings and those in authority, and appealed to him that it was their constant practice. They represented, in strong terms, the miseries they suffered by the seizure of their goods, long and painful imprisonments in various parts of the kingdom, in which many had died and left their widows and orphans destitute. The 'learned (clergy) of this land,' they tell his majesty, 'procure your temporal sword to persecute us by casting us into prisons, where many of us have remained divers years in lingering imprisonments, deprived of all earthly comforts, as wife, children, calling, etc., without hope of release till our God—for the practice of whose commandments we are thus persecuted—persuades the heart of your majesty to take pity on us, our poor wives and children. God is the lord of men's consciences, and the only lawgiver in matters of religion.' To this petition they subjoined ten short chapters, in which they endeavored to prove—

1st. That the Scriptures are the only rule of faith, and not any church, etc.

2d. That the interpreter of this rule is the Scriptures, and Spirit of God, in whomsoever, etc.

3d. That the Spirit of God, to understand and interpret the Scriptures, is given to every person that fears and obeys God, but not to the wicked.

4th. That those who fear and obey God, and so have His Spirit to understand the Scriptures, are most commonly the simple, poor, despised, etc.

5th. That the learned in human learning do most commonly err, and know not the truth, etc.

6th. That persecution for the cause of conscience is against the doctrine of Jesus Christ, the King of Kings."

7th. Perscution for cause of conscience is against the profession and practice of famous princes.

8th. Persecution for cause of conscience is condemned by the ancient and later writers, etc.

9th. It is no prejudice to the commonwealth, if freedom of religion were offered, etc.

10th. Kings are not deprived of any power given them of God, when they maintain freedom for cause of conscience."

These are only the titles of the chapters of this interesting appendix to their petition. You can find it in full in Crosby's History of Baptists, vol. 2, appendix pp. 10 to 51. All Baptists would profit by reading it thoroughly and prayerfully.

Says Taylor's History of the General Baptists, vol. 1, page 93: "From this abstract of the contents, it is plain that the petition maintained the same dignified sentiments, and showed themselves the undaunted supporters of the sacred rights of conscience, as when they published 'Persecuted and Condemned,' which they took this opportunity of reprinting."

Orchard's History of Baptists, vol. 255-6, says of this petition by the General Baptists to King James I: "In the most open and public manner, therefore, these Baptists avowed their peculiar sentiments and their assigned reasons for leaving the Church of England, which awakened their enemies to express themselves in reviling language from the pulpit, and to harass them in their spiritual courts."

Their petition, which was presented to his majesty, is divided into ten parts; each part is devoted to the illustration of doctrinal and the defense or explanation of their views and conduct. Their petition was rejected and their suffering continued; but notwithstanding the severities used against them, the brethren kept up their separate meetings and increased in numbers.

One of their enemies confessed that they were, in appearance, more holy than the members of the established church. From this petition, which was a bold appeal, it is demonstrated that there were Baptists in many parts of the kingdom, since this petition states they suffered imprisonment for many years in divers counties of England." Of the individual, who penned this petition for the oppressed General Baptists, and the manner in which it was written, Cramp's History of Baptists, page 298, remarks:

"The author of these arguments against persecution, says Roger Williams, as I have been informed, being committed, by some in power to close prison or to Newgate, for the witness of some of the truths of Jesus, and having not the use of pen and ink, wrote these arguments in milk, on sheets of paper brought him by the woman, his keeper, from a friend in London, as the staples of his milk bottle." See Wood's History of the General Baptists, page 108; Benedict's History of Baptists, page 331.

I will now call your attention to a famous work written by one of John Smith's and Helwisse's disciples, John Mortin; the book was found in demolishing an old wall near Colchester. Says Crosby's History of Baptists, vol. 1, page 277:

"The General Baptists were very fond of it, soon got it printed, and it has since received several impressions. The author of this book appears to have been a man of considerable learning and parts, one that understood the Oriental languages, and was acquainted with the writings of the fathers, but a very zealous Remonstrant or Armminan. It is entitled "Truth's Champion," and contains thirteen chapters on the following heads:

I. "That Christ died for all men.

II. Of his dying for all, to save all.

III. Of his power given to all.

IV. Of predestination.

V. Of election.

VI. Of Free-will.

VII. Of falling away.

VIII. Of original sin.

IX. Of baptizing or baptism.

X. Of the ministry.

XI. Of love.

XII. Of those that hold that God hath appointed or destined unavoidably all the actions, of men and the sad effect that follow.

XIII. Of the man Adam, and of the man Christ, with answers to divers objections to the same."

It is written in a very good style, and the arguments are managed with a great deal of art and skill, so that those who follow the remonstrant's scheme of doctrines do not value it without a cause."

From this statement of Mr. Crosby, you see clearly for yourselves that the doctrinal features of this book are similar to the doctrines set forth by the modern General Baptists, both in Europe and America. I invite your attention again to another book which was written in defense of the principles of these General Baptists that constituted Helwisse's church, and other churches of the same denomination in and about London at that time. It was in the form of a letter from a member of Helwisse's church, who had left the Church of England, and joining with such an heretical people, as they were then esteemed, wrote a letter to inform his relations of his real opinions, and what he had to offer in defence of it. This letter falling into the hands of a zealous son of the church, before it came to the person intended, he immediately published it with an answer to it. He says it was indited by a principal elder of that separation; and if so, in all probability Mr. Helwisse was the author of it. It bears date at London, the 10th of May, 1622, and contains, in a little compass, the state of this controversy. The spirit and management of the Baptists in those times, is very well represented by it.

Taylor's History of the General Baptists, vol. I, pages 93-94, in speaking of this production, says:

"In this letter, infant baptism is disproved—from the natural inability of infants to confess their sins, believe the gospel, etc., all which the Scriptures requires as pre-requisite to baptism—from their unfitness to be members of the visible church of Christ, which ought to consist of persons called out by grace from their natural estate, and separated from the world; from the impossibility of inheriting from their parents a fittness for gospel ordinances; showing at large that the covenant made with Abraham cannot entitle the children of believers, merely as such, to a participation of the privileges of a Christian church, and from the total want of command, example, or just consequence in Scripture, for baptizing them," This letter is signed "H. H."

As we have already seen, this letter was intercepted by a member of the Church of England, before it reached the friend to whom it was addressed. It was immediately published and an answer to it. Taylor's History of the General Baptists, vol. 1, page 94, says of this letter :

"Before it reached those to whom it was addressed, it fell into the hands of a warm advocate of the Church of England, who immediately published it, and an answer to it, under the title of "Ana-Baptism's Mystery of Iniquity Unmasked, by J. P., A. D., 1623."

This author says that the Baptists in those days wrote many books in defense of their opinions, and were in the habit of producing great numbers of Scriptures to prove their doctrines, and that they maintained an appearance of more holiness than the members of the established church, whose books and papers they avoided. He likewise informs us, that besides the denial of infant baptism, they also denied the doctrine of election and reprobation and final perseverance." Crosby's History of Baptists, vol. 1, page 139, in speaking of this same report, by J. P., adds: "And they had multitudes of disciples."

The letter referred to as being written by H. H., you can find in full, in Crosby's History of Baptists, vol 1, pages 133 to 139. Says Taylor's History of the General Baptists, vol. 1. page 95: "And J. P. assures us that their sentiments, both respecting baptism and predestination, gained, in 1623, multitudes of disciples, or in other words, that at that time the General Baptists increased rapidly in minds."

Says Crosby's History of Baptists, vol. 1, page 141: "In the year 1624, there came forth much great champions in the defense of infant baptism. The famous Dod and Cleaver united their strength and joined together in publishing a small treatise against the erroneous positions of the Ana-Baptists, as they termed them. In the preface they apologize for their engaging in this controversy, by alleging that those of the contrary opinion were very industrious and took great pains to propogate their doctrine; that divers persons of good note for piety, had been prevailed on by them."

Says Taylor's History of the General Baptists, vol. 1, page 96, in speaking of the sentiments of the Baptists as reported by this same Dod and Cleaver: "They bear the same testimony to the doctrinal sentiments of the Baptists, who they say agreed with the Arminians in some opinions, and asserted that all children dying in their infancy shall be saved through the merits of Christ." This book was called the "Patrimony of Children."

Cramp's History of Baptists, page 299, after refering to this book (Patrimony of Children) and the answer to the letter we have spoken of signed by J. P., says:

"It would appear, therefore, that the Baptists were an active and growing body."

Mr. Benedict, after reading and studying

carefully the works of these General Baptists, of which we have been speaking, in his History of Baptists, page 331, concludes in the following language:

"I have noticed striking traits of character in all the documents put forth by these Baptists, for a long time after their return to Holland, which shows that they had among them men of superior talents, who had made up their minds at all hazards to propogate and defend their peculiar sentiments, not only on the baptismal question, but also on the principles of religious freedom. Their remonstrances and petitions to civil rulers were not merely humble suplications for an abatement of their oppressions, for unrestrained toleration in their religious worship, but they were accompanied with expositions of their sacred rights of conscience, which we may well suppose would not be very graciously received by a monarch and a court who were under the influence of a bigoted and domineering priesthood.

We have seen from Taylor's History of the General Baptists, vol. 1, page 71, how the General Baptist church at Amsterdam, Holland, was formed: "That they first formed themselves into a church, and appointed two of their number—perhaps Smith and Helwisse—to baptize each other and afterward to baptize the rest;" which expedient Cramp's History of Baptists, page 287, and Crosby's History of Baptists, vol. 1, page 103, fully endorse. We have also seen that Benedict, in his excellent History of Baptists, page 450, endorses this principle, and on page 331 expresses his admiration of these people and the great work they performed for the cause of pure Christianity. While there are those among the United Baptist brethren who, from their peculiar and fanciful notion of the necessity of "succession" in order to the validity of the church and the dispensation of its ordinances, would have us believe that from the fact of the "lay baptism" or "informal baptism" of Smith and his church that it was not a genuine Baptist church.

Mr. Orchard, though a Close Baptist, makes this statement, in vol. 2, page 238: "The church over which Mr. Smith settled is said to be a 'Regular Baptist' church, by historians." So we challenge the Christian world to point us to a single Baptist church that endured the same privations, persecutions and imprisonments "as witnesses for the truth," and yet accomplished so much for the restoration of pure and genuine religion. Yes, that simple form of devotion to God, divested of that cumbersome appendage of human ceremonies which tends to supplant the ordinances which Jesus gave his people. The books written by this church would make a valuable and respectable library of themselves. While they were engaged in restoring this simple form of devotion, and writing in behalf of baptistic doctrine, they were actively employed in organizing local churches until the General Baptists became very numerous in and about London, and in fact through all England.

They were friends to soul-liberty and never lost an opportunity to present their claims before their civil rulers in behalf of the separation of church and State. So rapidly did they increase under these circumstances that from the date of their first church, which was organized at Amsterdam, in 1607, till 1660, their churches have increased to near one hundred, with a membership of twenty thousand. This brings us to the time when the General Baptists, after having endured many persecutions, privations and imprisonments, and after having appealed to the magistrates for redress in vain, presented King Charles II. with their petition and confession.

Orchard's History of Baptists, vol. 2, page 299, says; "So common were the sufferings and insults of the times that a narrative of their afflictions was drawn up, and with a confession of the brethren's faith, signed by many of the General Baptist ministers, on behalf of twenty thousand members, presented to the King. Mr. Thomas Grantham and Mr. Joseph Wright, by the help of a member of Parliament, presented them to his majesty, July 26," (1660).

On this same subject, Cramp's History of Baptists, page 324, remarks: "The Baptists saw the storm coming and took measures accordingly. They asked for no indulgence, no emoluments. They sought no office. All they wanted was freedom of worship. They recognized but one course of action in things civil. They were prepared to be obedient subjects. With these views they approached the throne.

"1st. A petition was presented to the King, July 26, 1660, setting forth the sufferings inflicted on the churches in Lincolnshire. 'We have been much abused,' they say, 'as we pass in the streets and as we sit in our houses; being threatened to be hanged if but heard praying to our Lord in our own families, and disturbed in our so waiting upon Him, by uncivil beating at our doors and sounding of horns; yea, we have been stoned when going to our meetings; the windows of the place where we have met have been struck down with stones; yea, we have been taken as evil-doers and imprisoned, when peaceably met together to worship the Most High, in the use of His most precious ordinances. * * * And as if all this were too little, they have, to fill up their measures, very lately indicted many of us at the sessions, and intend, as we are informed, to impose on us the penalty of £20, each, for not coming to hear such men as they provide us.' Accompanying this, was a confession of faith, drawn up by Thomas Granthem, said to be 'owned and approved by more than twenty thousand'."

Says Taylor's History of the General Baptists, vol. 1, pp. 185-6, when speaking of the same subject: "The Baptist were forbidden to assemble for the worship of God, without giving security for their good behavior. In the simplicity of their hearts they complied, never imagining that peaceably attending to their religious duties would be construed into bad behavior. Their enemies, however, esteemed this the height of their offending, and proceeded to still more violent outrages. The Baptists, finding no redress upon applying to the magistrates of the country, resolved to appeal to the king. Accordingly they drew up a narrative of their sufferings, in an address to his majesty, which, by the interest of an honorable member of parliament, their messengers obtained an opportunity of delivering into the hands of Charles II., on July 26, 1660. * * * * At the same time, these messengers presented the king a brief confession of faith."

This confession you can find in full in Crosby's History of Baptists, vol 2, appendix pp. 76 to 90.

The heading of this confession reads thus: "A Brief Confession or Declaration of Faith, lately presented to King Charles the Second; set forth by many of us, who are falsely called Ana-Baptists, to inform all men, in these days of scandal and reproach, of our innocent belief and practice; for which we are not only resolved to suffer persecution, to the loss of our goods, but also life itself, rather than to decline the same," &c.

I have read you the history in this case in detail, for the express purpose of showing that while the General Baptists suffered, perhaps, more than any class of dissenters, notwithstanding, in the language of Mr. Benedict, "their remonstrances and petitions to their civil rulers were not merely humble supplications for an abatement of their oppressions; for unrestrained toleration in their religious worship, but they were accompanied with expositions of the sacred rights of conscience."

You see, again, they set forth the idea that they were not Ana-Baptists—not in the sense of re-baptizing, but to show that they were not descended from the Ana-Baptists, or a part of that old denomination. This confession, while it differs in some of its features from the confession of 1611, is Arminian.

We have seen that the General Baptists in 1660 amounted, in number, to "more than twenty thous and." Notwithstanding the persecutions through which they passed, so wonderful was their success, so rapid their increase, that when William III. was declared king of England, Feb. 13, 1689, they amounted, in round numbers, to *thirty thousand.*

On this subject, says Taylor's History of the General Baptists, vol 1, page 302: "If the General Baptists, at the restoration, amounted to *twenty thousand*, they must, at the revolution, exceeded *thirty thousand.*"

"Says Woods' History of the General Baptists, page 145: "It is almost certain that the General Baptists were then (1689) more numerous than the other section of the body, their numbers being supposed to have exceeded *thirty thousand.*"

Both General and Particular Baptists seem to have prospered more, prior to 1689, when William III. was declared king, than they did subsequently. On this subject Woods' History of the General Baptists, page 145, remarks: "William III. was declared king Feb. 13th, 1689. A law was soon enacted in favor of dissenters, which has generally been distinguished by the appellation of the "Act of Toleration."

By this act a legal termination was put to the persecution of non-confomists; some respect was shown for the rights of conscience, and dissenters obtained liberty to worship God without exposing themselves to civil penalties; and again on page 146 "for some years after the cessation of persecution, some of the churches continued to flourish; in many others it soon became evident that the leaven of corruption was operating." Mr. Cramp in his excellent History of Baptists, bears evidence of the correctness of this statement, and says, on page 484:

"The Baptist (General and Particular) interest in England fell into decline after the revolution. Liberty did not bring life. The sunshine had for a time a withering effect," and again on page 500: "The backsliding and coldness had effected all religious communities in England," and on page 496, in accounting for this decline of Baptist sentiment in England, he quotes from Robinson: "Christian liberty," exclaimed Mr. Robinson, "thou favorite offspring of heaven, thou first born of Christianity, I saw the wise and pious servants of God nourish thee in their houses and cherish thee in their bosoms; I saw them lead thee into pubic view; all good men hailed thee; the generous British Commons caressed and praised thee and lead thee into an upper house, and there—there didst thou expire in the holy laps of spiritual laws." Now for the cause of the decline among the General Baptists; as I propose discussing their decline, especially, defering that of the Particular Baptists until I shall take up their history. I will refer you to what Cramps History of Baptists says:

"A sad degeneracy had taken place among the General Baptists (called Free Will Baptists, in the United States) who, as the reader is doubtless aware, adopt Arminian views, the Particular Baptists being denominated Calvinists. Arminianism had crept in among them and with it certain other errors. The loss of life followed the obscuration of light. Anti-evangelical sentiments and practices prevailed to such an alarming extent that the sound hearted of that denomination felt the necessity of withdrawment. They peaceably withdrew in the year 1770 and formed the New Connection of General Baptists.

The blessing of God followed the movement. The new body thus constituted, is now the General Baptist denomination, the Arianised churches having for the most part, fallen into Socinianism or become extinct."

This is a correct statement, and no General Baptists feels disposed to deny it. See Taylor's History of the General Baptists, vol. 1, page 463; Wood's History of the General Baptists, page 148.

I have given you this bit of history, to show you that the formation of the New connection of General Baptists was a matter of necessity and also to introduce the facts relative to the formation of this body, and to vindicate the General Baptists in the charge sometimes made against them by some authors and other parties, who have only partially studied their history, that they are not sound on the doctrine of the "*Trinity*."

Now for the organization of the New Connection. We have seen how Smith's church was organized at Amsterdam. How the most of the English Baptist churches were formed. We have glanced at the approval of this method by Crosby, Tombes, Spilsbury and Benedict, a method once acknowledged by very nearly all Baptist historians and scholars, to be both right and valid. We have also noticed the decline of the General Baptists, and its causes.

In speaking of this period and decline of the Baptistic sentiments, Wood's History of the General Baptists, page 158, remarks:

"It was unquestionable the most unevangelical period that had ever occured in this country since the reformation. At this gloomy crisis three facts present themselves to our notice, which bear indications of Divine Providence—the mission of Wesley and Whitefield to arouse the nation from its spiritual slumbers—the efforts of Andrew Fuller to reclaim the Particular Baptist churches from the errors of Antinomianism, under the influence of which they were fast declining—and the rise of individuals from apparent obscurity to receive and perpetuate the sentiments peculiar to the General Baptists, at the time when the scriptural character of the original body seemed almost at the point of extinction."

A number of persons in Leicestershire were awakened under the preaching of Wesley and Whitefield.

In 1745 they organized a church, consisting of only *seven* members. Of this church, says Taylor's History of the General Baptists, vol. 1, page 17:

"Their enemies, indeed, called them Methodists, but they had never been properly connected with that party and disapproved of several things in their doctrine and discipline;" on page 18: "They called themselves Independents."

Says Wood's History of the General Baptists, page 165: "Some of the preachers at an early period, entertained doubts on the subject of baptism; at length discovering from the Scriptures that immersion was the proper mode of baptism, they resolved to adopt it. A large tub was brought into the meeting-house in which, for several years they immersed their infants. * * * * The friends at Barton examined the Scriptures on the subject and found that the New Testament furnished no authority for the baptism of infants, but enjoined baptism on those who professed to repent and believe. After much consultation, it was agreed that Mr. Donisthrope should baptize Mr. Kendrick and then Mr. Kendrick should baptize him, after which they should unite in administering the ordinance to the rest of their associates.

"This was accordingly done, about the middle of November, 1755, when between sixty and seventy thus solemny devoted themselves to the service of the Savior." And again, on page 168: "The cause spread over a large tract of country. * * * After frequent discussions, it was agreed (1760) that the body should be divided into five distinct and independent churches, each having its own pastors or teachers. These prosperous churches united, in 1770, with the more orthodox part of the old connection of General Baptists, who had left their brethren on account of differences on the question of the Trinity, and the union of these two bodies formed the new connection of General Baptists. Their first association was held in London, on June 7th, 1770."

Continues Wood's History, on page 177: "After solemn prayer to God for His direction and blessing, a union was formed under the designation of 'The New Connection of General Baptists, formed in 1770, with a design to revive experimental religion or primitive Christianity, in faith and practice.' * * Six articles of religion were proposed, agreed upon and signed, as a declaration of their views on those points which had been the chief subjects of difference between them and the other body."

As we have no disposition to again, at this juncture, introduce the historic evidence of the right of this church to begin or restore immersion, but as we have seen already, it was an established principle among Protestants, and in particular among Baptists, "that an unbaptized person might warrantably baptize, and so begin a reformation," we shall now pass to the consideration of another subject.

I now call your attention to a custom among General Baptists, of the laying on of hands on baptized believers. If my memory serves me correctly, it was introduced among them between the years 1640 and 1650. The necessity of this imposition of hands was pleaded for from their interpretation of Hebrews, vi., 1-2.

Taylor's History of the General Baptists, vol. 1, page 410, says of this custom among them: "This doctrine spread rapidly and very extensively, but never appears to have been adopted by all the General Baptists."

I have introduced this doctrine of the General Baptists of England for the purpose of showing you that this custom was transmitted to the General Baptists of America by them, and we will, when we come to examine the history of these people in America, see that they, from the fact of this custom, were called Six-Principle, or General the Baptists, while

Particular Baptists, in contra-distinction from them and this custom, were called Five-Principle Baptists. Bear this in mind, for we shall speak of these principles as separating the American Baptists, and to show their true origin and descent, that the Six-Principle Baptists descended from the General Baptists, while the Five-Principle Baptists descended from the Particular Baptists of England.

The General Baptists of England, like the Particular Baptists, adopted several confessions of faith. While the confession adopted in Amsterdam, Holland, taught a possibility of apostasy and a possible salvation to all, some others indicate that the General Baptists of some localities had swung somewhat to the Calvinists on these principles, though the greater number seem to have adhered tenaciously to first principles.

COMMUNION AMONG THE GENERAL BAPTISTS.

We will again take up the communion question among the General Baptists. We have seen from Crosby's History of Baptists, vol. 2, appendix page 4, article 11 of the Smith confession, that the communion and baptism should be regularly kept up in all churches, to be dispensed by lay members in the absence of the pastors; and in article 15: "That the Lord's Supper is the outward manifestation of the spiritual communion between Christ and the faithful, mutually to declare his death until he come."

Orchard's History of Baptists, vol. 2, page 262, in speaking of the General Baptists, quotes Mosheim, vol. 2, page 218, in the following language: "There is," says Mosheim, 'much latitude in their system of religious doctrines, which consists in such vague and general principles as renders their communion accessible to Christians of almost all denominations. Accordingly they tolerate, and, in fact, receive among them of every sect, even Socinians and Arians; *nor do they reject any from their communion who profess themselves Christians, and receive the Holy Scriptures as the source of truth and rule of faith.*"

In following this quotation of Mr. Mosheim, Mr. Orchard willingly or unwilling does the General Baptists an injustice. This injustice is apparent when we come to notice the following, from Mosheim, in the same history of these people, he says:

"*After the manner of the ancient Menonites, they look upon their sect as the only true Christian church and consequently shun, with the most scrupulous caution the communion of all other religious societies.*"

You see these statements are not congenial with each other.

Mosheim had read Mr. Whiston's Memoirs, after he had joined the General Baptists, and consequently founded his first remark (quoted by Orchard) from Whiston's statement

You will perceive that much, or at least a part of these statements refer to receiving into church fellowship persons entertaining opinions not strictly taught or believed by the General Baptists, but yet they do refer to the Lord's Supper and show that the General Baptists were generally liberal on this question. When the question of the laying on of hands was pleaded for as a necessity or prerequisite to communion, they drifted in the direction of close communion but as this principle (laying on of hands) was more fully understood, they became avowed open communionists, and to-day are, perhaps, among the Liberal Baptists, the most free and liberal at the Lord's Table.

For proof of this, I refer you to the resolution passed by their General Association, held at Wisbech, in 1875, which I will now read you:

"On motion of the Rev. S. Cox, it was

"*Resolved*, That in the future, the communion service held during the meeting of the Association be open to all evangelical believers." See General Baptist Year Book, 1875, page 24.

They were soon enabled to cut themselves loose from ritualism and proscriptive principles and adopt the principle set forth by Crosby's History of Baptist, vol. 4, page 420, which says:

"For my own part, I make no scruple to declare, that it is my opinion that no faith ought to be explicitly required, in order to the communion of Christians, considered as such, but what is necessary to denominate a man a Christian."

Yes, the General Baptists drew inspiration from these principles and soon rose above sectarian principles and open communion was the result.

Perhaps you ask me in your minds, as I have said the first church of the General Baptist denomination was organized by John Smith, in 1607, if there were no General Baptists previous to this time? I answer in the affirmative. After stating the leading doctrinal features of the General Baptists, which I hope you have kept in your mind, I will proceed to examine the doctrines of the primitive churches, so as to see how they (the primitive and General Baptist churches) compare with each other. As I prefer particular Baptist proof on this subject I will introduce again, Mr. Crosby, vol. 4, page 407, who says:

"The English Baptists, though they are unhappily disunited, and distinguished by the title of *Generals* and *Particulars*, yet it is the only point I know of wherein they differ from the primitive churches."

IN ENGLAND AND EUROPE. 93

On pages 440-48-49, after giving the opinions of the Gnosties, which are foreign to the Bible, as he thought, he says:

"Where such principles as these are found among men professing Christianity, there are sufficient grounds for separation and distinction and such may deservedly be styled *Antinomians*. But I know of none such among the English Baptists. If they differ about the extent of Christ's death, free-will and the efficay of grace, this is no more than what has been common to the church from the beginning, and at most can be deemed but mental errors, and if they will continue to make distinctions and keep up separate communities thereon, let them remember who said: "A house divided against itself cannot stand."

Inter-communion among the English Baptists (both General and Particular) existed largely in the days of Mr. Crosby, and to-day the Association between them, known as the Baptist Union, welcomes irrespective of denominational peculiarities, all Baptists to the immunities of such an Association, of which we will say more before we are through with the English Baptists.

Again, on pages 414–15–17–18: "In the conduct of the primitive churches, it is observable, that as there ought to be, so there was a mutual intercourse and society fellowship and communion in all useful and regular ways, between their several respective churches, and congregations, being all Christians and believers."

"As to their discipline, though there might be a disagreement in some lesser and inferior points, yet they still retained peace and order, and one church did not imperiously claim and exercise jurisdiction over another, but whatsoever was regularly performed in one church was allowed to be valid and obligatory by all others. Whoever was baptized, ordained or the like, in one church, was not obliged to receive those things *de novo*, if his circumstances, and the Divine Providence should necessitate to be a member of another.

To advance proofs of this concerning baptism is needless, seeing it is well known that the baptism of heretics was valid and never reiterated." Knowing these principles to be largely practiced among both General and Particular Baptists, he delivers himself in the following, page 419: "And thus, my brethren, I hope in the course of this history I have made it appear that you are the only people who closely adhere to the *apostolical practice*, and the practice among the *primitive churches*;" and in the conclusion of his history on the same subject, page 420, he says: "In the happy days of primitive Christianity, the Christians, who were Baptists, were so eminent, above all other sects, for their moderation, the peaceableness of their temper and disposition, and for their mutual love and charity, that the world observed it with astonishment, and the very heathens cried out, with admiration, "*Behold, how they love one another.*"

While a majority of the Particular Baptists in England at the present time practice open communion, they have only returned to the practice of the early churches of Particular Baptists in England; that is in allowing each church to regulate its own affairs. This will the more clearly appear when we give you a quotation from the "Particular Baptists' Confession of Faith," known as the London Confession, adopted in 1689, and subsequently adopted as the Philadelphia Confession. At this assembly in London in 1689, Mr. Crosby says, in vol. 3, page 246:

"There were more than one hundred congregations of them (Particular Baptists) assembled together to consult of proper ways and means to advance the glory of God and the well being of their churches."

The same author, in the same volume, says, on page 249, that they declare in the following words:

"We disclaim all manner of superiority or supremacy over the churches, and that we have no authority or power to prescribe or impose anything upon the faith or practice of any of the churches of Christ.

And on page 250 they further declare:

"That in those things wherein our church differs from another church, in their principles or practices in point of communion, that we can not, shall not impose upon any particular church therein, but leave every church to their own liberty to walk together as they have received of the Lord."

These declarations have the true ring of Baptist principles, and may be read with profit by every lover of religious liberty and church independence.

Therefore, it appears that the authority exercised over the Baptist churches in America by the associations, is an innovation on Baptist principles and a departure from the practice of the early churches of English Baptists.

Now, my Christian friends, it is to be regretted that the United Baptists of the United States have so far apostatized from this original love and unity, which was so abundant among the primitive Baptists, and after rejecting the Calvinistical creed of their ancestors (the Particular Baptists), claim to be the only true church, and refuse to commune with the other Baptists at the Lord's table. But the General Baptists, as you see from these quotations, stick to primitive principles in regard to the *Lord's Supper* and *Baptism*. So you see from this the General Baptists are, in *principle*, what the primitive churches were.

Yes, in principle, and as a General Baptist denomination, we claim to be just what the Apostolic churches were.

Every Baptist historian recognizes the fact that the Baptist churches which existed prior to the organization of the first Particular Baptist church in London, Sept. 12th, 1633, were what would now be called General Baptists, and it is a most singular fact that Orchard, Graves, Ford, Ray, and all other Baptists who insist on the necessity of succession in order to valid baptism, include, in their line of succession, both General and Open Communion Baptists, who lived previous to 1633, and many who have lived since that time, bearing our name and holding to our principles of *soul liberty* and *free communion*. Yes, men who, if living to-day—notwithstanding they claim them as their ancestors—they would not commune with them at the Lord's table.

Yes, my General Baptist brothers and sisters, while we attach no importance to the theory of succession in order to the valid dispensation of the ordinances which Jesus gave his people, still we may console ourselves and rejoice to know that we have a regular historic line from the primitive churches down through the Baptist martyrs of old, in point of principle and not in name. In the language of Benedict, page 73: "We have good reasons to believe that Baptist sentiments have lived in every age, from the Apostles to the present time." Not the United or General Baptist denominations—but Baptist sentiments—for we, as denominations, are comparatively young.

In order to understand how to trace the line of the descent of these two denominations, and in order to know which has the best claim to antiquity, we must understand the names which were generally applied to them, respectively, and by them accepted. The Generals were called Arminians, and the Particulars, Calvinists.

I have already referred you to Crosby's History of Baptists, vol 1, page 173. In order to understand, I will repeat it: "Those that followed the *Calvinistical* scheme of doctrines, and from the principle point therein *particular election*, have been called 'Particular' Baptists; and those that have professed the Arminian or remonstrant tenets, and have also, from their chief of doctrines—universal redemption—been called 'General' Baptists."

With this explanation of Crosby's, I pass to a quotation from Benedict, to show the correctness of my statements. Page 325: "It is, however, very well known by the community at home and abroad, that, from a very early period, they have been divided into two parties, which have been denominated General and Particular; which differ from each other mainly

IN ENGLAND AND EUROPE. 99

in their doctrinal sentiments—the Generals being Arminians, and the others Calvinists."

With these definitions we are prepared to advance in our investigations. We will first see which of the two denominations is the older, and then we will look after the sentiments of those Baptists preceding the organization of either of the denominations. We have referred you frequently to the different Baptist authors who fix the date of the first General Baptist church in Amsterdam, Holland, in 1607.

I will now read you from an official report of the gathering at Kittering, to celebrate the fiftieth year from the formation of the Missionary Society, under whose auspices Cary and others, of the first Baptist missionaries were sent to India. Of this report Benedict says, page 304:

"As the narrative was published as an official document in connection with the doings of the Jubilee, the presumption is, that its statements were approved by the whole denomination."

Now what does it say in reference to the age of the two denominations? Let us see.

"The first regularly organized Baptist Church of which we possess any regular account, is dated from 1607, and was formed in London, (Amsterdam) by a Mr. Smith, who had been a clergyman in the Church of England. It was formed on the principles of the General Baptists. In the year 1633 the first Particular Baptist church was formed in London under Mr. Spilsbury."

This statement, which Mr. Benedict said was *official*, was made at a Particular Baptist gathering. It cannot be otherwise than correct.

With these facts from creditable authors, I will give you the statement of Mr. Cramp in his History of Baptists, page 302, which is as follows:

"In the year 1633 an event occurred which requires specific notice. This was the formation of the

Particular or Calvanistic Baptist Church in England. Hitherto the Baptists favored the Arminian views."

This settles the question of the age of the two denominations and conclusively shows that all Baptists in England, especially, were General or Arminian. But let us see if we have no further proof on this subject. Were these sentiments confined to England? We think not. Let us see. Benedict, in his History of Baptists, says:

"It is evident that the Dutch and German Baptists have, generally speaking, been of an Arminian cast."

But is this all? Let us hear Cramp, on this subject, page 233:

"But they could not put down the Baptists, who grew and flourished, in spite of them. Congrega—

tions were discovered in Bocking, in Essex, at Feversham, in Kent and other places. Their number must have been considerable, as four ministers were arrested when the discovery was made. The names of the ministers were Humphrey Midleton, Henry Hart, George Broadbridge and ——— Cole. At the time of their apprehension they were assembled at Bocking. Besides the ministers, about sixty members of the congregation were assembled. Their christian organization appears to have been correct and complete. They met regularly for worship and instruction, the ordinances of the gospel were attended to, contributions were made for the support of the cause, and so great were their zeal that those who lived in Kent were known to go occasionally into Essex to meet their brethren there—a journey of fourscore miles—which, in the sixteenth century, was no small undertaking. When they were brought into the ecclesiastical court they were examined on forty-six articles and charged with Pelagianism and other errors. Their religious sentiments, or those imputed to them, would now be called Arminian."

Continuing his narative of these people, he says, on page 242:

"We cannot but regret that so little is known of this interesting band of disciples. Strype asserts that they 'were the first that made separation from the reformed Church of England, having gathered congregations of their own.' As they confessed that they had not communed in the parish churches for two years, their separation must have taken place about the year 1548, which was before the Presbyterians or Independents were known in England. The Baptists were the vanguard of the Protestant dissenters in that country."

The quotation is lengthy but interesting on many accounts.

1st. It shows us that these people in sentiment, were General or Arminian Baptists.

2d. It shows that they were the first to separate from the establised Church of England.

Orchard's History of Baptists, vol. 2, pages 204-5 says:

"It is probable that many Baptists were in Kent, and that the General Baptist church did exist at this time, (1548) at Canterberry, with the church at Eythorn." "Among the Baptist, in Kent, stands the name of Joan Baucher.

Ford's Origin of Baptists, page 46, in speaking of Joan Boucher, or Joan of Kent, says: 'She was a Baptist, a member of a Baptist church then existing at Canterbury, and which exists to this day and hour."

This, he said, in tracing the succession of the Baptists (United Baptists.) For an elucidation of the facts in regard to the religious opinion of these people, I will now read you what Wood's History of the General Baptists says upon this subject; and as he is an English author, he is entitled to great credit upon this particular subject. In speaking of these same people of whom we have been reading from Cramp's History of Baptists in Kent and Essex, he says, on pages 98-9: "Congregations were discovered at Feversham, in Kent, and Bocking, Essex, and in other towns and villages." Four of their teachers, with a considerable number of the people, were seized. Mr. Humphrey Middleton was the most eminent of these ministers. He appears to have been in prison until the end of Edward's reign. Yet the Baptists became very numerous. Five hundred are said to have resided in one town. The clergy endeavored to check their progress by publications on baptism, but the Baptists replied that "children are of Christ's kingdom without baptism." Luke xviii, 16.

"As books did not silence them, a commission was issued and a Protestant inquisition established, under the especial direction of Cranmer. Joan of Kent, supposed to have been a member of the General Baptist church at Canterbury, or Eythorne, fell a victim to the misguided clergy." It is computed that during three years, "two hundred and seventy persons were burnt to death at the stake, besides those who were punished by imprisonments, fines and confiscations."

Taylor's History of the General Baptists, vol. 1, page 57, says:

"Tradition says that Joan of Kent was a General Baptist, and a member of a General Baptist church which, at this early period, existed at Canterbury." Ivimy's History of Baptists, page 138.

These people, with their church organization, did not belong to the General Baptist denomination, because, as we have seen, there were neither General or Particular Baptist denominations at this time, but they were, in principle, what the General Baptist denomination was when organized. And we find the church at Eythorn afterwards belonged to the General Baptist denomination. John Knott, the pastor of this church, assisted at the formation of the new connection of General Baptists in 1770. This church afterwards embraced the Calvinistical doctrines and joined the Particular Baptists.

Now we have heard these several authors, and they are a unit on our side of the question. They bore abundant evidence that those professing Baptistic principles were what would now be called General or Arminian Baptists. While we believe their church organizations were broken up, under the proclamation of Elizabeth during the latter part of her reign, which commanded all heretics to depart the land, to which we have already referred, we have no doubt but they returned during the reign of King James I., and reorganized many of their churches.

We find many of these churches afterwards in the General Baptist denomination, and bearing their denominational name. This is, I suppose, why authors of church histories have called them General Baptist churches prior to their union with the General Baptist denomination. And here, perhaps, is the point at which Mr. Ray, in his Succession, finds that the General Baptists received their baptism from another source than John Smith and his church, with their "informal" and "lay" baptism.

So Joan of Kent, with her numerous brothers and sisters in the gospel, were, in principle, General Baptists. But this is not all. I have said the General Baptists were in historic line with the Baptist martyrs of old. Now, if we are to credit the various Baptist authors from whom I have been quoting, we will find that we are inevitably driven at once to the conclusion that William Sawtree, who was the first to suffer death in England, and Edward Wightman, the last, for their religious opinions, were both General Baptists. Orchard's History of Baptists, vol. 2, pages 148-252. Edward Wightman was a member of the General Baptist church which Smith and Helwisse organized. He was a near relative to the Wightmans of America, who were General Baptists.

Time would fail us to speak, in particular, of the different martyrs among the General Baptists. Yes, my friends, they were numerous. They suffered death in its most horrible forms rather than abjure their religious principles.

There are others of whom I will here speak. Says Benedict's History of Baptists, page 327:

"Among the most distinguished ministers of this order in early times, the General Baptists mention Smith, Helwisse, Lamb, Denne, the Jeffrys, Barbar, Grantham, Russell, Gosnold, Plant, Ives, James, DuViel; and at later periods, their men of eminence have been Gale, Emlyn, Whiston, the friend of Sir Isaac Newton, of Lord Chancellor King, and of Queen Caroline, wife of George I.; James Foster, eulogized by Pope for his eloquence as a preacher; Toulmin, commentator of Neal's History of the Puritans; Dan. Taylor, John Evans, author of a work of great currency on religious denominations; J. G. Pike, of Derby, (yet living) Secretary of their Foreign Missionary Society, and author of several most excellent treatises widely circulated both in England and in our own country." John Milton, the poet, was a General Baptist. John Gosnold, of whom we have spoken, was a true friend of Hansard Knollys, and was the most eloquent divine of his day, his congregations in London numbering three thousand.

But in reference to succession, I will, in conclusion, present you with the theory of the General Baptists on this subject, and will read you from Taylor's History of the General Baptists, page 1, for proof. He says:

"A General Baptist who understands the true principles of his profession, does not esteem it necessary to trace his tenets through the several ages of the church. He is persuaded—however early and however generally the contrary opinion may have prevailed—that those doctrines which distinguish him from other professors of Christianity are expressly taught and enjoined in the grand commission which the Adorable Head of the Church gave to his Apostles immediately before his taking his seat at the right hand of God."

This is sufficient evidence to all. Now we have proven, as we conceive, among others the following facts:

1. The General Baptist churches are, in point of principle—not in uninterrupted succession—one with the apostolic or primitive churches.

2. The General Baptists place no kind of reliance on uninterrupted succession, to prove the correctness of their position, but that those doctrines which distinguish them from other Christians are taught and enjoined in the Scriptures—yet they are in line with those ancient churches.

3. The General Baptist denomination is twenty-six years older than the Particular Baptist denomination —the former having been organized in 1607, the latter in 1633.

4. Prior to the organization of the first Particular Baptist church in 1633, in London, all Christians professing baptistic principles in England were what were called Arminian or General Baptists, which is equally true of other countries.

5. That open or inter-communion, among all Baptists, both General and Particular, in ancient days, was the general rule, and close communion the exception.

6. That the General and Free Will Baptist churches of America are the legitimate offspring of the General Baptists of England and Europe, and they of the original or primitive churches, in point of principles and practice.

CHAPTER II.

EARLY HISTORY IN THE UNITED STATES.

In our pursuit of knowledge concerning General Baptists in England, Mr. Adam Taylor's History of the General Baptists was the first that gave us anything like a connected history of these people. Subsequently, we obtained the history of J. H. Wood, which fully corroborates everything that Mr. Taylor says, and fully agrees with the detached fragments gathered from many other histories. In pursuing the several Baptist histories of the United States, we found the frequent mention of Mr. Richard Knight's History of the early General Baptists in America.

This work was diligently sought after by the writer for several years. Meanwhile other General Baptists in the West were looking after our history, and finally, through the indefatigable efforts of Jeff. Holeman, M. D., formerly of Clayville, Kentucky, but now of Evansville, Indiana, Knight's History was obtained of Rev. A. H. Heath, of Providence, Rhode Island. This work takes up the history of the

General Baptists, or the principles of Christianity promulgated through the General Baptists, from the days of the Apostles to the beginning of the present century, or 1827. In doing this Mr. Knight condenses Taylor's History of the English General Baptists into the space of about two hundred and forty pages.

He then takes up the rise and progress of the General Baptists in the eastern part of the United States, as organized by Roger Williams, in 1637, and traces them on down to 1827. Mr. Knight had also heard of some General Baptists in Virginia, North and South Carolina, but of these he could gather no particular information, only Elder Jno. Comer, a member of the same association of which Mr. Knight belonged, had met one Paul Palmer, a minister, belonging to the Kehukee Association of General Baptists, in North Carolina, who reported that said Association consisted of twenty churches and eighteen ministers.

During the late civil war, however, ——— McClure, a son of Brother Joseph P. McClure, of Princeton, Indiana, while in the South, found the history of the said Kehukee Association, written by Burkitt and Reed, which brings the history of these people down to 1794, when most of them were transformed nto a Calvinistic or Regular Baptist Association.

We will now briefly notice the history of the General Baptists in the New England States and then give an account of the Kehukee Association in North Carolina and then pass to the history of the General Baptists in the West, as organized by Elder Benoni Stinson and others.

"The oldest Baptist churches in the United States were General Baptist in sentiment and usuage."

This is the general expression of historians in America. Mr. Benedict says:

"They were generally inclined to those doctrinal sentiments which in England, would have denominated them General Baptists."

Mr. Wood says: "They were unanimous in rejecting the Calvinist doctrines and were, in fact, a body of General Baptist churches," and as such had correspondence with the General Baptists of England, in 1824.

Mr. R. Knight, Pastor of the Scituate church, in Rhode Island, and their historian, denominate them General or six-principle Baptists. He also connects their history with the English General Baptists, and blends their history with the General Baptists of North and South Carolina and Virginia, who were organized and pastored by General Baptist ministers direct from London, England.

As a further and final proof of those early churches

of General Baptists in the United States, being the direct descendents of the English General Baptists, we quote from Crosby's History of English Baptists, vol. 1, page 111, in speaking concerning the first settlers in New England says:

"That some of these were Baptists, appears from Mr. Cotton Mather's Ecclesiastical History of New England, where I find the first settlement of the English in this part of America, was in the year 1620."

Speaking of certain pious Non-Conformists who had left England for Holland, and finally come to America in 1620, in vol. 1, page 111, further says:

"Among these, some few were Anti-Pedo-Baptists, so that Anti-Pedo-Baptism is as ancient in those parts as Christianity itself."

These Anti-Pedo-Baptists were, evidently, General Baptists, as it is certain that the Particular Baptists, (at this date, 1620) were not in existence in England, until 1633. Therefore these Anti-Pedo-Baptists could not have been Particular Baptists.

The sixth principle refers to the practice of laying on of hands on the newly-baptized, based on Heb. vi., 1, 2, 3. "This practice," says Mr. Taylor, vol. 1, p. 411, "caused much confusion in England about 1670," and the "imposition of hands on the baptized, as such, appears to have been unknown to the Confessors of 1611. If we credit D'Anvers it was first introduced in 1645 by Frances Cornell into the churches in Bishopsgate street, which afterward removed to White alley. During the protectorate it spread rapidly in various parts of the kingdom. In 1659 it was defended by William Jeffreys in Kent, and in 1660 was inserted in the famous confession presented to the king. In 1672 the churches in Bucks and the neighboring counties introduced it into their creed, and it was held by most of the LincolnshireGeneral Baptists. In London it formed a principle band of union among the five churches, though there were several flourishing societies which opposed the practice. Mr. Griffiths, indeed, quotes the pious Gosnold as an advocate for the practice, but it was not adopted by the church in Paul's Alley. The General Baptists in the west of England, it is probable, did not approve of it, and there were many churches in Lincolnshire who have a decided testimony against making it essential to communion. W. Jeffreys, Thomas Grantham, J. Griffiths plead for the necessity of this barrier between brethren in the seventeenth century.

Mr. Benedict, referring to this question, says:

"The General Baptist churches are not all properly united in one close body any more than the Particulars. Some believe more and some less of the leading maxims of the general creed, and this may be said of all sects and parties whatever."

It does not appear that the practice of laying on of hands ever caused much trouble in the new connection of General Baptists in England. We find nothing of the kind in their confession at the present time. While the first General Baptist churches in the United States were strenuous for laying on of hands, it does not appear that they made it a test of fellowship or essential to communion for a long time, for we find some of these churches practicing open or free communion for upwards of one hundred years after their organization, and at least one, to-wit: the second church in Newport, planted in 1656, has never practiced anything else but open communion. Of the church in Swansea, in Massachusetts, Mr. John Callender, who was one of its pastors, says:

"Union with Christ was the sole ground of their communion with each other, and they were ready to accept of, receive to and hold church communion with all such as, in the judgment of charity, were fellow members with Christ Jesus, though differing in such controversial points as are not absolutely and essentially necessary to salvation."

From the remarks of Mr. Backus and several other historians, we conclude that the most of those early churches endorsed the above sentiments as set forth by Mr. Callender.

Of these early churches, historians generally do not give us any particular account of but a very few of them. Mr. Wood says, on page 234, that: "In 1824 they had fifty-seven able, laborious and useful preachers. The publications which were issued prove the authors to have been men of real talent and of considerable literary attainment."

Mr. Knight, who was not writing a general history, but giving an account of the General Baptist churches in the early history of the United States, gives us a very clear account of thirty-seven of these churches, which were associated together in the same bonds of union.

In Rhode Island, Mr. Knight mentions, "Providence, settled in 1637; New Port, in 1656; North Kingstown, 1665; South Kingston, 1680; Smithfield, 1706; Sictuat, 1725; Warwick, 1725; Richmond, 1725; Cumberland, ——; East Greenwich, 1743; Fulling Mill, 2nd., 1785; Gloucester or Burrilville, 1749; Cranston, 1764; Coventry, 1768; Foster, 1780; Gloucester, 2nd., 1780; Cranston, 2nd., 1816;

In Massachusetts, Dartmoth, 1684; Swansea, 1693; Rehobath, 1732; Rehobath, 2nd., 1753; Cheshire, 1771; Lanesbourough, 1772; Rehobath, 3rd., 1789; Springfield, 1796.

In Connecticut, Groten, 1705; New London, 1625; Thompson, 1750.

In New York, New York City, 1724; Otsego, 1792; Amsterdam, 1807; Deuryter, 1811; Willitt, 1823: Brookfield, 1810.

In Pennsylvania, Abbington, 1821.

In Vermont, Shaftsborough, 1768.

In Virginia, Burley, 1715; Surry, 1725.

Mr. Knight then mentions eighteen churches in North Carolina, an account of which will be given at another time.

Those early churches began to associate themselves together in a yearly meeting, about the close of the sixteenth century, and as early as 1729 it consisted of twelve churches and eighteen ordained ministers and two hundred and fifty communicants.

Mr. Backus, in his history, says that John Comer, who was a member of this yearly meeting, and who had a manuscript history of those people, represents that all of those eighteen ministers held to general atonement.

Mr. Benedict agrees with Mr. Backus and believes that they were all of the General persuasion, and Mr. Knight bears these authors out in this belief. All of those writers had access to Mr. Comer's manuscript.

"Besides these," says Mr. Knight, "There were at that time but four Baptist churches in New England: viz., one in Boston, one in Swansen, and one in Newport, that held to the Calvinistic doctrine, and one in Westerly, and a few persons in New Port called Sabbatarian Baptists."

In 1769 they concluded to alter the name of their yearly meeting, and call it an Association, but made no change in the rules or regulations. At this date the Association "consisted of the following churches, viz: Providence, New Port, Swansea, North Kingstown, Richmond, Dartmoth, Rehobath, Groton, New London, Smithfield, Scituate, Warwick, South Kingston, Cumberland, East Greenwich, Groton, Coventry, and perhaps some others."

These churches are represented by Mr. Knight, as being in a prosperous condition from 1764 until 1774 or until about the beginning of the trouble that caused the Revolutionary war, on account of which the annual Association ceased to meet. However, about the same time, 1774, "a number of Elders and Messengers, delegated from said churches, met in General Conference, at Elder Samuel Winson's meeting house, in Johnston, and agreed to constitute and form themselves into a semi-annual General Meeting. "Most of said churches appointed delegates and united with them, and in a short time this Yearly Meeting numbered about fourteen churches." In 1788 they agreed to hold but one General Meeting in each year. In 1802 the Yearly Meeting consisted of twenty-one churches. In 1807 they organized Amsterdam church, in New York.

The prosperity of these people in New York, was so great that in 1813 they were set off into a new Association or Conference.

Mr. Benedict, in speaking of these people, page, 508, says:

"It is now (1813) eighty-four years since this great Association, as it was then esteemed, was held. Very considerable changes have taken place in most of the churches of which it was then composed, but the same body, on the same plan of doctrine and discipline, still exist under the name of the Rhode Island Yearly Meeting. This meeting, on account of its making the laying on of hands, a term of communion and its inclination to the Arminian system of doctrines has no connection with any of the neighboring churches. It contains thirteen churches, twelve ministers and over eleven hundred members; eight of these churches are in this State, (Rhode Island) the others are in Massachusetts and New York."

It appears that at the organization of the semi—

annual yearly meeting, in 1774, that not all of the churches united with them. Providence now (1871) belongs to the old Warren Association. At just what time she united with that body I am not prepared to say, and of the other thirty-six churches of which Mr. Knight gives us an account, eleven had then (1827) become extinct. Four others were then in a very low state, two had become Calvanistic, and one had gone to the Free Will Baptists, which, in 1827, would leave them eighteen working churches. This old body is now (1882) still extant.

It appears that about the time of the organization of this semi general meeting, in 1774, that some of the churches had become so strenuous and presistant in the doctrine of laying on of hands, that they made it a barrier to the communion.

In 1771 the Richmond church entered into an agreement not to commune with or admit any members that did not hold strictly to the doctrine of laying on of hands on the newly baptized." Knight, page 263.

When this old body or yearly meeting had become so strenuous in this doctrine as to plunge herself into close-communion, Mr. Bachus says, on pages 414 and 415:

"The churches which held to mixed (or open) communion began a yearly meeting in 1785, under the name of the Groton Conference, and it now (1795) includes the Baptist churches of Dartmoth, New Bedford, two in Rehobath, two in North Kingstown, one in South Kingston, New Shoreham, two in Westerly and one in each of the towns of Groton, Stonington, Lyon, Saybrook, Sutton, Preston and Canterbury, extending over part of three States."

In 1785 a majority of the Groton Association; consisting of about forty churches, located in Connecticut, Rhode Island and Massachusetts, held to open communion and general atonement. But the pressure was so great from the restrictive brethren that most of them afterward limited their communion to members of regular Baptist churches. From that time to the present the close-communion party have zealously pushed their sentiments while the liberal have inclined to make concessions for the sake of union and peace. As a consequence, the restrictive party absorbed "almost the entire element of liberal or open-communion Baptists."

But the leaven has been constantly working and now the major part of the Baptists in this country believe that Christ made an atonement for all men; that man is endowed with the power of choice, and is under obligations to choose life and live. On the communion question they are greatly changed. Very few churches make an occasional communion of their members with Pedo-Baptists a disciplinary offense; many of them quietly admit Pedo Baptists to to the Lord's Supper in their churches, hundreds of their ministers give no invitation to the Supper because they regard an invitation to those of the same faith and order as an unwarranted exclusion of others. A respectable and an increasing number of ministers are open communionists." Baptist Union, January 14, 1873.

We have given the above to show that notwithstanding nearly all of the early churches or organizations of General Baptists in America have been absorbed by the Calvinistic and Close Communion Baptists that our principles of liberty have not been lost. But to-day the great majority of the Baptists in America are teaching the doctrine of a general atonement, which doctrine, in the early history of the English Baptists was the distinguishing features between the General and Particular or Calvinistic Baptists, and that open communion, which was the practice of the earliest Baptist churches in America, is a fundamental principle of General Baptists everywhere at the present time, and the increasing tendency in the whole Baptist family in America, to open communion is such, at this time, that if each individual church influenced by the ministry was allowed a vote on this question an overwhelming majority, would decide in favor of open communion.

The Rev. J. D. Beugless in an address "delivered at the opening of the Central Association of Baptists at Buffalo, New York, August 27th, 1872," on "Fundamental Baptist Principles and their History." In speaking in reference to the "Groton Union Association," of which we have been speaking he says:

"From these churches there migrated a large number of Baptist families and settled in Western New York, where they have ever since steadfastly maintained their glorious principles of religious liberty, fellowshiping at the Table of the Lord all those who have fellowship with Christ, their Head, regardless of difference on questions not absolutely essential to salvation."

Since the above article appeared in the Golden Rule, in the spring of 1881, some exceptions have been taken to my statement in regard to the Free Communion Baptists being the direct descendants of of the Old General Baptists in New England. Since then I have taken considerable pains to look into this matter and I am thoroughly convinced that my previous statements are correct.

It will be observed that the Groton Union Conference was originally organized on the open communion element of the Old General Baptists of New

England, and that the two churches at Westerly, Rhode Island, and the one at Stonington, Connecticut, were members of that Association, and Mr. A. D. Williams, D. D., author of the Memorials of the Free Communion Baptists, fully corroborates my statement. In speaking in reference to their origin, page 20-21, he says:

"Near the middle of the eighteenth century a church was organized in the town of Westerly, Rhode Island, and on the hill above the present village of Westerly, for a long time better known as ' Pawcatuck Bridge.' The church was really Baptist, but its members so strongly sympathized with the Separates that its first Pastor, Oliver Babcock, was ordained April 4th, 1750, by David Sprague, a Baptist Minister, in connection with Solomon Paine, a Pedo-Baptist or Separate Minister."

Now, it must be remembered, that David Sprague belonged to the General Baptists at that time, but as a Pedo-Baptist Minister, assisted at the ordination, this does not exactly prove my point.

But you will bear in mind that Benajah Corpe, who was the founder of the Free Communion Baptists, was a member of the General Baptist church at Westerly, Rhode Island, and moved to Stephentown, New York, probably, about 1780, and began to preach, and through his influence a number were converted and desired to be organized into a church. Accordingly, Elder Simeon Crandall, who was Pastor of the Stonington church, in Connecticut, which was a General Baptist church, together "with a member of Elder Babcock's church, (in Westerly, Rhode Island,) being sent from their churches from home," did, on the 13th of September, 1783, organize the first Free Communion Baptist church in New York. And about two years after, or October 15th, 1785, this same Elder, Simeon Crandall, and an Elder Davis, from the Stonington church, in Connecticut, ordained Elder Corpe. See Memorials of Free Communion Baptists, pp. 26-53.

These facts are also fully corroborated by Mr. Bachus, and the Rev. J. D. Bengless.

Mr. Williams, in his Memorials of the Free Communion Baptists, does not seem to fully comprehend the fact that the Westerly and Stonington churches were General Baptist churches, and says:

"An impression somewhat extensively prevails in New York that the Stonington and Westerly churches were 'Free-Willers.' It is, however, sufficiently certain that the prevailing sentiment of the churches of the Groton Union Conference, including those of Westerly and Stonington, were Calvinistic. There was, indeed, considerable diversity of belief on this point among individuals, and there were, probably, times when a large number, if not a majority, of some of the churches were strongly tinctured with Arminian sentiments. This appears to have been the case with the Westerly, and probably, also, with the Stonington church at the time Mr. Corpe moved to New York," but he admits that those Arminian tenets may have been derived from those Old General Baptist churches. See pp. 23-24.

It is proper here to state that the probabilities amount to almost a certainty, that notwithstanding the original churches in the Groton Union Conference were General Baptists. That many of the Separate or Pedo-Baptist churches, originating from the Whitefield revivals, which subsequently became Separate Baptist churches and were strongly tinctured with Calvinism, also became members of the Groton Union Conference, which took pace under the Old Union, in 1785, "the basis of which was that the preaching of a general atonement or particular redemption should be no bar to fellowship.

With this explanation the reader can better understand the condition of affairs in the Graton Union Conference at the time of the organization of the Free Communion Baptists in New York.

After Mr. Corpe's ordination, in 1785, he continued faithfully preaching the gospel, the church continued to grow and other ministers were ordained, such as Nicholas Northrup, March 20th, 1793; Geo. Elliot, February 6th, 1794; Cary Rogers, April 9th, 1795; John Howard, December 3d, 1795; John Strait, ———; Thomas Tolman, (who had been a soldier in Burgoyne's army and may be termed the somnambulistic preacher, because he sometimes preached in his sleep), October, 1796, and John Wilson, 1797; And, says Mr. Williams:

"We have now reached what may be regarded as the close of the first period in the history of the denomination. It has existed about thirteen years and a half and consists of seven ministers, nine churches, with one, and only one, house of worship, the 'Log Meeting House,' of the third Stephentown church, and probably about five hundred communicants."

"Hitherto everything had centered at Stephentown. But a change soon took place. New and modifying influences arose and additional, and somewhat different characteristics were developed." See William's Mem., pp. 82-83.

In 1802, these people engaged in a great revival, and another in 1808, and another in 1812. Other ministers of influence had been raised up among them and they began to hold yearly meetings as early as

1802 and probably earlier, and in 1825 they had two yearly meetings. In 1835 they organized a General Conference. In the meantime churches had been planted in Pennsylvania and Canada, and considerable prosperity followed the labors of the whole fraternity. Many drawbacks and discouragements to some extent retarded their progress, but still they moved forward and success followed their labors. In 1820 these people numbered 1400. In 1840 they numbered about 3000. Mr. Williams says:

"Considering that this denomination in the then wilderness country, and that its ministers had none of them enjoyed the advantages of the schools or of any considerable culture, this is a gratifying result, and manifests that it possessed many elements of christian vigor and efficiency."

You will observe that this was fifty-seven years after their first church was organized. If these results were gratifying to our Free Communion Baptist brethren, it certainly ought to be a matter of great encouragement to General Baptists to know that just fifty-seven years after the organization of their first church they number nearly 13,000 members. Mr. Williams, speaking further of these members, says:

"Neither was there any one of these ministers especially endowed as an organizer or a leader. They led men to God and organized churches."

But there was no one who had the peculiar gifts to use these materials of denominational power in the most effective way. One man, gifted, especially, as a master builder, would have made the denomination occupy a much larger place in the public eye, and would have led it forward to become a much larger numerical and actual force."

But about this time (1840) these people began to take advanced steps in education, and in a few years after, or in 1844, established Whitstown Seminary, which has proved of incalculable value to the Free Baptist cause in the United States. They also soon after engaged in mission enterprises and assisted in sending the first Free Will Baptist missionary to the heathen. After a correspondence of several years, the Free Baptists united with the Free Will Baptists (North) in October, 1841, while the general conference was in session at Topsham, Mass.; and, says Mr. Williams:

"Since that time, these Free or Free Communion Baptists have remained a contented part of the Free Will Baptist denomination, and nearly all (except historical) traces of their separate origin and denominational life have long since disappeared. These people engage in supporting all the general enterprises of the Free Will Baptists, and at the same time cultivate their own distinctive field where they first planted churches."

We have been informed that the Free Communion Baptist element now constitute about one-half of the Free Will Baptists' general conference. Rev. G. H. Ball, D.D., of Buffalo, N. Y.; Rev. R ꞏnsom Dunn, Professor of Biblical Theology in Hillsdale college, Mich., and Dr. Bates, President of Ridgeville, college, Ind., are representative men of the Free Communion Baptists. I mention these names because they are well known to General Baptists in the West, having been among us several times. Dr. Ball is a recognized champion of religious liberty. Rev. A. B. Miller, D.D., of Evansville, Ind., a Close Communion Baptist, is the only man of that faith bold enough to meet Dr. Ball in open discussion on the communion question. In that discussion Dr. Ball has given the Open Communion Baptists weapons sufficient to put the enemy to flight upon any ground they may chance to meet. I have mentioned these facts to show that when the old Rhode Island yearly meeting ceased to "maintain those glorious principles of religious liberty," the liberal element was drawn together into the Groton Association, and when that body suffered itself to be driven into close communion its direct descendants came forth in New York under the name of Free Communion Baptists, and are now a growing and an influential people, whose power is becoming very great throughout the United States.

130   EARLY HISTORY

We have shown that the first Baptist churches in America were General Baptists; that the Groton conference was organized from the old Rhode Island yearly meeting, and that the Free Communion Baptists, as they exist to-day, are the direct descendants of the Groton conference.

We now turn to the history of the General Baptists in Maryland, Virginia, North and South Carolina. We will begin with the church at Chestnut Ridge, in Maryland. It was founded this wise: Henry Saytor, a layman, who belonged to the General Baptists in England, came to America in 1709 and settled in the northern part of Maryland. He soon "invited Baptist ministers to preach in his house, by which means a few, from time to time, were proselyted to his sentiments. Among the ministers who officiated with this infant community as pastor, or supplies, in early times, were George Eaglesfield, of Pennsylvania; Paul Palmer, whose name will appear among the General Baptists in North Carolina; Henry Loveall, and probably others."

All of these ministers were probably won over to the General Baptists through the influence of Mr. Saytor, for we find that Mr. Eaglesfield was preaching to the first Baptist church in Philadelphia in 1723-4. Paul Palmer must have belonged, at one time, to the old Welsh Track church, in Delaware, for he was baptized at that church by Owen Thomas, pastor thereof. Elder Palmer was ordained in Connecticut; was some time in New Jersey; then in Maryland, and then went to North Carolina, where he spent a useful life.

The covenant of the church at Chestnut Ridge was as follows:

"We, the humble professors of the gospel of Christ, baptized upon a declaration of faith and repentance, believing the doctrine of general redemption (or of the free grace of God extended to all mankind). * * * And further, we do bind ourselves to follow the pattern of our brethren in England to maintain order, government and discipline in our church, especially that excellent directory of Rev. Francis Stanley, entitled, 'The Gospel Honor and Church Ornament, dedicated to the churches in the counties of Lincoln, Nottingham and Cambridge'."

This church was not constituted until 1742. Paul Palmer first baptized nine persons. Afterwards came Henry Loveall and baptized forty-eight more and constituted a church. This church increased very fast, and began to spread over the country, and soon extended over to Opeckon and Ketockton, Virginia, insomuch that in four years the number of communicants amounted to 181."

In this state of prosperity Mr. Loveall was found to be of unsound character, and the church gradually went down. Mr. Saytor, who may be considered the founder of this church, bore an excellent character and was a very liberal supporter of the gospel.

The church at Opeckon, or Mill Creek, was constituted in 1743, and originated from the General Baptist church at Chestnut Ridge, whose history has just been given. This church was finally absorbed by the Calvinistic Baptists.

We will now notice one church in Massachusetts—the second in Boston, which was founded on this wise:

"In 1794, Mr. Healy and wife, Matthew Heuse and wife, Wm. Lynes and wife—all members of the General Baptist church of Friar Lane, Leicester, England—having resolved to go to America, covenanted together before they departed, to remain together as a religious society. They reached New York, October, 1794, and remained there until in the spring of 1795. Then they went to Boston, where they commenced meeting, and in 1797 they built a house of worship 40x27. Like many others, their church was finally swallowed by Calvinistic Baptists."

GENERAL BAPTISTS IN SOUTH CAROLINA.

We find an account of only one General Baptist church in South Carolina. About 1733 a number of members withdrew from the Charleston church, and constituted a General Baptist church at Stono. In 1736 they sent to England, and secured Rev. Robt. Ingraham for pastor. Henry Haywood, from Farnham, near London, was their second pastor Daniel Wheeler was the next. Caleb Evans was their fourth. This church continued for about fifty years and then became extinct. The account of the General Baptists in Maryland, Massachusetts and South Carolina has been taken almost entirely from Mr. Benedict's histories.

We will now begin with the General Baptists in Virginia and North Carolina, and show a continued line of succession down to the present time. On pages 316-17 of Mr. Knight's history, he says:

"It appears that as early as the close of the 16th century (or about 1700), a number of General Baptists emigrated from England and settled in and about Burly, in the county of the Isle of Wight, in the State of Virginia. These formed themselves into a band, but being destitute of a teacher, they sent a request to England, about the beginning of the 17th century for assistance in the ministry, whereupon the English General Baptists called and ordained to the ministerial office Robert Noron and Thomas White, in London, to come over and labor among the people. They, soon after their ordination, started for America. Elder White died on his passage out, but Elder Norton landed in America in the autumn of 1714, and commenced his ministerial labors with them at Burly.

Elder Nordin's labors were blessed in that quarter and a flourishing church was soon formed at Burly. He exercised his functions as their pastor, with zeal, activity and usefulness, for about twelve years, and the church increased under his care until death called him to his reward, in consequence of which they were left destitute of an administrator, and again sent their solicitations to England for assistants, who sent to their aid Elders Casper Ments and Richard Jones, who arrived at Burly in 1728. Elder Jones was installed their pastor, and Elder Ments went into the county of Surry and gathered a church where a number of the Burley members then resided. These churches continued to increase and there are traces of other churches having been formed in those parts."

Mr. Benedict, on page 642, of his new work says:

"Both of these ministers were living in 1756, as appears by a letter which this church sent, at that time, to the Philadelphia Association."

But owing to "a wasting pestilence" in that section of country which carried off many of the members of this church and in 1742 caused many to leave and emigrate to North Carolina. This church was so enfebled that it never recovered its former strength and finally become extinct, but in what way I cannot tell.

This now brings us to consider the history of the General Baptists in North Carolina. Morgan Edwards says that there were some Baptist families in North Carolina, as early as 1695. Knight says the General Baptists were there in 1690. It is certain, however that Paul Palmer organized the Perquimons church on the Chowan river towards the northeast corner of the State, in 1727, and "on account of the wasting pestilence" in Virginia, referred to above, "William Sojourner, who is said to have been a most excellent man and useful minister, removed, with many of his brethren, from Burly, in Virginia, and settled on Kehukee Creek, in North Carolina, in which quarter, it appears, there had existed churches of the same denomination from 1690 up to 1742, and that these societies and those in Virginia, had formed themselves into a yearly meeting as early as

1720 and Paul Palmer, one of their ministers, informed John Comer, of Newport, of their yearly meeting, as early as 1729.

In North Carolina the General Baptists increased very rapidly and in a few years after the removal of those from Burly to Kehukee Creek, there were sixteen flourishing churches in that quarter. The zealous labors of their ministers, Elders Paul Palmer, Jos. Parker, William Sojourner and many others among them contributed much to their prosperity and increase, for many years."

These churches are represented by Knight, Benedict and others, as increasing and prospering until about 1765, when most of them were transformed into a Calvinistic Baptist Association. However, some of these churches were not transformed until 1794, and some few of them never yielded to the proselyting influences of the transforming element, but maintained their principles and gradually added other churches and their unbroken lineage is in existence in North Carolina at this time, (1882) as will be shown hereafter.

We have before us a history of these people after they were transformed into the Kehukee Association of Regular Baptists and subsequently took the name of United Baptists. This history was written by Elder Daniel Burkitt and Jesse Read. The former was clerk of the Association for thirty years. I doubt not that these authors were faithful in writing the history of this body of people after 1765. But it is lamentably plain that they studiously avoided recording a satisfactory account of these churches which had been organized since 1690 or seventy-five years previous to their transformation into a Regular or Calvinistic Baptist Association. But we are thankful for what little information they have given us respecting their origin. Here is what Burkitt and Read have to say concerning those churches:

"Some of the churches which at first composed the Kehukee Association were the church at Toisnot, in Edgecomb county, the church at Kehukee, in Halifax county, the church on Fishing Creek, in Halifax county, the church at the falls of Tar river, in Edgecomb county, the church on Reedy Creek, in Warren county, the church at Sandy Run, in Bertie county, and the church in Camden county, in North Carolina. The most of these churches, before they were ever united in an Association, were General Baptists and held with the Arminian tenets. We believe they were the descendants of the English General Baptists, because we find from some original papers that their confession of faith was subscribed by certain Elders and Deacons and brethren in behalf of themselves and others to whom they belonged, both in London and several counties in England, and was presented to King Charles II." upon his assention to the throne.

This was the confession of 1660, presented by Elders Thomas Grantham and J. Wright, and is that after which the articles of faith of the General Baptists as organized by Elder Benoni Stinson and others in southern Indiana, are modled. Burkitt and Read further say:

"They preached and adhered to the Arminian or Free-Will doctrines and their churches were first established upon this system   *   *   *   * The churches of this order were first gathered here by Elder Paul Palmer and Joseph Parker, and were succeeded by a number of ministers whom they had baptized."

We can not learn that it was customary with them to hold an Association at all, but met at yearly meetings where matters of consequence were determined.

"This was the state of these churches until Divine Providence disposed the Philadelphia Baptist Association to send Messrs. Vanhorn and Miller, two ministers belonging to that Association and lived in New Jersey to travel into the Southern colonies and visit the churches and preach the gospel. When they came to

North Carolina some of the members belonging to these churches seemed to be afraid of them. * * But by the greatest part of the churches they were cordially received."

We do not wonder at those General Baptists appearing shy at the appearance of those Calvinistic Baptists, for it has ever been the work of these brethren to follow closely after the General Baptists with their intensely proselyting spirit, until the time has been, when the liberal element was almost entirely absorbed. But the principles of General Baptists are founded upon Freedom and Liberty, and though held in check for a while, will come forth with renewed energy and vigor. Though transformed in Virginia and North Carolina, in 1765, they burst forth in New England, in 1780, under the name of Free-Will Baptists, headed by Elder Benjamin Randal, and in Western New York, about the same time, under the name of Free Communion Baptists, led on by Elder Benijah Corp, and in Southern Indiana, in 1823, under the leadership of Elder Benoni Stinson, under the name General Baptists.

Burkitt and Read have the following, in regard to to the ministers who went into the Kehukee Association:

"The principal ministers which belonged to the

Association, on its first establishment, were Elders Jonathan Thomas, John Thomas, John Moore, John Burgess, William Burgess, Charles Daniel, William Walker, John McClamer, James Abington, Thomas Pope and Henry Abbot, all of whom, except Elders John McClamer and James Abington, we believe, were baptized by ministers of the Free-Will order."

The reader will observe that these authors use the names General and Free-Will interchangeably. We find on pp. 234-35 of Burkitt and Read's history, the following account of the Reedy Creek church, above referred to:

"Dr. Josiah Hart was the first preacher of the Baptist pursuasion, who preached here. He came about the year 1750 and preached, and baptized soon after, William Washington, James Smith, Samuel Davis, William Walker, and others joined in the work of preaching and baptizing all, upon what is called the Free-Will plan, and many came and were baptized. William Walker was chosen from among the rest and called their pastor. Things went on thus until 1755. In May, of that year, Elder John Gano, from the North, visited this place and seeing the situation of affairs, probably represented the case, on his return, to the Philadelphia Association, who, the fall following, delegated Elder Peter Peterson

Vanhorn and Benjamin Miller to attend and settle churches upon the doctrine of Free Grace and according to the Gospel order."

This took place ten years before the Kehukee Association was organized or transformed.

On page 298, of Burkitt and Read's history, we find the following, in reference to the "church on Muddy Creek, Duplin county, North Carolina. Elder Jobe Thigpen moved into the neighborhood in the year 1781. At that time there were none of the Baptist Society in these parts, only himself and his wife. He had then just began to preach a little more than one year bofore and it appeared that the Lord blessed his labors insomuch that a considerable number were brought to the knowledge of the truth and by him were baptized. But as he was a minister of the Free-Will order, and the members received on that plan, it was thought advisable for the church to come under re-examination. Accordingly help was called for, who were Elder Robert Nixon and others. The members in this place were received into fellowship with the Particular Baptist churches, and finally in 1793 united with the Kehukee Association.

"Thus by means of those ministers, who visited the churches, several were reformed and the work of reformation progressed until the greater part of what few churches were gathered in North Carolina, both ministers and members came into the Regular Baptist order.

"Elder Palmer, we believe, died before the reformation took place, and Elder Joseph Parker, we cannot learn, was ever convinced of his errors or receded from them but continued in his way, and we cannot understand that he was very successful, because all the ministers of that party were brought over to embrace the Calvinistic scheme, except Elder Winfield and Elder William Parker, and, we presume, but a few either ministers or members except the members of their churches."

The churches here referred to, we have no particular account of except

"The church on Meheren, Hartford county, North Carolina. This church was originally gathered and constituted on the Free-Will plan. Elders Joseph Parker, William Parker, Winfield and others of that order, frequently preached here."

Elder William Parker was preaching to this church in 1773 and probably continued until about 1793, for he died about that time, after which Elder Burkitt preached for them for some time. Finally, in 1794, being left destitute of a pastor of their own order, they, too, were pursuaded to come under re-examination and united with the Kehukee Association. Burkitt and Read have had a good deal to say about "reformation and re-examination" and the lamentable condition of these General Baptists.

There is no question in my mind but what the General Baptists, about whom we have been writing, had become somewhat indifferent and remiss in duty, but the charge that they did not require a change of heart, or conversion or regeneration, before baptism, is not well enough authenticated to bear scrutiny, from the fact that, with only one or two exceptions, all of their members were received into the Kehukee Association of Regular Baptists upon their baptism, and their ministers on their baptism and ordination, and it would seem a little strange that a people who had only the form of godliness, without the power, could become true and genuine Christians by the simple avowal of a belief in the doctrines advocated by the Calvinistic Baptists. And yet this was the manner in which most all of those unconverted General Baptists, as they were termed, were received into the Regular Baptist church. "Oh! Consistency, thou art a jewel."

We have traced the General Baptists of North Carlina down to 1765, when most of their yearly meeting were transformed into the Kehukee Association of

Regular Baptists. We have also seen that the church at Meheren continued under the pastoral care of Eld. William Parker until about 1793, at which time he died, and that through the influence of Elder Daniel Burkitt, a Regular Baptist, that church was also induced to unite with the Regular Baptists. Burkitt and Read refer to some other churches under the care of Elders Joseph Parker, William Parker and Winfried that did not yield to the transforming element.

Concerning those few churches, Rev. I. D. Stewart, author of the History of the Free Will Baptists, says:

"I wrote the History of the Free Will Baptists and have now looked up the correspondence, and find that the letter sent by Elder Buzzle to Rev. J. Heath, April 23, 1627, was not published in the Star, but an allusion to it. Bro. Heath wrote, May 29, 1827, and it was published June 28. He speaks of the people in North Carolina, and the Free Baptist faith and practice. He says they have a 'book of discipline.' Buzzle's letter was printed with the minutes of that year. He says: "Twenty-five years ago (1807, only thirteen years after the transformation of the Meheren church) when I first came to the ministry, there were but three ministers and five churches. Number of members now, about 800; leading ministers, Frede ick Fonville, Isaac Pipkin, Henry Smith, Levi Braxton, Nathaniel Lockhart, Reading Moore, Jesse Alpin, Jeremiah Heath, Jere. Rome, James Moore and Robert Pond.' He adds, the ministers are 'all men of families, of little property, and not a single scholar among us'."

On December 13th the Star speaks of another letter from Jesse Heath. Nineteen ministers attended the last conference, recently held, and about as many churches represented by letter. Refreshing revivals. He said Buzzle's letter to him was laid before conference, and "every part of it approved." Thirteen copies of the Morning Star were taken in North Carolina in December, 1827.

The above letter is of very great importance in establishing a connection between the four churches of the old General or original Free Will Baptist that escaped the transformation and continued steadfast in their original doctrines, and the present original Free Will Baptists in North Carolina.

The reader will bear in mind that in 1807, when Elder Jesse Heath, became a minister among the General Baptists in North Carolina, that this was only thirteen years after the Meheren church, of which Elder William Parker had been pastor for many years previous to his death, had been absorbed, and these people then claimed to be the direct descendants of the English General Baptists as organized by Elders Paul Palmer, Joseph Parker, William Parker, William Sojourner and others; and Elder R. K. Hearn, who is now (1881) one of their old ministers and editor of "The Free Will Baptist," published at Free Mount, North Carolina, dates their origin to the same beginning. Elder Hearn wrote a sketch of the "Origin of the Free Will Baptist church in North Carolina," and published it in the "Toisnot Transcript," edited at Toisnot, N. C. This sketch commenced May 20, 1875, and closed June 17, of the same year. In regard to the correctness of these articles, Elder E. R. Ellis, the editor, gives the following:

"We begin this week the publication of the 'Origin of the Free Will Baptist church in North Carolina,' by Elder R. K. Hearn. This is the most truthful account we have of the origin of the church in North Carolina, and doubtless it will be read with much interest by a great many members of the church. Elder Hearn is fully competent to write the history of the church, and we would be pleased if he would undertake the task, of publishing it in book form."

Bro. Hearn does not intend publishing a book, and we have his consent to use these articles in our work. The first of these are substantially the same as given by us, but we prefer giving Bro. Hearn's articles entire, for they are very valuable testimony, coming, as they do, from an old and respected father of our brethren in North Carolina. These articles clear up the obscurities of the history of those people, and set forth, in a clear and satisfactory light, that which for a long time has been a matter of conjecture to us in the West. It will be more interesting when we tell you that the different branches of these people in North Carolina and other Southern States amount to near 10,000 communicants.

ORIGIN OF THE FREE WILL BAPTIST CHURCH OF NORTH CAROLINA.

BY R. K. HEARN.

I now make the feeble attempt, as I promised a few weeks ago, to show by whom the Free Will Baptists of North Carolina were organized. The account will be very imperfect, owing to our forefathers having kept no record of the proceedings, and as all the facts concerning the Free Will Baptists that we can get are derived from our enemies and tradition.

The limited circumstances and education of the writer—I say limited circumstances, because I have to work hard and have no time to read or write only of a night, after my day's labor is finished, precludes a thorough examination.

Sometime in the year 1727, a minister by the name

of Paul Palmer, a native of Maryland, moved to North Carolina and settled at a place called Perquimans, on Chowan river. Mr. Palmer commenced preaching, and the same year organized a church at that place. Mr. Palmer was called General or Liberal Baptist, in opposition to the Particular Baptist. According to Mr. Benedict, he was baptized at Welsh Tract, in Delaware, by Owen Thomas, the pastor of the church in that place; was ordained in Connecticut, then went to New Jersey, then back to Maryland —his native State—and then to North Carolina, where he gathered the church above mentioned, with which he continued until his death. He was contemporary with Mr. John Comer, of Newport, Rhode Island. Benedict saw a letter written by Palmer to Comer, dated 1729, stating that the church which was gathering there two years before, at that time consisted of thirty-two members. Among the first converts of Mr. Palmer was Joseph Parker, who soon commenced preaching, and by the labors of Mr. Palmer, or Joseph Parker—I am not prepared, at this time, to say which—William Parker and a Mr. Winfield were raised up to the ministry. I shall refer to Elder William Parker again, to prove that we sprung from this church, and that this church was the first Baptist church in North Carolina. Such is history as recorded by Morgan Edwards, Burkitt, Read, Biggs and Benedict; and if I prove that this church was our mother, it will prove that we were the first Baptist church in North Carolina. This is the reason why the title page of our book of discipline calls us the "Original Baptist Church," holding the doctrine of General Provision, and this is our true name, and I will, before I get through, show why we are called Free Will Baptists. It is an error that we are the same as the Northern Free Will Baptists—as a great many may suppose, and, as I suppose, your correspondent W. thinks. I do not recollect, at this time, when the Northern Free Will Baptist church was organized; but Elder Benjamin Randal, its founder, never commenced preaching till 1775—so says his biographer—and our mother church was organized in 1727, some forty-seven or forty-eight years before.

Thus I have given an account of the first Baptist church in North Cirolina. I will now speak of the progress of the church. The ministers that I have mentioned, and others who were raised up under their ministry, traveled and preached considerably, and in the course of a few years organized several churches. In the year 1742, William Sojourner, who is said to have been a most excellent man and useful minister, removed with many of his brethren from Berkley, Virginia, and settled on Kehukee creek, in Halifax county. In the same year he planted a church in that place, and with the assistance of Palmer, Parker, Sojourner and other ministers, many were added to the church, so that they had by the year 1752, increased to sixteen churches. These churches had, according to Mr. Benedict, an annual interview, or yearly meeting, in which they inspected or regulated the general concerns of their commnity. These churches enjoyed great prosperity, and increased in number until about the year 1751, when a Mr. Robert Williams, a Calvinistic or Particular Baptist minister of Welsh Neck, South Carolina, visited some of these churches and preached among them. This was some twenty-four years after the organization of the first General Baptist church in North Carolina.

Through the labors of this minister there the commencement of the breaking up and remodelling of the churches, it is not known whether or not he went among them by invitation from some of their members, nor can the extent, character and results of his efforts be given, as no record of them has been found.

William Wallace, a layman, commonly called the sleigh maker, also took an active part in the matter, and his conversation and efforts were attended with considerable success. The time when his labors were performed is not named, but probably it was some time after the commencement of the mission of Rev. Mr. Williams. In the summer of 1754, Rev. John Gano was sent by the Philadelphia Association, with general and indefinite instructions to travel in the Southern States. Under these instructions he visited the General Baptist churches in North Carolina. Morgan Edwards, says Benedict, thus decribes the visit:

"Mr. Gano, on his arrival, sent to the ministers, requesting an interview with them, which they declined, and appointed a meeting among themselves to consult what to do. Mr. Gano, hearing of it, went to their meeting, and addressed them in words to this effect: 'I have desired a visit from you, which as a brother and a stranger I had a right to expect, but as ye have refused, I give up my claim and have come to pay you a visit.' With that, he ascended into the pulpit and read for his text the following words: "Jesus I know, and Paul I know, but who are ye?" This text he managed in such a way as to make some afraid of him and others ashamed of their shyness. Many were convinced of error touching faith and conversion, and submitted to examination.

This visit, says Elder Elias Huchings was made about two years after Mr. Williams began his proselyting labors, and it seems evident from Mr. Gano's visit, and what followed, that the work was carried on in a very zealous manner; and, in some instances, in utter disregard of propriety and Christian courtesy.

The refusal of the ministers to have an interview with Mr. Gano, when he requested them to meet him, was an act of disrespect towards him; but it is presumed that they intended nothing of that nature. Their course shows that they were utterly opposed to the object of his visit, and they probably refused to see him, not on account of intended incivility, but through desire to avoid discussion on an unwelcome subject with one who possessed abilities far superior to theirs. Most ministers, on being regarded and treated as intruders, would probably have ceased from further effort at proselyting, and departed from the place, but Mr. Gano took a different course. He went to a meeting of those who, as he well knew, had met for consultation, and did not desire his presence. Not content with this, he obtrusively entered the pulpit and preached a disparaging sermon to the dissatisfied and simple-hearted auditors. Being thrown into confusion by his great ability and ingenious handling of the words of an "evil spirit" as a text, they seem to have lost their independence, and were made to believe that their doctrine was unsound, and that their hearts were unrenewed. This led some of them to renounce their former faith, and to receive his opinion of their spiritual state as decisive on that subject. Mr. Gano's efforts seem to have unsettled the minds of a considerable number of the ministers, and finally led to the defection of most of the churches and ministers to hyper-Calvinism. On his return, he represented what was regarded as their deplorable condition to the Association, who appointed Messrs. Miller and Vanhorn to complete the work of proselyting them. These men engaged zealously in the work assigned them, and a great change was effected among these people, which, it is asserted, consisted not only in reforming their creed and purifying their churches, but also in reviving the power of godliness among them, and in the awakening and conversion of many who needed such a change.

What was left unfinished by these two men, was zealously carried on by the newly converted ministers, who were anxious to lead others to adopt their views. The work was prosecuted so energetically, that about four years after Robert williams commenced his efforts among these people, all the ministers, except Elders Joseph and Wm. Parker, and an Elder Winfield, and all the churches except those under their care, had embraced the views of those who had taken so much pains to convert them to the Calvinistic faith. Thus it is seen, that in some less than thirty years after the commencement of their denominational existence in North Carolina, these people were so much scattered that it seemed nearly impossible for them to survive their calamities, and it was feared by the remnant, and hoped by their enemies, that such would be their hard lot.

It has already been stated, that about the year 1752, some thirteen years before the revolution above named was completed, this title branch of Baptists had increased to sixteen churches. Probably some others were organized during the thirteen years just named, but if so, no account of them is now to be found. Benedict states that the ministers were considerably numerous, but their number is not given. This unfortunate body of Baptists commenced its existence in North Carolina fifty-three years, and was mostly absorbed by the Calvinistic Baptist denominations twenty-eight years, before the rise of the Free-Will Baptists at the North.

The enemies of the Arminian Baptists in North Carolina were greatly elated at the revolution, and regarded it a great and beneficial change. Indeed, Benedict seems to think that, on account of the lax views and dicipline of the churches, the innovation, or reformation, as they called it, was necessary and useful. But considering the manner in which the revolution was brought about, and the unhappy result of it, there is much room to doubt the propriety of the measure.

Had the zealous and well-meaning New Lights, as the Calvinistic Baptists were then called, been invited to visit and remodel these churches, no objection could, probably, be made to their course, but going among them uninvited to proselyte them, was obtrusive and provoking. There was surely work enough to be done in North Carolina by the Baptist ministers without interfering with the few churches who felt that they had a right to organizations, and to labor unmolested in the fields they entered peaceably and had occupied some twenty-five years without molestation.

It is asserted that these churches were so lax in their discipline, and held such erroneous views of conversion, that they actually needed the revolution through which they passed. There is reason to fear that they were negligent in discipline, but in this respect they seem to have been as well off as the Episcopalians, who were their only religious neighbors when the churches were organized. The relation of a Christian experience was in no case required as a condition of admission to membership in the Episcopal church, and there was nearly or quite as much laxity of discipline in that large and popular sect as there was among the General Baptists.

The Episcopalians were as lukewarm, formal, and destitute of the power of godliness as were the Free-Will Baptists. Why, then, did the energetic New Lights pass by this larger body and obtrude themselves upon the weaker? The proselyting of this body is justified on the ground that it needed a thorough renovation. If this view of the case is correct, the Philadelphia Baptist Association should have looked after the spiritual interests of the Episcopal church, as well as after those of a far smaller body. Dr. Gano ought to have sent to their leading "ministers, and requested an interview with them;" and on their declining, he should have treated them as arrogantly as he did this feeble band of Baptists. Similar efforts should have been made for the renovation of these. But nothing of the kind was done. Dr. Gano knew full well that the ministers of the Episcopal church were his equals in learning and talents, and if he attempted such a thing that he would more than meet with his match, but as the Baptist ministers were men of very limited education, he could succed with his powerful eloquence in proselyting them and their members.

The divisions and secessions of the Free-Will

Churches, which were caused by proselyting members of another denomination, left the adhering remnant in a sad state of discouragement, distraction and ill will towards those who were the authors of their troubles. Their most active, intelligent and efficient ministers and members had seceded and were laboring zealously against them. Though a considerable number of the members retained their original views, and would not go with the seceders, they were only the scattered and unorganized remains of the churches that had left them. They were not disciplinarians, and were in some sense like fragments of a routed and dispirited army after its principal officers and soldiers had gone over to the enemy.

Public opinion was pretty strongly against them, as it is often against the weak and unfortunate, they were regarded by many as deceived and deceivers in regard to the matter of religion; they were also considered as heretics and classed with Universalists.

A deep seated dislike, amounting almost to abhorrence, was created between the two parties formed by this division. Each body regarded the other as holding damnable errors—the extremes of Calvinism and Arminianism—and each cordially hated the tenets of the other.

To the Arminians the name of New Lights was

odious, and the name of the Free-Will was equally odious to these. The relation of a few incidents may serve as an illustration of the views and feelings of these two opposing bodies of Baptists.

In 1784, as Elder Wm. Parker was reading his text, he was stricken with palsy, and falling in the pulpit, he is reported as saying:

"Blessed be God, I have fallen in a good cause." His reason then departed to return no more, and two or three days afterwards he "breathed out his soul into the hands of the Redeemer." So say Messrs. Burkitt and Read.

Some seven years after this incident occurred, a Baptist minister, whose name was Frost, "came from Europe," (probably from England) and commenced preaching in the Calvinistic Baptist church in Portsmouth and Norfolk, Virginia. He soon began to "preach the doctrine of free-will, supposing, it is alleged, by the New Light writers, that man has power to work himself into a state of favor with God. A committee was appointed by the church to convert him; failing in this, another was chosen to silence him, but with no better success.

Shortly after that, he went to a place to preach, but while reading his text, his voice faltered, he cried "let us pray," fell on his knees speechless, and died in less than three hours.

Thus, say the historians named above, "did God avenge his suffering church in these towns, for the fox was spoiling the tender grapes."

When, in 1812, Elder Joseph Smith died, who was the pastor of the church at Pungo River, a Calvinistic minister asked a colored member of that church, "Now your *plaster* is gone, what will you do?" Some twenty years later, several copies of a selection of hymns, by Elder John Buzzle, were sold to the North Carolina Free-Will Baptists. One of the hymns commences as follows:

> "Come all who are New Lights indeed,
> Who are from sin and bondage free'd;
> From Egypt's land we've taken flight,
> For God has given us a New Light."

The hymn, which commends all New Lights, and refers to all true Christians, was read by the purchasers with grief and almost indignant astonishment. It was supposed to be a commendation of that order of Baptists who had, nearly three-quarters of a century previous to that time, broken up the Free-Will Baptists; and caused them a great amount of distress, an act which they had not forgotten nor forgiven. They were pacified only with the assurance that the obnoxious hymn was not a commendation of their New Light enemies, but was designed to approve and encourage faithful Christians of all orders.

At the time of the invasion and the scattering of the Free-Will Baptists in North Carolina, the uncharitable, and in many instances malevolent feelings between the two bodies were general and mutual, A lapse of over one hundred years has somewhat softened the acrimony of these feelings, but it has not eradicated them, for up to this time there is a deep-seated dislike of both parties against the other. At this distant period, the Free-Will Baptists have heard so much of the breaking up of the early churches, that they can hardly regard the decendants of those that did it as Christians, and were but little disposed to fraternize with them. The views of the two sects in regard to doctrines and church building, are nearly as variant as at the commencement of the separation, each party being confident that its views were right, and those of the other ruinously wrong.

Had the New Light Baptists been more prudent in their zeal to proselyte this people, and sought to accomplish their end in a less overbearing manner, it would have prevented much mutual ill-will and also a great amount of distress among those whom they failed to convert to hyper-Calvinism.

Burkitt and Read regarded it as very wicked in Elder Frost to attempt to proselyte the churches in Portsmouth and Norfolk, Virginia, to his Arminian views. Their sympathies were much awakened in behalf of those "distressed" and suffering churches, and the sudden death of that minister was considered by them an act of Divine interference in their behalf. But no pity was felt for the Free-Will Baptist churches, which were overwhelmed with confusion and distress by the unfraternal efforts of the misguided men who subverted them. The long continued hatred and contentions which followed subversion, leave but little room to doubt that, on the whole, its results were more injurious than beneficial to the cause of morality and religion.

But little is known of the church discipline of the early Free-Will Baptists in North Carolina, than the assertion of their enemies, that it was very negligent.

The following statement, made, perhaps, twenty-five years ago, to Mr. Benedict by Dr. Wheeler, of Murfreesboro, North Carolina, probable contains the most that can now be learned on the subject, and it is much to be regretted that no historical sketches of any of these churches can be found, except those gathered by Elder Paul Palmer, which is the first Baptist church that was organized in the State. As this church was organized in 1727, the records named below stopped thirty-one years short of its commencement; but they, no doubt, describe the state of things in the church before its defection to Calvinism. Dr. Wheeler's statement is as follows:

"I have procured the records, which go back to 1758, when John Burgess was pastor, and the business of the church was managed by elders or overseers, while the private secular matters of the members were under the direction of the ministers and six members, who were constituted the "Court of Union." The churches had several arms or branches in the adjoining counties, to which the ministers, attended by the overseers and the clerk, regularly repaired.

"In a few years the Court of Union was dispensed with, but the churches being dissatisfied with its extinction, nine members were chosen, who were considered to be permanent elders, if found faithful, while the former overseers or elders were elected annually."

Such, says Benedict, "was the complex machinery in ecclesiastical affairs at that early period with this well-meaning people."

This statement rests on the supposition that the ecclesiastical machinery of the other churches was as odd and cumberous as that contrived for the government of the Perquiman church, and there seems no reason to doubt that such was the case.

I have said that there were sixteen churches of the Free-Will faith before the breaking up and remodeling by Gano, and only six are recorded by the historian, and I suppose that these six embraced the doctrine of hyper-Calvinism. The other ten are left without any written account, and it is unnecessary for me to follow these six, as they belong to other denominations. I will return to my promise of refering to William Parker, and see if tradition cannot tell us something of a few of the other ten churches.

The old settlers of this part of Pitt county, knew Parker well, when they were children, and many anecdotes are told concerning him, which I deem unnecessary to relate, but as a faithful soldier of the Lord Jesus Christ, he ceased not to travel and preach, (often on foot) free salvation to his fellow-man, until, like a faithful soldier, he fell at his post.

An old Free-Will Baptist sister, who lived to be considerably over a hundred years old told her son, and he, also a Free-Will Baptist, told the writer of this that she knew Elder William Parker well, that she well recollected when he first came to the neighborhood and when he preached his first sermon on the plat of ground whereon old Gum Swamp Church now stands. The writer lives within about three-quarters of a mile of said church, and was raised within two miles of it. The old sister referred to was named Teel, by marriage. I think her maiden name was Pollard. She was raised within a few miles of

Gum Swamp and lived and died in the neighborhood and was a faithful member of the Free-Will Baptist Church at that place up to the time of her death. I do not recollect whether she was baptized by Elder Parker, or by some other minister who was raised up under his ministry. She said that he soon raised up a church, and was pastor up to the time of his death. It will be borne in mind that Elder Parker was a member of the Perquimans church—the first Baptist church in North Carolina—at the time he organized the Gum Swamp Church, and if so, this proves that the Perquimans church is our mother, and that we are the original Baptist church of North Carolina holding the General provisions.

Elder William Parker also traveled and preached in Green and Lenoir counties, and organized churches in both of these, and according to the best information we can get, he organized the churches at Jones', now called Little Creek, and Grimsley, in Greene county, and Louson Swamp and Wheat Swamp in Lenoir county. This accounts for five more of the original sixteen churches, the other five I suppose, at this late day, cannot be accounted for.

Gum Swamp, in Pitt county, has stood the shocks of proselyting, and remains firm to the Free-Will Baptist cause up to the present time.

Little Creek, in Green county, has at one time

been divided, but while their pastor and a large number of its members turned from the old path, a few remained firm, and like one of the seven churches in Asia, did not defile their garments.

Louson Swamp went with the Rev. Mr. Hunnicut in his raid on the churches of North Carolina, and Wheat Swamp, I think, died for lack of ministerial labor.

The writer of this, in company with Elder Joseph Sauls, visited this church in 1867 and found a few old members still strong in the faith of the old Free-Will Baptists, but the old house was very much decayed, and the seats and all of the floor had been destroyed by the United States soldiers, during the war. The Disciples have a good building in the same yard, and a large number of members.

The next point under consideration is, why are we called Free-Will Baptists? A religious interest commenced, by whom, or what means, it is not said, in the valley of Flat Swamp, and the Conetoe settlements, in Pitt county, about the year 1766, and some ten years afterwards, a New Light church, called Flat Swamp, was organized there. Sometime subsequently, says the New Light Historians, the love of some of the members waxed cold, and the seeds of discord were sown in the church, "which caused the *Arminians* and Universalists to look out of their dens, where they had been driven by the refulgent beams of gospel truths."

It is added that Arminianism prevailed but little among them, as it was an old doctrine they were well acquainted with it before their conversion.

From this statement it is manifest that there was a people in this section that gave them considerable trouble, who, according to the figurative language of their enemies, were driven into seclusion by the glorious light of Calvinistic decrees, election, reprobation, etc., and owing to the trouble this people gave them, they called them, by way of reproach, "Freewillers." But it is not intimated whether or not there had previously been a church there, of these hated Freewillers, and the fugitives from the New Light effulgence, named above, were members of that church who could not be admitted into the new organization, or else they utterly refused to join it.

Who were these people that troubled these New Lights in the Flat Swamp and Conetoe settlements? The answer is, Gum Swamp church and its pastor, Elder William Parker. Gum Swamp church is in the Conetoe settlements in Pitt county; Flat Swamp church is fifteen miles from Gum Swamp, near the line of Pitt and Martin counties, on the road that Elder Wm. Parker would have to travel from his home to Gum Swamp church. No doubt, that as he traveled by Gum Swamp to his appointments, he preached often in the Flat Swamp settlements, and the members from Gum Swamp, meeting him there, gave these New Lights the trouble they speak of.

It was nothing uncommon, in that day, for people to travel fifteen or twenty miles on foot, to hear the gospel preached; unlike they are in our day, who can not go five miles to hear, unless on extraordinary occasions.

As I shall not have occasion, perhaps, to speak of Elder William Parker again, I cannot leave this part of the subject without saying, that, according to tradition, he was a man of wonderful muscular power, slow to resent an insult, but when fully aroused he feared not the face of man; otherwise he was as gentle as a lamb. He was untiring in his efforts as a minister, often traveling long distances on foot, to preach the gospel, and when he fell he was at his post. What a glorious death! The writer of this greatly desires to be at his post, when death shall come, as a faithful soldier of the Lord Jesus. How uncharitable and unchristian in his enemies, to ascribe it to an interference of Divine power, to take him away from troubling them. Had he embraced their extreme views of hyper-Calvanism, they would have praised him as a great minister, dying a triumphant death.

I have now shown that the name "Free-Will," was given us by way of reproach. Elder Elias Huchens, of Dover, New Hampshire, says we were called Ana-Baptists, Baptists and General Baptists, until the year 1828, when we adopted the name of Free-Will Baptists.

The historians, all of whom were our enemies, as I have already shown, say these early churches were very lax in their discipline but have failed to show wherein the looseness consisted, only in one point :

"They did not require an experience of grace from their members, when they received them into the church."

If this is all they could say, at this late day, most of the christian denominations are lax in their discipline. These early churches took the Bible for their guide, they practiced its sacred teachings, and as the Apostles never required an experience, and as it was nowhere authorized in Holy Writ, they practiced what they found the gospel required, that is faith in the Lord Jesus Christ, repentance towards God, and Baptisim by immersion; and baptised their members on a profession of their faith in the Lord Jesus Christ, and not by experience.

Every Free-Will Baptist will see that this is his doctrine, and the true doctrine of the New Testament, and that it is our practice to the present day to baptize members on their profession of faith in the Lord Jesus Christ. They may call it lax in discipline, if they choose, we cannot, for we find no warrant in the New Testament, for an experience of grace, as they term it.

I have shown, that according to Mr. Benedict, these early churches had an annual interview, or yearly meeting, in which they regulated the general concerns of their churches, and if Mr. Benedict is correct, our Conference was organized by Palmer, the two Parkers, Sojourner and others, long before I was born, instead of Elder James Moore, myself, and others, as brother Nash would have us believe. Our Conference is nothing more than an annual or yearly meeting, where we meet to regulate the general concerns of our churches.

It is true that these churches were broken up, in part, but there were three ministers who stood firm and unshaken, and the churches that they were pastors of, stood firm, and, of course, they continued to hold their Annual as well as their Monthly and Quarterly meetings, at all events, our enemies have failed to show that they did not, and I defy any person to show to the contrary.

I heard, when I was a small boy, the old people say, that the Ana-Baptists or Free-Will Baptists, held a Conference at Gum Swamp when they were children. I have in my possession an old hymn book with the title page torn off, to the back part of which is tacked one leaf of a Minute without date. On that leaf it is stated that the Conferance was held at Wheat Swamp, in Lenoir county, and a resolution that the next Conference be held on Contentney, at Grimsley. There is another resolution upon the same leaf which I will give:

"*It is Resolved*, That the ordinance of the anointing with oil, shall not, by the Elders of the church, be administered to any but members of the society; and at their discretion a part, or the whole man may be anointed.

The contribution was only fourteen dollars and twenty-five cents, and only two hundred copies of the minutes were ordered to be published. There are only four ministers' names attached to it, although there might have been others on the next page, as the four are at the bottom of the page. But in the appointment to preach on Sunday, there is no other name mentioned, but three of those whose names are on the leaf.

The four names were, F. Fonvielle, Isaac Pipkin, Levi Braxton and Jesse Heath. Elder Braxton was pastor of the Gum Swamp church, as long ago as the writer of this can remember, and succeeded Elder Roach, who had resigned or died before my recollection. Elder Heath is well known by the old people of Green county. Elder Pipkin, I have been informed, is the father of Elder Isaac Pipkin, whose name is at this time on our minutes. Elder Fonvielle I know but little about, only I have heard him spoken of as one of our old ministers. After giving the text the minister preached from, on Sunday, it is added that a large, attentive and polite congregation waited on a faithful dispensation of the Gospel, and we pray that the happy effect may be long felt and enjoyed in the regions of Wheat Swamp. May God grant it, for Christ's sake, Amen.

This book and leaf bears the mark of age, is printed in the old style, but we cannot give the date. An old brother, in Martin county, presented it to me several years ago and told me that it was the hymn book in use when he was a boy.

I have now traced the origin of the early Baptists a far as I can from history and tradition. I have passed over many things that could be said, but thought it unnecessary and would stop here, as I think I have fulfilled my promise, but on account of what has been said about us in modern days, I think it necessary to peruse the subject farther, and, if it should give offence to some, I cannot help it, "for truth is mighty and will prevail." I feel certain that every old Free-Will Baptist knows these things to be so, and will take no offence.

After the breaking up of the churches as I have described, in a few years the Free-Will Baptists commenced increasing and they soon spread over fifteen counties, mostly in the eastern part of the State, and numbered over two thousand members, and about forty ministers. They enjoyed peace and prosperity, until the Conference became large and it was thought best to divide and hold two Conferences, one bearing the original name, the other, the name of Bethel Conference. I cannot give the dates of what I am going to relate, but it is true and there are living witnesses to the truth of it besides myself. I have had the Minutes that gave the date, but I have loaned them out or misplaced them so that I do not know at this time where they are.

Some time between the date of 1839 and 1843, Elder J. T. Latham and other ministers of the Free-Will Baptist Conference, embraced the views of Alexander Campbell and withdrew from the Free-Will Baptists and carried with them the most of the Bethel Conference and did all they could to proselyte the members of the original Conference, and like the new lights of old, succeeded too well.

In 1839 our Conference numbered 2006 members and 32 preachers, in 1843 we were reduced to 1440 members and 22 preachers. Such was the success of those that embraced the views of other denominations. Having recovered from this innovation, prosperity again crowned us with success and our increase in about four years was from 1440 to 2563 members, 58 preachers and 49 churches. It is seen from this statement that we soon recovered the ground that we had lost numbering in 1847 more than we did in 1839. But this state of prosperity did not last long, for at the Conference of 1847 the foundation of another division was laid which took place in a few years. The subject of our members uniting with secret societies had been discussed, and much opposition to it, and in some churches members had been excommunicated for joining them. At this Conference it was known that several ministers had united with them, and Elder John F. Jones offered the following resolution :

"Shall this Conference be a Conference with Free Masonry; or a Conference without Free Masonry?"

Voted that it be a Free-Will Baptist Conference without Free Masonry.

After the passage of this resolution several ministers withdrew from the Conference, and this subject continued to disturb the Conference, until 1853, when Elder Alfred Moore introduced a resolution the purport of which was, "that no church belonging to this Conference *shall be at liberty* to reject any person applying for membership, or excommunicate any member on the grounds that he belongs to the Order of Free Masons or Odd Fellows."

Brother Henry Stancill proposed to amend by adding unless a majority of members shall so decide."

Article 3rd, Section 1st, of Rules of Church Discipline says:

"After every matter regularly discussed, then it shall be put to vote, and a majority shall carry the point."

Elder Alfred Moore refused to accept the amendment to his resolution, upon which Elder James Moore introduced a resolution giving to each church its own key—privilege of transacting its own business. Both the resolutions being put to a vote; Elder Alfred Moore's resolution without the amendment, received 36 votes, and that of Elder James Moore, received 66 votes. After this vote was taken there was some confusion, and it was found impossible to harmonize or unite upon those resolutions so the conference divided, each party claiming the old name. And as some of the officers went with each party it was necessary for both to reorganize, and both did reorganize choosing officers to fill the vacancy, I suppose this to be the reason of brother Nash falling into the error of saying, that the original Free-Will Baptist Conference of North Carolina was organized by Elder James Moore, R. K. Hearne and others. If this construction be placed upon our organizing at that time, it can be said that we organize every year. I have shown who organized the original Free-Will Baptist Conference of North Carolina, or who were its founders. Are we that Conference or not? I say we are. I suppose it is not denied but we are up to the Conference of 1853 and owing to division at that Conference both claiming the name, it is said we are not. Then if we are not, where are they, have they become extinct? There is no man living in eastern North Carolina, who has any acquaintance with the Free-Will Baptists that would pretend to say they have become extinct. They know we are the original Free-Will Baptists of North Carolina, although they may not be honest enough to own it. The other party bore the name a few years, then a portion of them united with Rev. Mr. Hunnicut, under the name of Union Baptist.

A few years ago that denomination became extinct, and a portion of them changed their name to Baptist, of which Brother Nash became their leader.

We bear the same name, we have the same book of discipline, we preach the old doctrine, we receive members the same way without an experience of Grace, we commemorate the Lord's Supper the same way, we wash the saints feet the same way, we are the same persecuted old Free-Will Baptists that was organized in 1727 by Elder Paul Palmer.

The old Conference, at the time of division in 1853 adopted the following resolutions:

"That by the help of God we will adhere to, and abide by, and keep inviolate the articles of faith, the rules of discipline and the constitution of the original Free-Will Baptist church. That we believe the rules of discipline gives to each individual church its own key—the privilege of transacting its own business independent of the General Conference."

Since the adoption of the resolutions we have had peace and harmony and great prosperity, and so long as we continue in the old paths we will have peace. God in his wisdom placed these despised people in eastern North Carolina for a purpose, and they will continue, notwsthstanding they may be surrounded by false teachers, persecuted like the saints of old. The time may come when some of them may have to seal the truth with their blood, but God in the providence will not leave himself without a witness of the truths of the Gospel.

The reader must not suppose from what has been said that these people do not believe in experimental religion or the operation of the Holy Spirit on the individual conciences. For their ninth Article of Faith fully settles this question, which is as follows:

"We believe that sinners are drawn to God the Father, by the Holy Ghost through Jesus Christ the son, and that the Holy Ghost offers his divine aid to all the human family, so as they all might be happy would they give divine teaching * * * * *

The only difference between the General or Free-Will Baptists and the Particular Baptists is that the General require answers to leading questions, while the Particulars require the candidate for church membership to relate the experience attending his conviction and conversion, which is termed an "experience of Grace." Both alike believe in faith, repentence, true and genuine conversion and they are both sound alike on the doctrine of experimental religion.

A HISTORY OF THE RISE AND PROGRESS OF THE GENARAL BAPTISTS IN THE WEST, AS ORGANIZED BY ELDER BENONI STINSON AND OTHERS.

As Elder Benoni Stinson was the leading character in organizing the General Baptists in the West, it becomes necessary for us to give a brief sketch of his life. Elder Stinson was born in North Carolina, October 11th, 1798, and came, with his father, Elijah Stinson, to Wayne county, Kentucky, when he was quite a boy, where he had but little opportunity to attend school. In fact the writer has heard him say that what little education he did receive he obtained it by the light of a burning pine knot. However, he was a man of a robust constitution and in the possession of extraordinary natural powers of mind.

He professed religion in 1820 and joined the United Baptist Church, in Wayne county, Kentucky, and was baptized by Elder Mathew Floyd. Soon after, he was licensed to preach the Gospel of Christ and was ordained in November, 1821, by Elders Mathew Floyd and Richard Byers.

Elder Stinson was called to the pastoral care of Liberty Church in Wayne county, Kentucky. But shortly after, he moved to Vanderburgh county, Indiana, where a work of grace was commenced under his ministry and a church, called New Hope, was organized, in which he and his wife deposited their letters. Elder Stinson was then appointed by this church a delegate "to go to what was then called The Wabash District Association, which was held at Patoka Church, near Princeton, Gibson county, Indiana."

"It must be noted that up to this time this body of people were working under the old Union, which had been formed in Kentucky, the basis of which was:

"That the preaching that Christ died for every man, should be no bar to fellowship."

"But a majority of the controlling ministers in this body were Calvinistic and their articles of faith savored strongly of unconditional election and reprobation. Elder Stinson first tried to have this article so modified that he would be allowed to preach that Christ died for all, or free salvation, which doctrine was as dear to him as life." In this he was disappointed. He and his wife then took letters from New Hope Church and united with Liberty Church, in Vanderburgh county, Indiana, one mile and a half below Evansville, which had been organized on thirty-three members, who believed in a general atonement. This was in the fall of 1823.

Elder Stinson now felt like he was a free man, and began to preach from house to house and from one neighborhood to another and his labors were abundantly blest to the conversion of many precious souls and by September, 1824 three other churches had been organized, to-wit: Union, Black River and Providence. These churches met in September, 1824 and organized Liberty Association of General Baptists, with a membership of two hundred and one. Rev. Thomas Goadby, President of Chilwell College, near Nottingham, England, who is a member of the General Association of the New Connection of General Baptists in England, in a private letter to the writer, asks "why Elder Stinson and his adherents took the name General and not some other name." The question is easily answered. Elder Stinson, though a mere boy, was not without a knowledge of ecclesiastical history and in pursuing his studies in this direction, he found a people denominated General Baptists, who held to, and promulgated, what he conceived to be the doctrines taught by Jesus Christ and his Apostles. It will be seen, by reference to Mr. Knight's history, that the English General Baptists sent missonaries direct from London to America, about the begining of 1700, and Burkitt and Read's history developes the rise and progress of this people in Virginia, North Carolina and South Carolina. Among these people was found a confession of faith signed by Elders and Deacons in and around London and Liverpool, in England. This was evidently the confession of 1660, presented by Grantham and Wright to King Charles II., upon his assention to the throne.

This is the confession after which our articles of faith are modled. Therefore, it will be seen, we are not only genuine General Baptists but "we are the direct decendants of the English General Baptists."

We will now speak a little further of the life of Elder Stinson. At the time Liberty Association of General Baptists, in Indiana, was organized, Elder Stinson was only twenty-six years old. "At this period of the life of this great and good man, he met with much persecution from many sources" and nothing short of a firm convicton of being in the right and that, backed by an iron will, could have sustained him in this conflict. He was frequently called upon to meet the strongest men in the old Calvinistic Baptist denomination. Unfortunately, only one of those debates are left in print. We console ourselves, however, that the discussion with Elder Joel Hume, embodies, to some extent, the logical powers of his mind, though this discussion was held in his declining years.

We have had, in our denomination, men that could talk with more fluency, but for a systematic arraignment and forcible and impressive delivery, he had but few equals in all our land. He had that peculiar force in delivery that indelibly impressed his sermons upon the minds of his hearers. With peculiar clearness the writer can call to mind those wonderful sermons on the atonement communion question and the eternal judgement.

Notwithstanding the many fiery trials through which he was called to pass, he traveled much in Indiana, Kentucky and Illinois, and his eloquence drew thousands to hear him preach on his favorite theme, the general atonement or that salvation is possible for all men.

The following account of Elder Stinson's life and labors, are taken from the "Biographical Sketches," published in the General Baptist Herald, in 1877-78, by Captain Wm. Reavis, of Evansville, Indiana, who in the early part of his life was a prominent minister of the General Baptist denomination and of whom frequent mention is made in this work.

Brother Reavis says: "While I carefully note the fact that he became a great favorite among the people and that he was very popular, both as a man and a preacher, truth compels me to say that he had his enemies. * * * * The idea that a young man, with but little beard on his face could gather such crowds to hear him preach, and then hold them enchanted with his peculiar eloquence, grated somewhat harshly upon the sensibilities of some of the older Elders, especially the Calvinistic portion of them.

"Had Elder Stinson been but an ordinary man he might have lived and died in the old Calvinistic Baptist church, and, groaned under the 'yoke' of bondage which the doctrines of unconditional election and reprobation would have imposed upon him. But Elder Stinson was a man of principle, he had been soundly converted and felt it his duty to preach, and he was ready to preach and declare the whole counsel of God, as he understood it, on all proper occasions.

"We see him, now almost a beardless boy, with a little handful of brave spirits around him, and five to one of the Baptist preachers around him opposed to the doctrine he preached, still he was firmly planted upon 'the Rock of Ages' and unfurled the banner of the Cross, and proclaimed the glad tidings of salvation, that 'Jesus Christ, by the grace of God, had tasted death for every man.'

"During the summer of 1824, Elder Stinson had continued in the field, laboring for his Master, and his labors 'were not in vain, in the Lord.' The doctrine of a general atonement began to gain ground very rapidly and it was not long until other Baptist ministers came to his assistance.

"Among those, I will mention Elders John Almon, Jesse Lane, sr., and Berry T. Dunn, all of whom now engaged in preaching the doctrine of 'Free Salvation to all men on the terms of the Gospel.'

"While this work of organizing churches was going on right in the midst of the Predestinarian Baptists. They looked upon him with suspicion and on one occasion, at least, the officers of a Calvinistic Baptist church, in Posey county, locked the doors of the church against Elder Stinson and the cengregation that had assembled to hear him preach. The people seemed determined not to leave without hearing him and the weather being warm Elder Stinson mounted a log for a pulpit and preached a powerful sermon as well as administering a scathing rebuke to those who had shut him out of the church. This circumstance was related by David Stephens and Daniel Miller, who were both members of the old Liberty Church. However, there is no such record against Elder Stinson. He was never known to debar a minister of any denomination from preaching in his pulpit.

"In the meantime God blest the labors of Elder Stinson and there were many glorious revivals followed the preaching of himself and those that stood connected with him, and particularly at Enon Church, near Princeton. The exercises of those meetings deserve a passing notice. There you could see the gray haired and the young bowed down together, asking the prayers of christians in their behalf. I remember, on one occasion, at the time of an Association there, that Elder Stinson had occasion to preach at the popular hour, on Sunday, to a large congregation, perhaps two thousand persons were present; he preached on his favorite theme, the atonement of Christ. His text was, Luke 24th chapter, 46 and 47 verses.

For two hours, Elder Stinson held that vast audience spell-bound, being, at this time, in the prime of life, his reasoning powers and eloquence were so great that the people seemed rivited to the spot. He seemed to have such perfect control of his audience that they hung on to his lips as if enchanted. The silence was so profound that it was almost painful, and it was only broken by an occasional sob, an ejaculatory prayer or a shout. Tears were seen coursing down the cheeks of many a bronzed face. I remember to have seen two distinguished citizens, on that day, who were men of good sense and culture, both of them were believers in the Bible but neither of them were religious. Those men sat close to each other in front of the stand or rostrum. While listening to the bursts of eloquence as they poured forth from the lips of the enthusiastic speaker, I saw them spring to their feet more than once and lean forward as though they were afraid they would lose one word of the discourse, while the tears rolled down their cheeks in profusion.

"After this sermon was over the friends, not only of the General Baptist church, but of other churches, crowded around him and shook him by the hand congratulating him on his fine effort on the atonement.

"I have only given one specimen of the manner and ability of Elder Stinson in the pulpit on great occasions. I could, from memory, give many, but this will suffice, at present.

"In this connection, I wish to say, that after one of those great efforts which seemed to fill the minds of christians with thoughts too large for utterance and with that joy which is unspeakable and full of glory the people were so full as to want to give expression in some way to their feelings and it was on such occasions that Elder Jesse Lane, sr., was called out for exhortation. Then the long pent up feelings would give an expression and such shouts would follow as would seem to the listener that if the walls of old Jerico had been there they would have fallen before the victorious host of the Lord.

"We now propose to speak of Elder Stinson as a theological debater. Having all his life been a close Bible student and a constant reader of ecclesiastical history, and being naturally gifted with a fine voice and great reasoning powers, it was natural that he should attract considerable attention as a disputant upon theological questions.

"It is a very rare thing to find in the same man great talent both as a revivalist and disputant. But Elder Stinson possessed, in an eminent degree, this rare combination. It really seemed that he always had a reason ready for any and every body who inquired of him concerning any point of doctrine which he taught, and then his reasoning was generally so clear and convincing, and his logic so sound that he was not only very forcible but was, really, quite formidable as a debator. His fame, in this regard, was such as to naturally attract the attention of some very powerful divines who differed from him on doctrinal points, and this was the occasion of several debates between Elder Stinson and the Regular or Calvinistic Baptist Elders.

"These discussions were principally in reference to the extent of the atonement. I will not say that Elder Stinson gained the mastery over any of his opponents in his debates with them. I will say, however, that as a doctrinal preacher he was regarded, not only by his own people, but by other denominations, as a very strong man. It will be safe to say that, considering his limited education, he had but few equals, and no superiors, on this point. It is also worthy of note, to say of him that his manner toward those with whom he debated was so courteous, gentlemanly and christian like, that he and his opponent became more friendly after, than before these discussions.

"His first debate was with Elder Ezekiel Saunders, of the Regular Baptist church. This took place in Posey county, Indiana, but as it was not publised I do not now know what the propositions were which were discussed on that occasion. I only know that after this Elder Stinson and Elder Saunders were the best personal friends. Elder Saunders was a man of limited education, but he was strictly honest and much beloved, and highly respected both in and outside of his church relations. He was possessed of good common sense and a sound judgement and was very useful in his day, both as a minister and citizen.

"Some years after this Elder Jeremiah Cash, a Regular Baptist minister, brought a charge against Elder Stinson, before the public, to-wit: That Elder Stinson had been excluded from New Hope Church of Regular Baptists, before he united with Liberty Church of General Baptists. Now as this old slander against Elder Stinson was circulated by Elder Cash in the vicinity of Owensville, and many other places and believed and reiterated by many persons not familiar with the facts. The Owensville church of General Baptists had Elder Cash set a day to meet Elder Stinson at Owensville and prove his charges, which he (Cash) had boldy said he could do, or forever after hold his peace. The day was set and Elder Cash and Stinson met accordingly. Elder Stinson produced a certificate from Elder Ezekiel Saunders, who was clerk of New Hope Church, at the time Elder Stinson and wife were lettered off, and with whom Elder Stinson had before held a public discussion. This certificate showed that Elder Stinson and wife were in good standing in that church. Fortunately, I now have in my possession, the original certificate, which was written and signed by Elder Ezekiel Sanders, in his own hand writing, and as a matter of justice to the General Baptist people and the illustrious dead, I will place it on record as a matter of history, which is as follows:

VANDERBURG Co., Ia., Dec. the 13, 1842.

"This is to certify that Elder Benoni Stinson and wife were both members of New Hope Church, of which I was clerk, and that they were both dismissed by letter, and joined Liberty Church.

Given under my hand, this day and date above written, E. SANDERS.

"It was conceded, very generally, I believe, by a majority of those present at this interview, that Elder Stinson triumphahtly refuted this old and often repeated charge and with all fair minded persons, forever settled that question. . I am told however, that there are a few of the Reguiar Baptist Ministers in Illinois, who either from ignorance or malice, still repeat the slander and for this reason I have fortified the General Baptists with the above certificate; several other charges were also at this same meeting investigated and successfully refuted by Elder Stinson.

"These charges were to the effect that Elder Stinson should have said many hard words against the Regular Baptists, and Elder Cash acknowledged that his informants would not testify to what they had told him. This was a signal victory for the General Baptists, and such a thing is not even hinted at in these parts at this date.

"I am sorry to say that after this investigation the personal relations between Elder Stinson and Cash were not as pleasant as had been hoped for by their friends.

"But now they have both gone to their reward, and it is hoped and believed by their respective friends that they have gone to that 'sun bright clime,' where there is no more prejudice, pain or sorrow, and where brethren will never fall out by the way, where all wounds made by sin in this world of sorrow, will be healed.

"I am rejoiced to record the fact that this is the only instance known to me of any personal estrangement between Elder Stinson and any of the other Regular Baptist Ministers with whom he often met in friendly discussions. For notwithstanding all the conflicts and controversies between the Regular and General Baptists, Elder Stinson continued on quite intimate terms with them.

"Passing by several debates and short investigations of minor importance, held between Elder Stinson and others, I will now speak of his debate with Elder Joel Hume, of the Regular Baptist church.

"This was perhaps the most important discussion of his life, and before doing this, I must be permitted to give a short biographical sketch or Elder Hume.

Should these lines fall under the eye of my venerable and highly esteemed friend, who is yet living, I hope he will pardon me for the freedom I have taken in using his name in this connection.

"Elder Joel Hume was born in Campbell, now Kenton County, Kentucky, on the 13th of June, 1807. He openly professed the Christian religion in December, 1829, and joined the Vermillion church, was ordained in December, 1835. Elder Hume is emphatically what may be considered a 'self made man,' in the sense in which that term is generally used. But having great natural ability, an indomitable will and an industrious disposition, he began very soon after his ordination to exhibit talent of a very extraordinary character from the beginning of his ministerial career, he espoused the doctrine of a rigid 'Predestinarian.' Therefore he has continued uniformly to preach that doctrine ever since.

"He is one of those independent thinkers, who takes the Bible itself for the man of his counsel in matters of doctrine and proclaims the gospel as he understands it without fear, favor or affections. In personal appearance he is very large, has a powerful chest and large head. While he firmly believes in the doctrine of Predestination, he just as firmly believes that the doctrine of a general atonement or that Christ died for all men, is false, and it is perfectly natural that while he is defending the Predestinarian doctrines, that he should make war upon Arminianism, and it was just as natural that he should come in contact with many strong men who held to the doctrine that opposed Predestination.

The doctrine of free discussion or free speech is strongly indorsed by Elder Humes. He is distinguished in kindly and courteous bearing toward those who differ in opinion from him.

"His manner of debating or preaching seems to be peculiar to himself, while he does not indulge in high flowing words of 'man's wisdom'; he takes the plain unvarnished word of God which he calls the "Artillery of Heaven,' and thunders away with a power and skill that is really surprising, nor does he use any surplusage. His words are few and well chosen, his reasoning close, his logic strong, almost irresistable.

"Elder Hume belonged to the 'Old School' Baptist church, and has been regarded for many years as one of the ablest men in that fraternity, and to my knowledge he has been for many years the leader, as to ability and influence of that people in this part of the country. His influence and popularity is about as great and he stands in about the same relaion to the Regular Baptist people that Elder Stinson did to the General Baptists.

"Although Elder Hume was not here at the time of the organization of the General Baptist church and did not at that time come in contact with Elder Stinson, yet they did meet soon after Elder Hume became a member of the Salem Association of Regular Baptists and notwithstanding they differed widely as to their doctrinal views, they became warm personal friends and this friendship continued unbroken, both being fond of controversy and each being leaders in their respective denomination it was but natural that they should engage in a debate which they did on two occasions.

The first one of these debates took place at Linnville, Warrick county, Indiana. This discussion was not written and published, and, I believe, neither of them was well satisfied with it, and they met again, by mutual agreement, at Owensville, Gibson county, Indiana, where they were provided with a stenographer who wrote up the debate, and it was published in book form, and had quite an extensive circulation and may be found in the libraries of many families in Indiana, Illinois and Kentucky. At this time, I will not hazard any opinion as to which one, or whether either of the disputants got the better of the argument. I will say, however, that there was quite a large attendance present who listened to the end with unabated interest, and while all felt edified the friends of each were satisfied with the efforts made by their respective champions.

"It is true that theological discussions do not often produce much good feeling between the contending parties but in this case I am glad to note an exception, for I have it from the mouths of the parties themselves, and those who were present, that the discussion was conducted with much decorum and courteous bearing by the disputants towards each other, so that the meeting had a tendency to edify and bring into closer relations, socially, the Regular and General Baptist people. May God, in his mercy, grant that all religious discussions end in that way.

"Elder Hume commenced his ministerial labors with Bethel Church, in Posey county, Indiana, April, 1840. He continued his labors with that church for about twenty-three years, and while doing this, he generally had the care of three other churches, and for many years he attended five churches and carried on his farm, besides.

"Elder Hume has always been opposed to ministers having stated salaries for their services. He is sometimes misunderstood in this regard and has been accused of advocating the doctrine that preachers should have no pay for their services. But to the contrary, he holds that it is the duty of every church to minister to the wants of their Pastor and that this should be done in proportion to the ability of each member, and that these contributions should be made not by any law by which members are taxed, but by the free will of persons who pay money on this account. He would not have one cent for his ministerial rervices if the collection had to be enforced by any law, ecclesiastical or otherwise, and it is with pleasure that I record the fact that his brethren, many of whom are wealthy, have appreciated his great services, and prompted by that law which the spirit of God writes on the hearts of his people, they have, at least, partially rewarded him so that, I am informed, he has a good home in Owensville, Gibson county, Indiana, and a sufficient competancy that enables him to spend the evening of his useful life in comparative comfort.

"The debates between Elders Hume and Stinson, at Owensville, was the last of the kind which has taken place between the ministers of the two denominations or between Elder Hume and any one in this portion of the country.

"In reviewing the conflicts which Elder Stinson had from time to time with that people, running over a period of nearly fifty years, it is pleasant to reflect that the contest which was somewhat bitter at first, ended in such good feeling; and it is also gratifying to know, that during all this long contest, whatever may have been said by the opposition as to the irregularities of Elder Stinson in matters of discipline and doctrine, no charge was ever made against his moral character and, I may further add, that Elder Hume, with all the opposition he has met with from time to time, has, also, maintained throughout his eventful life thus far, a good moral character, no charge has ever been made against him of any conduct unbecoming a christian or a minister, and although not so strong, physically, as formerly, he still preaches with much power.

"Elder Stinson has ended his earthly career, he has fought the good fight of faith and is, doubtless, resting from his labors.

"Elder Hume is growing old, his limbs which were once strong, now tremble with age and much labor. A few more days, or years, at most, and he too, will no doubt, be called from labor to reward, and then on the golden shores of the 'better country,' he will meet Elder Stinson where death is swallowed up in victory, where each in loving embrace, can join in singing the 'songs of Moses and the Lamb,' to whom they will ascribe all the glory and honor of their salvation to the Lamb that was slain and liveth for ever more.

"Elder Stinson's last preaching was on the second Sabbath in October, 1869, at the old Mt. Pleasant Church, in Posey county, Indiana. He come to the church while Elder Jacob Speer was preaching and after the discourse was ended the church requested that Elder Stinson preach a sermon, which he did, before the congregation was dismissed. After dismission he announced that he would remain in the neighborhood and that some one would preach at lamp-lighting. The people came out and Elder Stinson preached, which was his last sermon. On Monday he came, in company with Maj. J. B. Cox, to a point near his home, where they separated, Elder Stinson being, apparently, in good health, but was taken down sick in about two hours after reaching his home and lingered about ten days when he yielded up his spirit to God who gave it. Thus ended the life of the founder of the General Baptists in the West, who had continued incessantly preaching the gospel from the date of his licensing until within ten days of the close of his earthly existence, and it is remarkable that he had not another appointment at that time.

ELDER JESSE LANE, SR.

We have given a short biography of Elder Stinson as well as some of the strong men in the Regular Baptist denomination, we will now give from the same pen, Elder Wm. Reavis', short biographical sketches of some of the Ministers that were immediately connected with Elder Stinson in his labors.

The first we mention is Elder Jesse Lane, sr., who in usefulness and energy as an evangelist giving in- increase and strength to the denomination. It is but just to say that he did as much in this direction as any one man who was associated with Elder Stinson. Elder Lane had been with the movement from its organization and was ordained in August, 1824, and he was at all times a zealous, earnest working christian, with his whole heart in the work. He had only an ordinary common school education, but he was well read in both sacred and profane history, he was rather under the medium height but square built and athlete, with dark hair and eyes, he had a strong voice which was not only musical but it was full of tenderness and pathos, he was never regarded as a very good textuary preacher or able expounder of the mysteries of the bible, nor did he aspire to those kind of gifts. His great fort was to present the gospel in its simplest form, it was his great delight to give his hearers the sincere milk of the word, he delighted to dwell on the beauties of religion and he left to others the task of presenting controverted points. His great gift consisted not in preaching but exhortation, he brought to his work an enthusiasm which was truly sublime. I have never heard any man whom I thought to be his equal as an exhorter. He was therefore emphatically a great revivalist. It was his custom for many years to attend associations and protracted meetings in company with Elder Benoni Stinson, and after Elder Stinson had held a congregation spell-bound for from an hour and a half to two hours, Elder Lane was merely called out for an exhortation on such occasions; he would arise and occupy generally about twenty-five minutes in such exhortations and appealed to his hearers as no tongue or pen can describe; he poured forth one continuous stream of eloquence with such tenderness and pathos as to touch and melt the hardest heart on such occasions; he generally called for those seeking religion and asked them to present themselves at the altar of prayer. At such times I have seen as many as fifty persons present themselves for prayer, and before the meeting was over on some occasions nearly that many persons would make an open profession of religion. It was thus that Elder Lane lived and labored during his very useful life. He died in Warrick county, Indiana, at his home on the — day of ————, 1851. His last hours were spent in prayer and praises, and he sent word to his brethren that he died rejoicing, that his work was done and that he had been permitted to preach his great theme of free salvation for twenty-five years. It was thus this bold soldier of the cross fell in the midst of his usefulness, but it is a great consolation to know that he died with the harness on in the full assurance of faith and in hope of a glorious resurrection and immortality.

But never while memory lasts will he be forgotten by those who knew him. Hundreds who read this short sketch of his life with hearts swelling out with hopes of immortality can join me in this sentiment as to him.

> "My buried friend can I forget,
> Or must the grave forever sever;
> They linger in my memory yet
> And in my heart they live forever."

ELDER BERRY DUNN.

Elder Dunn was not an educated man, nor was he what might be called a doctrinal preacher, but he was a man of good sense and fine feeling; he was a revivalist and his exhortations were full of the deepest feeling and earnestness; he was equally able in prayer. I have often heard him on revival occasions in prayer and it appeared to me that he prayed with more emotion and earnestness than many others I heard.

He labored mostly in Posey county, Indiana, and was very successful in building churches and winning souls to Christ. His career was not a long one, as he died in the prime of life, but while he lived he was a bright and shining light in the church, and his labor will not soon be forgotton by those who knew him. I have no means of giving any particulars as to the time when he was ordained or the date of his death. He was truly a nursing father in Israel who lived and was faithful to his trust, and of him it may be truly said, 'he being dead yet speaketh.' He was a delegate when the old Liberty Association was organzed.

ELDER ALVAH PARKER.

I can not mention all the Ministers who were co-workers with Elder Stinson, who are now dead; but I cannot pass without mentioning in this connection Elder Alvah Parker. He lived most of his time in and died in Vanderburgh county, Indiana, and was therefore often thrown in the same company with Elder Stinson, and lived within half a mile of him when he died. Being among the first who became converted, he joined the old Liberty Association, and after it was organized he claimed Elder Stinson as his father in the Gospel and was strongly attached to him all through his life.

"They had labored together in the same church and same cause for nearly half a century and, united in life they were not long separated in death. When Elder Stinson died Elder Parker was near and caught his dying words and the writer saw him stand by the remains and preach Elder Stinson's funeral sermon, in company with Dr. Andrews. This, I believe, was Elder Parker's last sermon. There was a remarkable incident connected with this circumstance which seemed a little like prophecy. Elder Parker said that when Elder Stinson was dying he told him that he would be the next to follow him. Elder Parker spoke of this at the funeral with much emotion, and said he expected soon to join Elder Stinson in the 'better land,' and sure enough, he died within six weeks after this. They are both now together with the spirits of the just made perfect, to be separated no more forever. I have no means by which to enable me to tell the precise date of the death of Elder Parker. He died at his home in Vanderburgh county, Indiana, about November, 1869. So ended the career of one who had been a preacher for nearly thirty years, and he, too, has left a name which will live and ought to live on the brightest pages of the history of the General Baptist denomination.

"I will remark here, that I am speaking mainly of ministers who are dead and who were more immediately connected with Elder Stinson in his labors. I would be pleased to make honorable mention of each and all of the veterans in the ministry who have died while in the service, but it will be impossible to do so in the short space allotted to me in a work of this kind. Many will remember Elder John Wood, Jacob Hougland and James Blackburn, all of whom were good and true men. Elder Blackburn, I am informed, died full of trust and in the hope of a blissful immortality, and his mantle has fallen on two of his sons, Elders W. J. and Wilson Blackburn, who are earnest and useful ministers and reside in Posey county, Indiana.

ELDER THOMAS FULLER.

Sometime in 1825, Elder Stinson established a preaching point in the neighborhood of where Mt. Gilead Church now stands. He met with much opposition in that quarter but still a wonderful revival followed his preaching and many were converted. Among these was one convert whose conversion seemed almost like a miracle. This was Thomas Fuller, who, up to this time, had been one of the most incorrigibly hardened of all the men in that neighborhood. It was a strange thing to see him at meeting and surprisingly strange to see him bowed down as a mourner, asking the prayers of God's people in his behalf. However, he was converted, and this wild man, who had hitherto been fierce and almost a terror to the good people of the neighborhood was now clothed as with a garment of salvation, and like one of old, seemed to be sitting at the feet of Jesus in his right mind. Nor was this all; he had no learning. He did not know one letter from another. He could neither read or write a word. His wife could both read and write and she was a christian. He sat daily at her feet and listened to her read the Scriptures. He committed whole chapters, to memory, and what is more strange, he began to preach. He was, at the request of his churchs licenced in September, 1827, and ordained two years after. He took the field and preached with such power and success as to surprise every one. His quotations of Scripture were nearly always correct and his manner of explaining different texts was astounding. He continued to go on, and prosper, building up churches wherever he went, and among all the ministers that sprung from old Mt. Gilead Church, Elder Thomas Fuller was the most noted and useful of any of them. He was a large man, about five feet ten inches in height, a broad chest and weighed about two hundred pounds, had a fine shaped head and face and a very heavy brain. His memory was extraordinary and he had a strong voice. He was pastor of Mt. Gilead Church for many years or most of the time from September, 1834 to 1852, and also attended two or three other churches at the same time. He seldom ever failed to preach once or twice on every Sunday when he was well. He presided at the business meetings of the churches he attended with dignity, and exhibited much parliamentary knowledge. His manners were sweet and gentle and his company was sought by many of the learned and influential men of the country. In short, he was the most popular and influential man I ever knew, to be unlearned, as he was. He took great delight in performing the rites of baptism, and during his life he immersed many hundreds. He never received much pay for his pastoral services but labored on his farm with his own hands and not only made a support for himself and family but often gave money to other ministers who visited his neighborhood. His disposition was cheerful and happy; indeed, he was witty, and at times, a great jester. For many year before he died he had frequent attacks of inflamatory rheumatism, which were very painful. He bore all these afflictions with a courage and fortitude that seemed almost super-human. He was born July 6th, 1791. He died, after a lingering illness, on the 25th day of August, 1857, leaving behind him a testimony of a blameless and useful life, universally beloved and respected by hosts of friends. In all the relations of life, as pastor, husband, father and friend, he fulfilled his duty with alacrity and having received much kindness at his hands, while he lived, his memory will ever be dear to me. Such was the result of his labors in Warrick county Indiana, that his influence, for good, will not soon be forgotten.

It was by such means as this that Elder Stinson was spreading the doctrines of free salvation on the terms of the gospel. He went up into the wilds of Warrick county when the country was new and a great revival was commenced under his ministry and Thomas Fuller and scores of others were converted. It is thus the good work of a useful minister goes on and good influences are started afloat down the stream of time, and eternity alone can unfold the amount of good which may result from a begining like this. It is on this account that it may be said of a good man when he is gone, he, being dead, yet speaketh. W. R.

We now turn to trace the history of Liberty Assosiation, the first of the General Baptist's organized in the West. It will be observed that at the organization of the body in 1824, it consisted of four churches, two hundred and one members, and twenty-two delegates, which are as follows :

Liberty Church—Elder Benoni Stinson, John B. Stinson, Daniel R. Jacobs, Geo. B. Wagnon, Benjamin McNew, and James Slover. Seventy-four members.

Union Church—Thomas E. Casselbery, John Blair, Asa A. Robertson, James Marrs, Berry T. Dunn, and Rufus Williams. Sixty-two members.

Black River Church—Thomas Almon, John Almon, John Robertson, William Steel, and George Woolzey. Twenty-nine members.

Providence Church—Jesse Lane, Aaron Ellsworth, John Garrett, Abraham Fronsway, and Henry James. Twenty-six members.

This little band appointed a Committee to draw up a Constitution, By-laws and articles of Faith, which when reported were adopted, and the articles of Faith remain to-day as they were when adopted with the exception of article fifth and eleventh. Article fifth read at first as follows, to-wit:

"That the saints will finally persevere through grace to glory."

Elder Stinson never believed in this article, but some of the members in the organization of Liberty Association did, hence the fifth article remained unchanged for twenty-one years, when at the instance of Elder Wm. Reavis it was changed to read:

"We believe that he that shall endure to the end, the same shall be saved."

Also at the same meetings the eleventh article was amended by placing in parenthesis, as it now stands (Infants and Idiots excepted.)

We here insert the Articles of Faith of most of the General Baptist Associations in Missouri and Arkansas. The first eleven of these are the same as we find in the minutes of all the Associations in Illinois, Indiana and Kentucky. The twelfth and thirteenth are a little in advance and doubtless will soon be adopted by all of our Associations.

They have the true ring and upon this ground we can successfully meet every objection of close communionists. Upon this ground our people in Missouri and Arkansas are meeting close communionists and are wonderfully successful.

CONFESSION OF FAITH.

1. We believe that the Scriptures of the Old and New Testaments are the infallible Word of God, and the only safe rule of faith and practice.

2. That there is only one true and living God, in the God-head or divine essence—Father, Son and Holy Ghost.

3. That we are fallen and depraved creatures, and cannot extricate ourselves from our fallen situation by any ability we possess by nature.

4. That salvation, regeneration, sanctification, justification and redemption, are by the life, death, resurrection, ascension and intercession of our Lord and Savior, Jesus Christ.

5. We believe that he that shall endure to the end, the same shall be saved.

6. That the joys of the righteous and the punishment of the wicked will be eternal.

7. We believe that Baptism and the Lord's Supper are ordinances of Jesus Christ appointed in the church and none but true believers are the proper subjects, and the only mode of baptism is immersion, and feet washing is an example or pattern of piety and humiliation.

8. We believe in the sanctity of the first day of the week (or Lord's Day,) and that it ought to be observed and spent in the public and private worship of God, and on it we should abstain from our wordly concerns, except in cases of necessity or mercy.

9. We believe in the resurrection of the body, both of the just and unjust, but everyone in his own order, those who have done good to the resurrection of life, and those who have done evil to the resur-

rection of damnation; and God hath appointed a day in which to judge the world in righteousness by Jesus Christ.

10. That it is our duty to be tender and affectionate to one another, and to study the happiness of the people of God in general, and to be singly engaged to promote the honor and glory of God.

11. We believe Jesus Christ, by the grace of God, tasted death for every man; yet none can partake of his divine benefits only by repentance toward God and faith toward our Lord Jesus, (infants and idiots excepted, they being included in the Covenant of God's grace.)

12. We believe that the Lord Jesus Christ is the door into the Church and that baptism is a duty in answer to a good conscience.

13. We believe that the Lord's people are one in him and therefore should be one at His table.

The second meeting of Liberty Association was held with Union Church, Posey county, when four new churches were added to their number, to-wit.: Mt. Gilead, Mt. Pleasant, Concord and Hopewell. The two former are in existence at present, one in Warrick the other in Posey county.

The Association, at this meeting, numbered three hundred and eleven, forty of whom were delegates.

At the third meeting, two churches, Clear Fork, of Pigeon and Free Salem, in Kentucky, were added. They then had two hundred and fifty-eight members and twenty-nine delegates, a decrease of fifty three members and a loss of eleven delegates.

The fourth meeting was held with Providence church. They did not receive any new churches this year but had two hundred and eighty-four members and thirty-two delegates, a gain of sixty-six members and two representatives.

The fifth Association was held with Concord Church, Posey county, and numbered two hundred and fifty-four members and thirty-three delegates, a loss of thirty members, but a gain of one delegate.

Up to this meeting the General Baptists of Liberty Association had practiced close communion, or held communion with immersed believers only.. Elder Stinson was held to this practice by the same course that retained the article of "final perseverance." It seemed impossible to get everything arranged as he desired. At first some of those who stood the closest to him in his belief on the atonement were strong opposers of apostacy, and "free or open communion," but Elder Stinson lived to see the day that all of these barriers were removed.

At their fifth meeting they agreed to proclaim open communion.

The writer heard Elder Stinson relate the circumstance that caused him to break over the barriers of close communion. He said that he (Stinson) "was conducting a protracted meeting near the Ohio river, in Vanderburgh county, Indiana. when Alexander Downey, a Cumberland Presbyterian minister came to his assistance and did excellent service all the week in singing, praying, exhorting and preaching, which was gladly received and highly appreciated, but on Sabbath was a communion service; I did not say it in so many words, but our former practice said, we have been well pleased with you all the week, but now you will please take a back seat until after this solemn duty and binding service is over, then we will be glad to have you assist us in our services." He said: "I must confess to you brethren, that I felt mean, and there and then I told my brethren that I intended to invite all of God's people to the Lord's table," and he ever afterwards followed the injunction of Paul: "Let a man examine himself and let him so eat," and he lived to rejoice at and fully endorsed the proclamation of the motto of Mr. Spurgeon, which is: " There is not a saint on God's green earth from whom I would absent myself at the Lord's table." The Association sustained Elder Stinson in his determination to practice open communion, and to-day there is not a single General Baptist church in the United States that does not practice open communion.

The sixth Association was held with Mt. Pleasant Church, Posey county, Indiana. Seven churches were represented and twenty-five delegates with a membership of one hundred and ninety-five. This shows a loss of three churches, five delegates and fifty-nine members. This appears to have been the most depressing period in the history of Liberty Association. The enemies of the General Baptist cause lost no opportunity in taking every advantage of Elder Stinson and his people, they called him the Freewiller, they told the people that the name General Baptist originated with Stinson and his few followers, that their practices were contrary to the teaching of the scriptures and that in so preaching they lost their identity as Baptists. Elder Stinson and his adherents sorely felt the evil arising from such misrepresentations, therefore a committee of five were appointed to prepare a letter circular, setting forth the origin of the principles as taught by General Baptists. The letter is found in the Minutes of the sixth meeting and appears to have had the desired effect.

They also appointed quarterly meetings in different parts of the Association and appointed Elders

Benoni Stinson, John B. Stinson, Jesse Lane, John Davis, and Thomas Fuller and Brothers Geo. B. Dagon and Reuben Darby to attend said quarterly meetings.

This is the first time we hear of John Davis being called an Elder.

The seventh Association met with Free Salem Church, Henderson county, Kentucky, and reported one hundred and ninety-four members, a loss of one. At this meeting "Elder Elias Hutchison, a visiting brother of the Free-Will Baptists of the State of Maine" appeared and was invited to a seat in counsel with them.

The eighth Association was held with the Mt. Gilead Church, Warrick county, Indiana. It is proper to state at this point that about the time Liberty Association was organized, a like separation took place in many other Associations in the South and West, most of whom was finally overpowered or absorbed by the Mother Association or the Missionary Baptists. Many faithful men however that were driven out under these circumstances formed themselves in to separate Baptists, Free, Free-Will and Free Communion Baptists. Notwithstanding these different names they are all genuine General Baptists in faith and practice and many of them are adopting that name. In the year 1827, Elder Jacob Speer with a number of others, by mutual consent, separated from the United Baptists, in the State of Tennessee, some of them moving to central Illinois, some to Indiana and some to other States. Elder Speer came to Indiana and settled near Princeton, Gibson county, Indiana. This was within the bounds of the Wabash District Association of which Elder Stinson was formerly a member.

ELDER JACOB SPEER.

Elder Speer being yet alive and well, he has passed his four-score years, it will not be necessary for me to say a great deal about him here, but this much I will say: it is impossible to write up, correctly, the history of the General Baptist church in this part of the country without mentioning him, nor could I do justice to the life and services of Elder Stinson without the frequent mention of the name of Elder Jacob Speer, and justice and truth compels me to say that, excepting Elder Benoni Stinson himself, no man living or dead has done so much to build up the General Baptist Church in this country as has Elder Speer. He has now labored in the ministry for over half a century and most of that time he has had the care of four churches, preaching to each two days in each month and often holding protracted meetings every day in the week. He is now old, and nearing the other shore, and cannot labor so much as formerly, but he is yet very useful and labors much in the cause when the weather is not too severe from heat or cold. He is a large man and has been very strong and vigorous. His voice, which is now somewhat shattered and husky, was very strong when he was in the prime of life. His education was very limited, but having mixed in good society so much and possessing an enterprising mind he has become generally, very well informed, especially in the Scriptures. Here I will say, for the benefit of young ministers, that Elder Speer during all his long life in the ministry has never done any act that would bring reproach upon the cause of Christ, and to this day he commands the respect of not only his own people, but the people of all denominations, who know him.

He is a man of strong convictions and his sermons are delivered with extraordinary earnestness. As to his great success as a preacher, we will here give an essay read by Elder Speer before the fifty-eighth annual meeting of Liberty Association, on the 18th of September, 1881. This is a synopsis of his labors in the ministry, and is as follows:

"I embraced Christ as my Saviour in the time of the great revival in Tennessee, in 1817, which lasted about three years. I united with Brawley's Fork Church of United Baptists which was then working under the old union, the basis of which was: "The preaching of the doctrine that Christ died for all men should be no bar to fellowship," but the general atonement element was so hard pressed by the Calvinists that a mutual separation took place and I went with what was called the Browley's Fork Church of Separate Baptists, in 1824, who held to a general atonement and open communion and belonged to the Concord Association of Separate Baptists. In the summer of 1828 I was licenced to preach and left Tennessee and reached Gibson county, Indiana, on the 6th day of January, 1829.

"As there were no Liberal Baptists in Gibson county at that time, I held my letter and commenced preaching in the country south of Princeton. In September, 1829, I went back to Tennessee and was ordained by Elders Calvin Curlee and Elisha Bell, of the Separate Baptists, and returned to Gibson county and continued preaching. In January, 1830, I constituted Enon Church, on seven members, and the same day received two by experience. This church was constituted simply as a Baptist church, holding to the doctrine of a general atonement and open communion. This church continued to prosper and sometime during the year 1830 we heard of the General Baptists in Vanderburgh and Posey counties, Indiana. I visited one of their churches in order to meet Elder Stinson, but he failed to attend his appointment and I returned home disappointed. Sometime during the winter of 1830 I started to Vincennes to enter a piece of land. As I approached White river I discovered a man waiting on the south side of the river, which proved to be Elder Benoni Stinson, who was also going to Vincennes to enter land. During this trip we obtained a good understanding of each others' doctrines and finding them to perfectly harmonize, we, in the fall of 1831, attended the Liberty Association of General Baptists, which was held with old Mt. Gilead Church, near Boonville, Warrick county, Indiana, and there united with the General Baptists and my labors have been with these people from that day until the present time.

"The following statistics will, to some extent, show the success attending my labors from 1830 to 1881: I have preached, as pastor, for eighteen churches;

have preached nine introductory sermons for Liberty Association; have acted as Moderator seventeen times; have attended the Association, as a delegate, forty-nine years out of fifty; I have constituted and assisted in constituting seventeen churches, and assisted in constituting three Associations; have united in marriage about one hundred and fifty couples, and have baptized about nine hundred.

To-day I am eighty years old and I feel like my labors will soon end and that my reward is close at hand."

On this occasion the brethren and friends gave money and other articles, to the amount of twenty-five dollars to elder Speer, as a birth-day present.

Elder Speer was diligent in preaching the Word and soon he organized Enon Church of Baptists, near Princeton, Gibson county. About this time he learned that Liberty Association of General Baptists was to convene in the following October, (1831) with Mt. Gilead Church, three miles south of Boonville, Warrick county, Indiana. When this meeting come on Elder Speer and Martin Tennison, from Enon Church, of eleven members, appeared with a letter, asking to be admitted as a member of Liberty Association of General Baptists. This was a grand and profitable union. It not only gave new life to Liberty Association, but threw a protection around Elder Speer and his little church at Enon which animated them to new action. This, the eighth meeting, numbered two hundred and thirty-four members, a gain of forty members.

At this meeting Elder Benoni Stinson was appointed General Missionary.

The ninth meeting was held with Providence church Vanderburgh county, Indiana. Nine churches were represented, with a membership of two hundred and ninety-seven, a gain of sixty-three. Elder Stinson, who had been appointed missionary at their previous meeting, reported that he had witnessed about forty conversions and that there was a general awakening among the unconverted, and that about two hundred were mourning on account of their sins. At the same time he stated that his pecuniary embarrassments had been such that he could not give much of his time to the work until the first of June. Since that time he had devoted almost all his time to missionary work. This report so encouraged the delegates that they obligated themselves to raise $167 for the missionary work the following year. At this meeting the churches were requested to observe the following 25th day of December as a day of fasting and prayer. It is to be noted that from this meeting, at which Elder Speer and his two churches joined the General Baptists, they steadily increased in numbers and influence, except two years.

The tenth Association was held with Enon Church, Gibson county, it numbered three hundred and eighty-three members and thirty-one delegates, a net gain of eighty-six.

The eleventh Association, held with Concord Church, Posey county, Indiana, numbered three hundred and seventy-three members, a loss of ten members.

The twelfth Association, held with Providence Church, numbered three hundred and eighty-two members, a gain of nine. At this meeting a resolution was passed in opposition to intemperance. They also agreed to form a Home Mission Society, at Evansville, Indiana.

The thirteenth Association was held with Enon Church and numbered three hundred and eighty-five, a gain of three. Elder Lewis Gould, of the Free-Will Baptists, was present at this meeting.

The fourteenth meeting was held at Mt. Gilead Church, Warrick county, Indiana, and numbered four hundred and seventy-one, a gain of eighty-eight.

At this meeting they agreed to send Elder Benoni Stinson as a corresponding messenger to the General Conference of Free-Will Baptists, which met in the following October, in the State of Vermont. Also agreed to render aid to the American Foreign Bible Society. This ends the third chapter of our work.

CHAPTER IV.

In the third chapter we have traced the history of Liberty Association for fourteen years. In this chapter we begin with the fifteenth meeting which was held with the old Liberty Church, in Vanderburgh county, Indiana. The first General Baptist Church of Evansville and Black River Church of Posey county, was received at the meeting. Brother A. H. Polk was a delegate from the Evansville church. This is the first mention of his name in connection with Liberty Association. We intend in the closing chapters of this work to record biographical sketches of many of the Ministers of the General Baptist denomination, therefore they only will be mentioned in the general make-up of this work. At this meeting is the first mention we find of a public collection being taken to defray the expenses of the Association.

At this meeting we hear the following resolution in reference to mission work.

226   EARLY HISTORY

"Resolved, that we request the Home Mission Society to exert its utmost influence to support the preaching of the Gospel in our destitute churches."

In answer to a petition from old Liberty Church concerning an institution of learning is the following:

"That three of her members of the Association appointed together with two gentlemen not members of this Association are to procure a charter from the legislature of the State of Indiana at its ensuing session and to purchase a site, erect and furnish a seminary of learning and that Col. Joseph Lane and Chas. D. Bourne, Esq., gentlemen who are not members of this Association and that Elder Benoni Stinson, Jesse Lane and Charles S. Weaver be appointed the Committee.

General prosperity now began to attend the labors of this devoted people. They numbered this year five hundred and sixty-nine, a gain of ninty-eight.

The sixteenth session commenced with Concord Church in Posey county, and they have enrolled seven hundred and ninety one communicants, a net gain of two hundred and twenty-two, and one new church. In reference to the "Seminary of learning," we find this resolution :

"That this Association ratify the acts of the Evansville church with reference to the proposed 'Seminary of learning,' and that she now take the institution under her patronage.

"That the Board of Trustees appointed for the seminary last year, viz: Col. Joseph Lane, Chas. D. Borne, Esq., Elders Benoni Stinson, Jesse Lane and Brother C. S. Weaver be re-appointed and that Elder John B. Stinson and Brother Wm. Depriest be added to to the number.

"That Elder Benoni Stinson, Jesse Lane and Geo. W. McAndrew be appointed agents to solicit subscriptions for and otherwise to promote the interest of the seminary.

"That the seminary take the name of 'The Indiana General Baptist Seminary.'

"That each member of this Association be advised to do all in his power by way of patronizing and otherwise sustaining the Institution."

Urgent calls from Kentucky and Illinois came up to this meeting for Ministerial help and provisions were made to supply them.

It was also resolved to appoint C. S. Weaver to secure two hundred copies of "The Treaties of Faith of the Free-Will Baptists, for the use of this Association." This action, doubtless, was conducive of much good in systematizing and better organizing the forces of the General Baptists.

Elder John B. Stinson was called upon and reported that the Home Mission Society has become inoperative. It was immediately resolved that the officers of the Society meet at old Liberty Church, on the first Wednesday in November, 1839, and revive the Society, which was not in vain, as appears from the report at the next meeting, which show that much good had been accomplished and that the Society, at that time, (1840) was "in a flourishing condition."

The seventeenth Association convened with Enon Church, in 1840. This was a successful year. They received nine new churches, to-wit: Grayville, Harmony, Grass Creek, Caldwell, Sharon, Owensville, Bethlehem, Mt. Olive and Zion, their net gain was ninety-nine.

At this meeting the educational interest was still alive and one solicitor appointed in each church represented, to solicit funds for the seminary and report to Charles D. Borne, by the first of January, 1841, and the same trustees were continued. A committee consisting of Elders Benoni Stinson, John B. Stinson and Jesse Lane, were appointed to prepare a circular letter, setting fourth the fundamental doctrines of the General Baptists, and showing that their doctrines have been recognized as the doctrines of the gospel, by a respectable portion of the christian church from the days of the Apostles to the present time. Also requested the committee to present said circular to the next Association for inspection."

The design of this circular was to show to the world that the opposers of the General Baptists had misrepresented their origin, they claiming that the General Baptists were no older than Elder Stinson.

This old and false accusation has followed us into every new field in which we have endeavored to plant churches. But we rejoice that in Mr. Knight's history this matter is forever set at rest. Mr. Knight fully establishes everything which the above resolution or request called for.

At this, the seventeenth annual meeting, in 1840, the five churches south of the Ohio river were granted letters of dismissal "for the purpose of forming a new Association, and appointed Elders J. B. Stinson, B. Stinson, J. Speer and J. Lane, a committee to meet said churches, viz: Sharon, Caldwell, Grass Creek, Chalybeat Springs and Liberty, Kentucky, at Caldwell Church, on Friday, October 9th, 1840, to constitute said Association.

The history of this new Association, to-wit: Union, will follow, in its proper place.

At this meeting we find the name of Wm. Reavis, jr., mentioned as a licentiate from Enon Church.

The eighteenth meeting was held with Mt. Gilead Church, Warrick county, September, 1841, and owing to the fact that the churches south of the Ohio river had been lettered off, to form a new Association, for convenience, Liberty Association was reduced to six hundred and eighty-one members.

One of the most important moves connected with the history of this people, had it been carried out, was made at this meeting, which was this:

"Agreed, that a committee of one member from each church, be appointed to solicit subscriptions for the purpose of publishing a book entitled 'The History of the General Baptists.'

"And, it is further agreed, that Elders John B. Stinson, Benoni Stinson and Jesse Lane be appointed a committee to publish said book, provided a sufficient sum be obtained to justify the undertaking."

As regards the duties of deacons, we find the following:

"In answer to the request of Evansville Church, agreed that, in the opinion of this Association, the official duties of a deacon are, to attend to the wants of the poor, and pastor of the church, and, also, to prepare the elements of the Lord's supper, and to assist in the administration of the same."

It was further agreed, that:

"With the consent of brother William Reavis, jr., that he be appointed a missionary for nine months, commencing the first day of January, next."

This is evidence of the high appreciation in which

the Association esteemed his ministerial gifts in the very commencement of his ministry.

ELDER WM. REAVIS.

A short biographical sketch of Elder Wm. Reavis, written by himself, appeared in vol. 5, No. 47, of the old General Baptists Herald, in connection with the biographical sketches, which we have already copied, says Elder Reavis:

"I have already mentioned the circumstance of having joined Enon Church, in Gibson county, Indiana, in 1839. I was sometime after this licensed to preach and was recommended by my church to the presbytery for, and received ordination, within six months from the time I was licenced. I had been bred up by the 'old school Baptist denomination' and my father was a staunch Calvinistic, but my mother was always a believer in a general atonement. My father dying when I was young it was but natural that I should sympathize with my mother in my religious convictions, as far as I had any. From the time Elder Stinson began preaching in Gibson county, my mother encouraged me to go often and hear him and she often accompanied me to his meetings. I first heard Elder Stinson preach in the month of June, 1826.

"Although many years have since rolled by and I was but a boy at that time, an impression was, on that day, made upon my mind which I shall never forget. His sermon was on a funeral occasion and even the text is still remembered. Rev. 14th chap. and 13th verse: 'Blessed are the dead who die in the Lord, from henceforth; yea saith the spirit, that they may rest from their labors and their works do follow them.' Although I did not profess faith in Christ until the year 1839, I never forgot the lesson which I learned on that day.

"It was in the month of March, in 1839, within one quarter of a mile of the place where I had first heard Elder Stinson, while setting and listening to my good old uncle, Stephen Strickland, sr., in an old school house, that I first felt that God, for Christ's sake, had pardoned all my sins and although the old school house has long been removed, I often visit the place with pleasure, and think of my conflicts and triumphs there. It was there, in that neighborhood, where I spent my boyhood days. It was there that I learned that I was a sinner and there where I first viewed, by faith, that flowing stream which is constantly supplied by the bleeding wounds of our Saviour. O, hallowed spot! May I never cease to cherish the fond recollections it brings to my mind. The reader will excuse me for making mention of myself in this connection. My associations with Elder Stinson and the General Baptist denomination after this period were of such a character that I shall be compelled to make some allusions to myself occasionally.

In the Autumn of 1841, Liberty Association met at Mt. Gilead Church, Warrick county, Indiana. At this meeting I was appointed to take the field as a general Missionary for the denomination without being limited. My instructions were to begin on the first day of January, 1842, and continue in the field nine months. I accordingly entered upon the work at the appointed time and traveled and preached in Indiana, Illinois and Kentucky somewhat extentively. I had many sore trials and troubles during this period of my life being young and inexperienced, but taking these nine months altogether I look back upon them now as the most happy and useful nine months I have ever realized in all my life. During my efforts on this Mission I preached one hundred and thirty-two sermons, and witnessed the conversion of one hundred and seventeen souls at meetings where I labored."

As long as Brother Reavis remained an humble

Minister of the Gospel, he was one among the most useful men that ever belonged to the General Baptist denomination, but alas, he laid aside his Ministerial robes and suffered himself to be drawn into to politics. This was the great mistake of his life, and it soon brought other troubles, which caused Brother Reavis to quit the Ministry altogether. He was once Treasurer of Gibson county, Indiana, and once a candidate for Congress, but defeated by Hon. Smith Miller.

He subsequently served as a Captian in the United States service in the late war, after which he established himself in the legal profession at Evansville, Indiana, and is now living there in very comfortable circumstances. While it is much lamented that Elder Reavis has ceased preaching, it is gratifying to know thas he is still living and a humble Christian, and it is hoped by many that he may soon enter the field again as a minister.

The nineteenth meeting was held with Black River Church, in Posey county, when they numbered eight hundred and sixty-nine, a gain of eighty-eight, and two new churches were received, Union, Illinois, and Salem.

It will be observed that Union Association now occupies the territory in Kentucky, adjacent Liberty, so Liberty Association began to move eastward into

Warrick and Pike counties and westward into Illinois.

Elder Wm. Reavis, who had been appointed missionary a year before, reported his labors for the last nine months:

"Showing that he had traveled over a large portion of country, preached one hundred and thirty-two sermons and witnessed one hundred and seventeen hopeful conversions, besides giving much interesting religious information."

A very important resolution was passed, urging the necessity of family devotion, which is as follows:

"That the heads of families be exhorted to worship God in their houses and bring up their children in the nurture and admonition of the Lord."

The twentieth meeting was held with Union Church, Posey county. It had nine hundred and thirty-eight members, a gain of sixty-nine. Columbia Church received, T. M. Strain and J. H. Cochrum, delegates. This is the first mention made of Elder T. M. Strain.

In answer to a request from Union Church, the following form in dismissing members by letter was given:

"This is to certify that our brother A. B. is in good standing and full fellowship up to this date and is now dismissed from our watch-care."

ELDER GEORGE P. CAVANAH.

Among the most distinguished names in the catalogue of deceased Ministers stands that of the late lamented and much beloved George P. Cavanah. This man, like Elder Stinson, was a native Kentuckian.

He was born in Christian county, Kentucky, on the eighth day of February, 1823. He was the the youngest son of William and Ivy Cavanah, and brought up under their care until he was eighteen years old. I will now quote from Elder Cavanah's own words found in a manuscript which is before me. "When I was eighteen years old, my father, through misfortune, was reduced from easy to very limited circumstances. All of his property, except what the law allowed him, was taken from him. The old homestead was sold at Sheriff's sale, and the law granted him the privilege of redemption by paying ten per cent. interest within twelve months. His age and infirmity rendered it impossible for him to redeem it, and the purchaser gave me the privilege of redeeming the land. I was young and my associates being by no means calculated to encourage me in the undertaking, I resolved too seek employment in other parts, and accordingly I prepared to leave those parts rendered dear to me by scenes of my childhood. About the 20th of February, 1840, I left my fathers house in company with a young man by the name of Thos. Pool, who resided in Henderson county, Kentucky. Through his solicitations I made up my mind to try my fortune in that county. Upon my arrival there I was taken sick and after a weeks' confinement I was again partially restored to health. I heard of employment in Hopkins county, some ten miles distant and I immediately returned that far to apply for the place and was successful. I remained here some six weeks and returned again to Henderson county and engaged with Mr. B. W. Handley and Herbert Baldwin to make a crop. During the spring and summer my health was fully restored. I found my new home quite agreeable in some respects, in others rather unpleasent. These two men seemed to take a deep interest in my welfare and always gave me good advice.

The season was favorable and we raised a good crop of tobacco, but before we could get our tobacco in market the term for the redemption of my father's land had expired. My employers assisted me in borrowing the money and I went and redeemed the land in due time. This involved me in debt and feeling under obligation to my two friends, Baldwin and Handley, I set in with them for the second crop.

I became acquainted with a couple of ministers of the gospel, who were preaching in that section, by the name of George W. McAndrew and James Hunt. Under their labors I became concerned about my soul's salvation. My associations, to some extent, were unfavorable to religion. My employers were religious men and gave me all the encouragement that I could have asked but my favorite young men, with whom I associated, were very rude. From them I received no encouragement. I was for a long time vascilating, sometimes I was deeply concerned, at other times I felt indifferent. I continued in this state until some time in the summer of 1842. During that season there was a considerable revival of religion in the neighborhood where I lived. I attended these meetings and resolved that I would renounce all my sins and give my heart to the Lord. After I had formed this resolution I was very attentive to what I was told to be my duty. I was particularly attentive to secret prayer, so much so, that I settled down in a kind of stupor in my feelings and would sometimes reason with myself in this way: Well, I have done my duty and I guess the Lord will save me, ultimately; however, my soul became unusually burdened and attendance to secret prayer failed to bring that temporary comfort to my mind. I attended a meeting in the settlement. Mourners were invited and I distinguished myself as a seeker after the Word of Life. I then exhausted all my strength pleading and crying for mercy, and after my strength failed, yea, after prayers and tears failed to bring salvation to my poor agonizing soul, for want of strength, I began to look around for help. I could find no earthly power that could administer the balm. Last of all, I turned my eyes towards Him who was once a man of sorrow and acquainted with grief. To my great surprise, instead of looking on me with indignation I beheld a reconciled countenance, and instead of spurning me from his presence he seemed to speak in sweet accents of love and said: Thy sins are all forgiven thee; take my yoke upon you and you shall find rest for your soul. I found myself in an extacy of delight in a moment, under his smiles and felt myself united to his people by an indisoluble tie of love.

An opportunity was given, the same night, being the 6th of September, 1842, and I united with the General Baptist church and submitted to the ordinance of baptism some few days after my unition with the church, by Elder James M. Hunt. I was still enthralled for a portion of the money that I had borrowed to redeem my father's land, which confined me to constant labor and deprived me of the many privileges I might otherwise have enjoyed. During that fall and winter I attended with the brethren in weekly prayer meetings and was frequently urged forward in exhortation. Nothing so delighted me as to be engaged in those social prayer meetings. My desire to serve God for what he had done for me increased daily.

In the spring of 1843 the church recommended me to the presbytery. Accordingly I attended presbytery, was examined and licensed to preach on the 15th day of April, 1843, Elder Geo. W. McAndrew presiding, I proceeded immediately to the work of the ministry. I employed myself in teaching a primary school for a livelihood and preached what I could during the spring and summer.

In the fall the Union Association met in the settlement where I lived and I attended. Elder Benoni Stinson was there and he prevailed on me to go to school. It was with no small degree of embarrassment that I consented to do so on account of my pecuniary circumstances, but some of my brethren joined with Brother Stinson and promised to assist me. I now commenced making preparations to attend school the following winter. In the month of November, 1843, I set out for the State of Indiana and crossed the Ohio river at Henderson, walked some four miles up the river to the house of James Starnes, Esq., where I was kindly received by the family and hospitably entertained until the day following, which being church meeting day, I attended church and listened to Elder Benoni Stinson, who was pastor of the church. I accompanied Brother Stinson to his home where I remained a week, during which time I was agreeably entertained both by the family and the library of Elder Stinson, and here it was agreed that I should attend a district school taught by Brother W. W. Willard, who was a competent teacher and that I should board with Brother Starnes."

This is all the data I have from his pen as regards his life, but it is enough to give the outlines of a character so noble and so pure, that the reader will not be surprised to learn that Elder Cavanah became one of the brightest stars and ablest preachers, not only as compared with General Baptist Ministers, but with those of any denomination in this part of the country of whom I have any knowledge. He did not receive anything more than a good common school education, but he applied himself so closely that he was well versed in the English branches of learning and very well read in theology as a preacher, his style was not only dignified, but his reasoning was clear and convincing and his logic was irresistable, his gestures were fine and manly and his voice was full of pathos and tenderness. He was so kind, so loving and so affectionate in his manner that he won the affectionate regard not only of his own people, but of many who belonged to other denominations. I once heard a distinguished Minister of the Methodist Church remark, that for natural ability as a gospel Minister he had never heard any man, who was superior to George P. Cavanah. From the time that Elder Cavanah took the field next to Elder Stinson, he was certainly the most eminent and useful of all the General Baptist ministers known to me. His preaching was listened to by great crowds of people wherever he was known and his very name became a tower of strength to the denomination. After marrying a Miss Lydia Robb, of Posey county, Indiana, he settled down in Owensville, Indiana. He lived in Indiana from the time he crossed the Ohio river to receive a better education. He made his home a part of the time in Gibson and a part of the time in Posey county, and for some years he was pastor of Mt. Pleasant Church, in the latter and to Owensville Church in the former named county, where he was most distinguished for his usefulness, but beside this his ministrations took a much wider range. Being thoroughly imbued with a missionary spirit he often visited the out-posts of the denomination not only in Indiana, but in Kentucky and Illinois, also.

It was a great relief to Elder Stinson, as I have often heard him say, to know that he had such strong support as Elder Cavanah, who was his co-worker in every movement which was gotten up for the advancement of the Redeemer's kingdom.

Elder Stinson had taken this man by the hand when he had first set foot on Indiana soil, as a mere boy, assisted in his education, opened to him his house, together with his library, and it was there at "Goshen Farm," the name of Elder Stinson's old homestead, on the banks of the beautiful Ohio river, where young Cavanah laid the foundation for that brilliant career which afterwards gave him so much distinction, but so bright a star and so brilliant a genius was not destined to remain long on earth. Elder Cavanah began to decline in health soon after he began to preach. From his boyhood he had seen trouble; to see his aged parents suddenly plunged from a position of comparative wealth to dependence, their old homestead, dear alike to him and them, sold under the hammer of the sheriff, for the debts of another and then the struggle of young Cavanah, both physically and mentally, he toiled for years to restore to his parents their home. Although, like the hero he was, he gained the victory, yet it told heavily upon his constitution in so much that he never recovered from it."

It is true, Elder Cavanah rallied and went out cheerfully in the great gospel field and did noble work but it was also true that he did this work with great pain.

His young trouble and other earthly troubles, not necessary to mention here, so weighed upon his spirit that he, like our dear Saviour in that respect, was, indeed, a man of sorrows and acquainted with grief. Never shall I forget how solemn and grave he looked especially in the pulpit. His face betokened much thought and deep feeling, and great sorrows had left an imprint there which could be noticed by the casual observer. He was not always serious. He could occasionally enjoy a joke with his friends, but his general deportment was very grave and he gave much of his time to the work. It was his mete to do his Masters' will. He was thoroughly in earnest in the great work to which he felt himself called and but for pecuniary embarasment would have given his whole time to the cause of Christ. As I have undertaken to vindicate the truth of history, I must say our brethren did not support Elder Cavanah as he should have been supported. Many of the brethren, it is true, gave to him liberally but this spirit of liberality in support of the gospel was not as general towards him as it should have been. He had sometimes to quit the field in the midst of his usefulness and engage, for a time, in secular pursuits, such as teaching school or standing in a store, for subsistance. Nothing so discourages a good man engaged in an honorable calling as a want of a proper appreciation of his services and this is more keenly felt by the true minister of the gospel than any other class. I think that this neglect was one of the causes of deep sorrows which followed Elder Cavanah to the grave.

Before he died, Elder Cavanah compiled, for the General Baptists, an elegant hymn book which has gone through several editions and it has been the most popular hymn book ever used by our people and it is still in much demand by our denomination.

It is much to be regreted that he left no written sermons behind him. He was not in the habit of writing his sermons however. He occasionally used notes on special occasions, but generally preached without looking at his theme. His mind was so clear and his memory so good, that he did not need such help, but he is known to have been a good writer. He had the happy faculty of condensing much in a short space. If he had undertaken it, I am of the opinion he would have made an excellent editor. Among the men of culture among us he was, perhaps, the most prominent. His talents were of such an order that he could have interested learned audiences and profound thinkers, in any of the great cities on our continent. He was, indeed, a workman that need not be ashamed.

Pressed down with the weight and burdens of which we have already made mention, he lived on, a spotless life, never having, at any time, brought reproach on the cause which he had espoused. He recognized the hand of God in all his afflictions and never lost sight of the "work of the prize."

After suffering long and much he closed his eyes on earth to open his spiritual eyes in our Father's house, where there are many mansions. He died at Owensville, Gibson county, Indiana, on the 20th of September, 1863, aged forty years, seven months and twelve days. His remains now rest in the cemetry near White or Columbia Church, about three miles southwest of Princeton, Indiana.

Brethren of the General Baptist denomination, you cannot recall our beloved and lamented Cavanah to do any act of kindness to him, personally, but have we not young ministers amoung us who have families to support and some of them young men of much promise of usefulness as ministers. If so, let us see to it, that they shall not be neglected. Let them be paid for their services and their temporal affairs so arranged that they can lay aside all worldly cares and devote their entire time to their calling.

Notwithstanding Elder Cavanah was so popular, he was so good, loving and kind to all, that no minister could ever find it in his heart to hold any jealousies against him. I have seen many of his survivors in the ministry weep when the name of Cavanah was mentioned in connection with the enterprise of the church in his day. He believed that every truly regenerated person was one in Christ, their head, and as such had a right to commune together at the Lord's Supper. Probably through his instrumentality as much was done to firmly establish this practice among General Baptists as any other man in the denomination.

We have only written biographical sketches of such living ministers as are so connected with the organization of the several Associations that it is impossible to give the origin of the Association without making mention of the men in such movement.

Besides this, there are serious objections to writing up the history of ministers living. All men are susceptable of flattery and their future usefulness being destroyed, some who have gone out from us and afterwards did and said a great many hard things against the General Baptists, had, probably, by the flattery of the churches, placed too great an estimate on themselves and, therefore, brought reproach upon the cause, and as it is both as a man lives and dies that constitutes the true character, we will not write too many living biographies.

However, brother Reavis left a few on record, among which are the names of Elders T. M. Strain and I. H. Henry, which we will give a place in this work.

Elder Thomas M. Strain was born in Gibson county, Indiana, December 21st, 1815. His father and mother died when he was a small boy and he was left to make his way in the world the best he could. He managed to make a living, but as there were no free schools he neither had time nor means to educate himself. September 12th, 1839, he was married to Miss Mary Lagrange. In the spring of 1842 he became deeply concerned about the salvation of his soul and soon after made an open profession of religion.

He united with the General Baptist church at Enon, Gibson county, Indiana, and was baptized by Elder Jacob Speer, whom he claims as his spiritual father and was licenced by the presbytery, at Enon, in 1845, and was ordained to the full work of the ministry on the first day of November, 1847, at Owensville, by Elders Jacob Speer, G. P. Cavanah and Benoni Stinson.

Elder Strain's conversion and call to the ministry were noted events, and they marked an era of prosperity in the history of oldLiberty Association and the General Baptist cause generally, which I, as a faithful historian, cannot afford to overlook or ignore.

Like all other faithful ministers he had many struggles and great difficulties to overcome before entering the gospel field. He had but little education, a young wife and family dependent upon him for support and with all, he, like Moses, had a stammering tongue. But he had such love and zeal for the cause of the Master, that he overcome all obstacles, by the grace of God, which was freely bestowed upon him.

Thus by God's help the poor stammering boy became a fluent speaker and a successful preacher and for more than a third of a century he has labored sometimes as a pastor and sometimes a missionary preaching nearly every Sunday and sometimes many days through the week to large congregations and making himself useful to the denomination in many ways.

Added to his talents as a successful gospel minister Elder Strain is a successful business man and by his own exertions he, as a merchant, accumulated a good living and is not dependent on the church for a support.

It is his opinion, however, that they who preach the gospel should live by the gospel or be well supported in the work. By his urgent personal appea to the brethren at each annual Association, missionary meeting and church dedication he has raised more money for the General Baptist people than any living man in the denomination.

By his exertions more than that of any other man, the church houses of Columbia, (White Church) Enon and Ft. Branch, in Gibson county, Indiana, were built, besides, I don't know how many other churches he has assisted in building. Elder Strain does not pretend to be a deep doctrinal preacher nor does he use high flowing words of mens' wisdom, but for correctness, native eloquence and deep pathos he has few equals. His sermons therefore, partake more of the practical and experimental than the ornate. He has social qualities of the highest order and his company is so pleasant that it is sought for and enjoyed by all ages and sex. He has on hand a constant fund of wit and humor, together with anecdotes, by the use of which I have known him to convulse large congregations with laughter while taking up collections at annual Associations.

He is now growing old but if the prayers of his many friends can avail he will live long and enjoy the blessings which cluster around a life of usefulness.

At this meeting, in 1843, a letter was received from Elder Joseph Wasson, of the Wabash Christian

Conference, desiring a union with the General Baptists. Elders Jesse Lane, Wm. Reavis and Benoni Stinson were appointed to answer said letter. "Referred a letter previously received from Union Association on the subject of establishing a religious newspaper, to a select committee, consisting of brethren Depriest, Speer, Willard and Polk."

The commitee to whom this matter was referred, "reported unfavorable to the establishment of a religious newspaper."

The 21st meeting was held with Owensville, Gibson county, eight hundred and forty-eight members, loss ninety. Skillet Fork Church, in White county, Illinois, received.

Elders G. P. Cavanah and W. W. Jenkens were delegates from Union Association.

This is the first mention made of Elder Cavanah, that humble, talented, logical, eloquent and beloved disciple, and here we will insert his biography. (See biography.)

Touching fidelity to the church or church attendance, I find this resolution:

"That in the opinion of this Association, if any male member of any of our churches fails to attend the meetings of the church of which he ia a member for six successive meetings, except absent on business or in case of sickness, is unworthy of fellowship and should be dropped from the communion."

The Association recommended the churches to obtain "some suitable minister to preach once a year on the mode, subject and design of baptism, the duties of ministers to churches and the churches to the ministers."

Resolved, "That the Association procure a book and appoint some suitable person to transcribe into it all of the former minutes of our Association and that in the future we will keep a regular record of all our proceedings.

A. H. Polk was appointed to transcribe the same."

I presume that brother Polk did the work assigned him but I doubt very much if that work was followed up. I am of the opinion that there is but one complete file of all the proceedings of Liberty Association from the organization to the present and that has been preserved by Elder Jacob Speer and is before me at present. Too many throw our minutes aside and think that they are of no use after the first reading, but we should remember that it is from our minutes that we get our history.

The writer has in his possession all of the minutes of the General Association. He has made diligent inquiry and does not know of another complete file, except one kept by Major J. B. Cox, near Evansville, Indiana.

It appears that at this early period our people saw and felt the necessity of a concentrated effort, as at this meeting they made overtures to Union Association to hold a General Association every two years. Whether this was reciprocated or not does not appear. However, we know that the two Associations have ever continued to work with and for each other, and an almost unbroken correspondence continued between them.

The twenty-second meeting convened with Mt. Gilead Church, Warrick County, and had eight hundred members.

At this meeting Elder Benoni Stinson was appointed to superintend the organization of Sabbath schools throughout the Association. Also, the following resolution was passed in reference to a religious, tri-monthly paper, published at that time:

"That, in the opinion of this Association the General Baptist Herald, edited by Elders B. Stinson and Wm. Reavis, jr., is worthy of a liberal patronage and that we not only approve of it, but encourage its circulation and that the Association appoint a committee to take charge of the paper as their own property and, if possible publish it weekly."

This is the first effort made by the General Baptists in the West to publish a denominational paper.

The twenty-third meeting was held with Owensville Church, in 1846, reported eight hundred and thirty-four members.

A constitution for a Home Mission Society was adopted at this meeting.

Also, "Application was made by Elder Jacob Holeman, for ministerial aid to assist in constituting an Association at Caldwell Church, in Caldwell county, Kentucky," on Friday before the second Sabbath in October, 1856.

"Elders J. B. and B. Stinson and Jacob Speer were appointed for this purpose" and organized Cumberland Association.

This took place six years after Union Association was organized.

Further mention of this body will be made at the proper time.

On receiving testimony against an offending member we find the following resolution:

"That, in the opinion of the Association no evidence ought to be taken against members of our churches, from out of the churches, except circumstances corroborate such testimony; but when the evidence is clear, the circumstances strong and the character of the witness good, the church may exclude, but even then it should be done with great caution.

The twenty-fourth meeting convened with Enon

Church, Gibson county, in 1847, and reported seven hundred and fifty-eight members.

The twenty-fifth meeting was held with Zion Church Vanderburgh county, September, 1848 and numbered seven hundred and seventy-seven members; two churches were received, Sharon and Honey Creek.

The twenty-sixth meeting was held with Columbia Church, September, 1849 and numbered seven hundred and fifteen members.

The twenty-seventh meeting was held with Mt. Pleasant Church, Posey county, in 1850, and numbered six hundred and eighteen members. Two new churches, Bethany and Mt. Zion, were received.

At this meeting a letter of correspondence was sent to the General Baptists in the State of Alabama. Also, we note the death of Elder John B. Stinson.

ELDER JOHN B. STINSON

Was born in Virgina, March 1st, 1787, of English parents, and learned the coopers' trade, which was the vocation of his father. At the age of twenty years he started to the Territory of Indiana, but meeting some friend, he stopped near Sandy Ridge, in Kentucky, and followed his trade. Here he met Matilda Paine, and they were married and moved down the Ohio river to Henderson county, Kentucky.

In 1809, he came to Vanderburgh county, Indiana, and settled just below where Evansville now stands. In 1810, the Indians became so troublesome that he was compelled to seek refuge in a fort in Kentucky. Those were perilous times. The river was frozen over, but not strong enough to bear up stock and the family crawled over on their hands and knees, pulling their bedding after them. He remained under the protection of the fort for some time. He was living in Indiana, in 1814, when General Jackson's fleet of dug-outs passed down, to fight the battle of New Orleans. In the same year he enlisted in the 10th regiment of Militia of Indiana Territory and proved a good soldier. He was rewarded by being commissioned a Captain in the 10th regiment, on the 27th of June, 1814, by Governor Thos. Posey, and did good service during the indian troubles. In 1818 Governor Jonathan Jennings commissioned John B. Stinson sheriff of Vanderburgh county, bearing date of the second year of Indiana as a State, to serve until the general election. After retiring from the sheriff's office he run trading boats on the Ohio river and accumulated considerable property. In 1821 he was commissioned Major of the 10th regiment of militia by Governor Jennings. During the

Harrison Indian war he was a sturdy soldier and well beloved by his men and comrades. He was Probate Judge for several years, also Associate Judge with Judge Hall.

John B. Stinson united with Liberty Church of General Baptists, October 5th, 1823, this being the day that this church was organized. In October, 1824, he was licensed to preach the gospel of Christ, and was ordained to the full work of the ministry in April, 1825, by Elders Benoni Stinson and D. R. Jacobs, and Deacon Benjamin McNew. He was an able and efficient minister in the General Baptist denomination, and considered the best disciplinarian belonging to it, in his day.

While Jesse Lane, sr., was laboring continually in revivals and Benoni Stinson preaching those deep doctrinal sermons, John B. Stinson was following closely with bis organizing powers, which gave strength and permanency to the cause.

He died in Vanderburgh county, March 17th, 1850, being sixty-three years and seventeen days old. His wife died thirteen years later, in 1863, being seventy-two years old. They left seven children, viz: Berry T. Stinson, Benoni Stinson, H. Clay Stinson, Mrs. Nancy Calloway, Mrs. Saleta Evans, Mrs. Fanny T. Green and Mrs. Missouri Stinson.

We are indebted to Maj. J. B. Cox for the above sketch.

The twenty-eighth meeting was held with Mt. Gilead Church, Warrick county, in 1851, and numbered seven hnndred and sixty-two members, and Wabash Church was received.

Elder H. A. Greggs presented a plan for the compilation of a General Baptist Hymn Book, which was approved. This was the first Hymn Book publisbed by the General Baptists in the United States.

We note the death of Elder Jesse Lane, at this meeiing. Thus, in the short period of two years, two of the fathers of Liberty Association passed away in death.

The twenty-ninth meeting convened with Black River Church, Posey county, in 1852, and numbered nine hundred and ten.

At this meeting the Association was layed off into four districts, in which quarterly and other meetings were to be held. Elder Jacob Speer was to superintend the meetings in the first district, Elder G. P. Cavanah, the second, Elder S. Rhoads, the third and Elder Benoni Stinson the fourth.

"These superintendents were requested to meet for the purpose of consultation, at Columbia Church, on Saturday, before the first Sabbath in January, 1852 at Mt. Gilead Church, on Saturday, before the second Sabbath in March, 1853." This plan proved beneficial, as appears from their increase in membership in this year.

The thirtieth meeting was held with Owensville Church, in 1853, and numbered 1061 members. Three new churches were received, viz: Richland, Otter Creek and Keg Creek.

Elder B. Stinson was appointed General Missionary and the district remained unchanged.

Elder Price took the place of Elder Rhoades in the third district.

The thirty-first meeting was held with Union Church, Posey county, in 1854, and numbered 971 members and six new churches were received, to-wit: Barren, Providence, Bethabra, Hickory Hill, Arrington Prairie and Union.

"Corresponding letters were called for, whereupon Elders H. S. Gordon and R. A. Bradley presented a copy of the minutes of the Free Communion Baptist Association and desired to open a correspondence with us."

"Elder Benoni Stinson, Alvah Parker, James W. Gwin, were appointed as corresponding delegates to the Free Communion Baptist Association, in Illinois and empowered to make any arrangement they may think proper, to effect a union between said Association and our denomination."

260   EARLY HISTORY

We presume a union was effected and the Free Communion Baptists adopted our articles of faith and took the name of the Southern Illinois Association of General Baptists. This took place in 1854 or 1855.

Elder Speer was appointed General Missionary from April 1st to the next meeting, in 1855.

The thirty-second meeting was held with Columbia Church, Gibson county, and numbered 1108 menbers. Barren Fork Church was received at this meeting.

The thirty-third meeting was held with Enon Church, Gibson county, in 1856, and numbered 1109 members and one new church, Bethlehem, was received.

At this meeting the Ohio Association of General Baptists presented a petition for correspondence with us, and after satisfactory examination as to their faith and practice, their representatives, Elders John Gregory and John Onyet, were invited to seats in council with us and we agreed to correspond with them."

It was further resolved, at this meeting :

That, "The churches can dismiss members by letter, only, and that in all cases where they cannot consistently give a letter, there is no alternative but to exclude."

The following, touching the reception of members

into the visible church, it having been presented to the church a year before, for their endorsement:

"That persons are received into any branch of the visible church by a manifestation of fellowship, upon satisfactory evidence of christian experience and a pledge of submission to the ordinance of baptism, at the earliest convenient opportunity, and a failure to comply with their pledge forfeits their connection with the church.

The thirty-fourth meeting was held with Owensville Church, Gibson county, in 1857, and numbered 1157 members, and one new church was received, viz: New Liberty.

At this meeting we note the death of "Elder Thos. Fuller, who had been preaching for over thirty years."

For the want of means, the Academy, of which we have frequently spoken, in the preceeding pages of this book, went down. At the meeting in 1857, we find our people laboring to revive this interest again.

"Elders T. M. Strain, Jacob Speer, G. P. Cavanah, B. Stinson and brother Henry Ayers, were appointed a committee to select a site and solicit subscriptions for an institution of learning, to be called the General Baptist Academy, and report at our next meeting."

The thirty-fifth meeting was held with Mt. Pleasant Church, Posey county, in 1858, and numbered 1375 members. One new church, Patoka, was received.

At this meeting we find our people laboring in behalf of a denominational paper, viz: "The General Baptist Banner." At the same time they were endeavoring to concentrate their forces into a general Association.

At this time, (1858) they numbered five Annual Associations, to-wit: Liberty, Union, Cumberland, Southern Illinois and Ohio, also the work on the Academy was continued. The Association requested Elder Cavanah to compile a General Baptist Hymn Book.

The thirty sixth meeting was held with Mt. Gilead Church, Warrick county, in 1859, and numbered 1383 members. One new church, Cynthiana, was received.

The United Association of General Baptists, which had been organized in Pike county, in August, of the same year, (1859) on our articles of faith, made application through her Messengers, Elder R. Voils and Temple Woolsy, for a correspondence with us, which was heartily reciprocated, and the following churches, "Mt. Olive, Bethabra, Otter Creek, Mt. Gilead, Richland, Bethany and Sharon dismissed by letter from this Association, when joined to the United Association of General Baptists."

The thirty-seventh meeting was held with Columbia Church, Gibson county, in 1860, and numbered 1110 members. Four new churches, Union Chapel, Mt. Pleasant, Clear Creek and Johnson Prairie were received.

Again our people embarked on the enterprise of publishing a denominational paper and elected a board of managers for that purpose, consisting of Elders T. M. Strain, J. P. McClure, Solomon Reavis, Richey Summers and Newton Skelton.

We are informed by Elder Strain that after each member of the committee had made a considerable sacrifice of money and time they were compelled to cease publishing their paper.

The thirty-eighth meeting was held with Owensville Church, in Gibson county, in 1861, and numbered 1133 members. Two new churches, Princeton and Pleasant Grove, were received.

At this meeting a letter of correspondence was received from the Shelby Association of Separate Baptists, in Central Illinois, by the hand of their Messenger, Elder Willis Whitfield, who was from the same Association in Tennessee, to which Elder Jacob Speer formerly belonged.

This correspondence was gladly received and Elder Benoni Stinson appointed to visit those brethren, in order to form a more perfect union. Elder Stinson visited Shelby Association and a friendly correspondence has been carried on ever since. The writer has been intimately acquainted with many of these people for about thirteen years. Many of them desire to take the name, General Baptists, and are of the opinion that the time is in the near future when Shelby, Ambraw, Central Indiana, White River, Sand Creek and some other Associations of Separate Baptists, will unite with our General Association, and take the name General Baptist. This is much to be desired, because the General and Separate Baptists are one and the same people.

The thirty-ninth meeting was held with Ft. Branch Church, Gibson county, in 1862, and numbered 1118 members. One new church, Baren Chapel, was received.

The fortieth meeting was held with Johnson Prairie Church, Wayne county, Illinois, in 1863, and numbered 1213 members. Two new churches, Willow Branch and New Salem, were received.

Elder T. M. Strain was appointed General Missionary for the ensuing year, he to depend on the liberality of the churches for support.

The forty-first meeting was held with Oakland City hurch, Gibson county, in 1864, and numbered 1200 members. Two new churches, Union Bethel and Palestine.

At this meeting resolutions were passed on the state and condition of our country, setting fourth the integrity of this Association in support of constitutional liberty.

Johnson Prairie, Mt. Pleasant, Illinois, Arrington Prairie and Willow Branch Churches, were dismissed from this Association, by request, and Elders Jacob Speer and Benoni Stinson appointed to organize them into a new Association. Thus originated the Union Grove Association, in 1864.

The following resolution was adopted:

That, "This Association learns, with deep and heartfelt sorrow, of the death of Elder G. P. Cavanah, and that Elder Benoni Stinson is hereby appointed to preach his funeral, to-morrow, at eleven o'clock."

The forty-second meeting was held with Barren Chapel Church, Gibson county, in 1865, and numbered 1128 members.

"Elder A. H. Polk was appointed General Missionary for the ensuing year, and Solomon Reavis J. P. McClure, Newton Skelton, R. B. Richards and L. L. Montgomery were appointed a committee to raise means" to pay brother Polk.

The forty third meeting was held with Mt. Pleasant, Posey county, in 1866, and numbered 1310 members. Three new churches, Wabash, Hazleton and Franklin Chapel were received.

At this metting "a letter of correspondence was received from the Wayne county, Illinois, Quarterly Meeting of Free-Will Baptists, and her Messengers, Elders M. A. Shepard and John Rhoads, were invited to seats in council."

The committee appointed in 1865, on Domestic Missions, reported that they had collected $371 20 and paid out the same to Elder A. H. Polk and T. M. Strain, for missionary labor.

The 44th meeting was held with Enon Church, in 1867 and numbered 1412 members. Three new churches, Bethlehem, east of Owensville, Mt. Moria, in Posey county, Independence, in Evansville.

The writer was a delegate to this Association from Owensville Church, and learned, at this time, that Oakland Institute was under consideration at this meeting.

The following resolution was adopted at this meeting:

That, "We invite the various Associations and other bodies of christians, who hold and teach the doctrines of general atonement and moral agency, and accountability, and who administer baptism by immersion only, and are liberal in their communion, to meet, by delegates, at Ft. Branch, on Thursday, before the fourth Lord's day, in May, 1868, for general consultation, and especially to consider the propriety of permanently organizing a general association for more thorough co-operation in spreading the gospel."

At the appointed time and place, quite a number of liberal Baptists, holding to the doctrines set fourth in the above resolution, met and the consultations were harmonious and pleasant and promised to be beneficial.

This convention adjourned to meet with Liberty Association, in September, 1368.

At this, the forty-fourth meeting of Liberty Association, of which we are now writing, (1867) the mission board reported that they had collected and paid Elder Polk $482 30 for missionary labor.

The forty-fifth meeting was held with Columbia Church, near Princeton, in 1868, and numbered 1653 members and three new churches, Mt. Olive, Beech Grove and Atioch, Wabash county, Illinois, were received.

We had at this meeting the most extended correspondence of any in our history. Besides Southern Illinois, Union and Cumberland, of Kentucky, and United, of Indiana, all of which were General Baptists, the following Free-Will Baptist bodies were represented:

"From the Wayne county Quarterly Meeting, Elders J. Rhoads and R. P. Lee ; from Maine Westerly Yearly Meeting, Rev. J. O. Libby; Ohio and Pennsylvania, Yearly Meeting, Rev. Dunn, Professor of Bibilical Theology, in Hillsdale Colege, Rev. L. P. Thompson and Rev. G. P. Blanchard; Wisconsin Yearly Meeting, Rev. E. D. Lewis."

After the Association had become fully organized it "yielded to the convention of Liberal Baptists, which adjourned its May session to this time and place." "The convention adjourned, and the Moderator called the Association to order. The President of the Convention, Rev. C. O. Libby, reported to the Association a resolution adoped by the Convention, which, after amendment, was adopted by the Association, as follows:

That, "The object contemplated in the original resolution calling the convention, can best be accomplished by the various Associations sending delegates and applying for membership in the General Conference of Free-Will Baptists, to be held in Buffalo, New York, commencing October 8th, 1868, and generally co-operating with them, retaining such names and usages as they may prefer."

"Upon the adoption of this resolution the Association proceeded to the election of a delegate to the Conference, which resulted in the choice of Elder A. H. Polk."

Elder T. M. Strain volunteered to go with Elder Polk. They went to the Shelby Association of Separate Baptists as delegates from Liberty Association, and that Association appointed Elder Joseph Peryman a delegate to the Free-Will Baptist General Conference, and from Shelby Association they all went together to the General Conference, at which a mutual union was formed, on the basis of the above resolution, and I doubt not, that had it not been for two things that that union would have remained unbroken to-day; but unfortunately, a committee was appointed, during General Conference, to draft resolutions setting forth the sentiments of that body on the state of the country, at this time, which was only a few years after the civil war. Some of their very best men used their influence to suppress them and supposed that the committee appointed for this purpose would not be called upon to make a report. However, near the close of the Conference, when many that opposed those bitter partisan resolutions were gone home, the committee was called upon to report. These resolutions were of such a character that Elder Stinson, and many others, who believed, as the great majority of Free-Will Baptists did, on political questions, "looked upon these resolutions as a political platform to govern the Free-Will Baptist denomination." Therefore, in a spirited letter to "The Christian Freeman," a paper published at Chicago, Illinois, in the interest of the Free-Will Baptists and which Liberty Association had recommended to her churches, Elder Stinson entered a protest against Liberty Association belonging to a body that would pass resolutions placing such political strictures upon any people.

Answers to this letter were written by Revs. Chase, W. E. Whipple and Ransom Dunn, also one by Elder A. H. Polk. This matter became so heated that the second article of Elder Stinson was not published, and the controversy suppressed. However, another thing occurred, which if possible, caused the breach to widen.

Rev. J. S. Manning of the "Ohio and Pennsylvania Yearly Meeting, who was a delegate to the Convention held with Liberty Association, in 1868, was then, or shortly after, stationed at Cairo, Illinois, laboring among the colored people, under the auspices of the Free-Will Baptist Missionary Board. This over zealous man, together with Rev. O. D. Patch, of the Free-Will Baptists, began to visit our Annual Associations in Illinois, trying to persuade our people to drop the name General Baptist and adopt the name Free-Will, and finally not finding any of our Associations willing to bring forward any such a resolution, Elder Manning offerered one himself, which was declared by the Moderator of Mt. Olivet Association, Elder John Onyet, to be unchristian, and out of order.

We must here state, that the General Conference of Free-Will Baptists, as a body, did not approve of the conduct of Elder Manning in this matter and he was finally warmly rebuked by some of the Free-Will Baptists for his indecorous and disastrous work, in defference to General Baptists.

Nearly all the General Baptist Associations east of the Mississippi river, had gone into this union, but all except Liberty, withdrew immediately after they understood the motive of the resolutions above reported. This matter continued to confuse and harass our people for many years, until finally, in 1877, the Association, while in session with Behlehem, three miles east of Owensville, resolved to withdraw her connection from the Free-Will Baptist General Conference. Notwithstanding, Liberty Association, on account of the things mentioned heretofore, passed through many turbulant and boisterous meetings, yet this work was not all in vain. It has brought about a better acquaintance of liberal Baptists generally, and there are strong ties of personal relationship existing between many of the Free-Will Baptists, who have visited us, and the whole General Baptist denomination. Through those visits the General Baptists have caught a spirit of enterprise and a consecration of their means that otherwise would have taken many years for them to have reached, and a possibility of a closer union is not yet forever destroyed.

The forty-sixth meeting was held with Mt. Olive Church, Posey county, in 1869, and numbered 1786 members. One new church, Mt. Pisgah, was received.

This is the highest number ever reached by this body. So far there has been a continual drain from it in forming new Associations.

The forty-seventh meeting was held with Mt. Pleasant Church, in Posey county, in 1870. Bethsada and Springfield Churches, in Posey county, were received, and 1433 members were reported.

At this meeting Liberty Association was called upon to record the death of three of her old and tried ministers and fathers in the gospel. In reference to them, we find the following:

"Whereas, Revs. Benoni Stinson, Alvah Parker and James Blackburn, since our last Association, have died, therefore,

"Resolved, That we deeply sympathize with the bereaved families, and further.

"Resolved, That their funerals be preached on Sabbath, in the following order:"

Rev. Jacob Speer, preach that of Elder Benoni Stinson; Elder J. G. Ensle, that of Elder Parker, and Elder J. G. Lane, that of Elder Blackburn.

The forty-eighth meeting was held with Owensville Church, Gibson county, in 1871, and numbered 1448 members.

At this meeting Elder Joseph Peryman, from Shelby Association, and Elder J. W. Vahn, of Ambraw Association of Separate Baptists, presented letters of correspondence, with a view of effecting a union with us, which was accomplished, allowing them their own choice of name, (General or Separate Baptists.)

At this meeting the following resolution, in reference to the "Baptist Union," a paper edited by Rev. Dr. G. H. Ball, of Buffalo, New York:

"That we cordially approve the course of the Baptist Union and we hail with gratitude, to God, the good fruits of its labors in gathering into one, the scattered members of the great body of liberal Baptists in the United States."

The merging into or consolidating this paper with the Morning Star, was greatly lamented by General Baptists everywhere. However, it sowed seed that will eventually bring forth an abundant crop.

The forty-ninth meeting was held with Columbia

Church, in Posey county, in 1872, and numbered 1662 members. Welborn Chapel Church, in Posey county, was received.

At this meeting a correspondence was commenced with Cumberland Association of Free-Will Baptists, in Tennessee, and the General Baptists, in Missouri.

The fiftieth meeting was held with Fort Branch Church, Gibson county, in 1873, numbering 1670 members. Mt. Vernon Church, in Mt. Vernon, Posey county, was received.

At this meeting we find the following, in reference to Home Missions:

"Whereas, The Home Mission Board, of Liberty Association, (as appointed by the Central Home Mission Board of the General Association) consisting of Elders D. B. Montgomery, F. M. Kerr and Bro. R. B. Richards, have been laboring since December 10th, 1872, to build up a permanent Home Mission fund and have, by the aid of the brethren, generally, throughout the Association, succeeded in securing subscriptions to the amount of three thousand dollars upon which ten per cent. interest is due, as soon as Liberty Association shall have taken said fund under her control. Therefore, be it

"Resolved, That Liberty Association of General Baptists, located in the States of Indiana and Illinois, receive said subscriptions and donations and incorporate and control the same, according to the constitution under which said subscriptions and donations have been obtained." See constitution.

It will be remembered that our people have encouraged the missionary work all through our history. Some years they were successful and would plant several new churches. Probably the next year, for the want of means, we would lose what we had done the year previous. Brother R. B. Richards, who had worked with the Missionary Board for several years, was convinced that the plan of making each year provide for itself, was not the right one, so he, being a member of this board, insisted on building up a permanent fund, and at the first meeting of the Board, December 10th, 1872, at his house, he proposed to be one of twenty men to give $100 each, for a permanent fund. D. B. Montgomery, a member of the Board and J. S. Mead, who was in the council with us, agreed to the proposition. Thus $300 was secured at the first meeting of the Board and $3,000 before September 1873. Since then several voluntary contributions have been made. The Board is in a healthy condition at present and consists of Elders Wm. Clark, President; Elder D. B. Montgomery, Secretary, and Brother J. P. McClure, Treasurer, and the following brethren are members of the Board:

J. S. Mead, Charles Mead, Charles Epperson, Elder Wilson Blackburn, G. B. Young, H. C. Daugherty, R. B. Richards, Julius Spore, James Brown, and John Hollis. Bros. Newton Skelton and Henry Clark, were members at their death, which occurred in the winter of 1880.

The fifty-first meeting was held with Bethlehem Church, Posey county, in 1874, and numbered 1714 members. Oak Grove Church, in White county, Illinois, and New Liberty, in Gibson county, were received.

Elder D. M. Shoemacker, and brethren J. B. Blythe, Samuel Boren and Samuel Carter, presented a letter of correspondence from the Union Christian Conference, which was gladly received, and the correspondence has been kept up ever since.

The fifty-second meeting was held with Oakland City Church, in 1875, and numbered 1679 members.

The fifty-third meeting was held with Mt. Olive Church, in Posey county, in 1876. Mt. Zion Church, in Posey county, was received.

We find the following, in reference to the death of Elder J. G. Ensle:

"Resolved, That in the death of Elder J. G. Enslee, we have lost an efficient pastor, a truly devoted christian, a man true to his convictions, and bold to declare the gospel of Christ, and as a tribute of regard for his labors, we appoint Elder Wilson Blackburn to preach his funeral at the stand, on Sabbath, at ten o'clock, A. M.

ELDER JAMES G. ENSLE.

The subject of this sketch was born in Vanderburgh county, Indiana, April 9th, 1830, and licensed to preach the gospel of Christ, by the Baptist church of Helena, Ark. and, I believe, was educated at a Missionary Baptist School in Arkansas, and afterwards moved back to Vanderburgh county, Indiana, where he united with the General Baptists and was ordained at old Mt. Pleasant Church in Posey county, Indiana, by the Presbytery of Liberty Association, consisting of Elders Benoni Stinson, A. H. Polk and T. M. Strain. At this time it was remarked by one of the shrewdest men in the General Baptist denomination, that this is the man the General Baptists have prayed for. He was not only promising then, but made an excellent preacher, sometimes becoming quite eloquent. He was acknowledged to be one of the best sermonizers in Liberty Association. He was a close student, very systematic, and logical. In the midst of his usefulness the question of a union between the General and Free-Will Baptists was agitated among us. He opposed the union, because he believed the Free-Will Baptist General Conference dabbled too much in politics. In the heated discussions which followed, he became somewhat estranged from a part of the Association, which, to a very considerable extent, limited his labors to the Southern part of the Association. He was modest and rather diffident, but true as steel to his convictions, and when once he took a decided stand on a question, he was not easily persuaded to a compromise. He knew nothing underhanded or undermining in working to carry a point.

He first settled questions as to right or wrong, in his own mind, and when satisfied that he was in the right he would contend for it in opposition to friend or foe. On first acquaintance he was rather distant, but when you became acquainted with him, you loved him.

He was a good writer and was senior editor of the General Baptist Herald, at one time, for about six months. But alas, when only about forty-six years old, he died, on February 20th, 1876. Of course, it was his gain, but the General Baptists sustained a great loss.

Zion Church house, as well as the membership at

that place, were chiefly built up by his labors. He prepared most of the heavy timbers of the house with his own hands, besides rendering much financial aid. He had the full confidence of all his community. He was, generally, the arbitrator of all difficulties arising between parties near him. May his mantel fall upon some of our young men.

The fifty-fourth meeting was held with Bethlehem Church, in Gibson county, in 1877, and numbered 1357 members.

The following resolution was passed at this meeting:

"Resolved, That a Board of three members be appointed to raise funds for our superanuated ministers, with power to mature a plan, and organize, under the law, to collect funds, appoint agents, and report at our next meeting."

Elders D. B. Montgomery, Wilson Blackburn and Wm. Tennison, were appointed, and J. B. Cox requested to assist them.

Elder Wilson Blackburn was appointed to preach a funeral discourse to the memory of R. B. Burlison, who had died since 1875.

The fifty-fifth meeting was held with Mt. Pleasant Church, in Posey county, in 1878, and numbered 1408 members.

The committee appointed on the superanuated

fund, in 1877, reported a constitution, (see constitution) and the Association appointed a Board of Managers, consisting of Elders Wilson Blackburn, brethren John Wilson, G. B. Young, Wm. Fairchild, H. C. Daugherty and W. C. Allyn.

The fifty-sixth meeting was held with Columbia Church, Gibson county, in 1879, and numbered 1483 members.

Elder Jacob Speer was advised by the Association to retire from the active duties of a pastor and visit the different churches when health and weather would admit, and also advised the churches to remunerate him for his services when he visited them. Elder Speer has been the faithful pastor of various churches for over fifty years, and was never known to miss an appointment when it was in his power to meet it.

The fifty-seventh meeting was held with Owensville Church, Gibson county, and numbered 1333 members.

At this meeting the Mission Board made an encouraging report.

The Association endorsed the Golden Rule, edited by Elder J. E. Cox, and published at Mt. Vernon, Indiana, and entered heartily into the work of endowing the College at Evansville, and her members have subscribed several thousand dollars to endow this much needed and deserved institution.

Liberty Association, in all her history, has never had a more promising corps of young ministers than she has at present, to-wit: Elders J. E. Cox, H. C. Cockrum, Josephus Latham, Felix Polk and Francis Wood. These have all been licenced within the last three years.

This ends the history of this Association for fifty-seven years.

EARLY HISTORY

The table below exhibits the date, Moderator, Clerk, new Churches received, total members, and the death of Ministers of Liberty Association. In the column of new churches, p. c. stands for Posey county, g. c., for Gibson county, v. c. for Vanderburgh county, w. c. for Warrick county, showing the county in which each new church is located.

Date.	Churches.	Moderator.	Clerk.	New Churches.	Members.	Death of Ministers.
1824	Liberty, v. c.	Benoni Stinson	T. E. Casselberry	Union, p. c., Black River	201	
1825	Union p. c.	do	do	p. c. Providence, v. c., Mt. Gilead, w. c., Mt. Pleasant, Concord and Hopewell, p. c.	311	
1826	Black River, p. c	do	D. R. Jacobs	Clear Fork, v. c., Free Salem, Ky.	258	
1827	Providence	do	do		284	
1828	Concord	do	J. B. Stinson		254	
1829	Mt. Pleasant	do	do		195	
1830	Free Salem, Ky.	J. B. Stinson	Jesse Lane		194	
1831	Mt. Gilead, w. c	do	do	Bethel and Enon, g. c.	234	
1832	Providence	do	W. Depriest		297	
1833	Enon	Benoni Stinson	L. W. Handley	Mt. Olivet and Bethlehem	383	
1834	Concord	Jacob Speer	Wm. Depriest		373	
1835	Providence	do	do		392	
1836	Enon	Jesse Lane	do		385	
1837	Mt. Gilead	do	do		471	
1838	Liberty	do	do		569	
1839	Concord	Benoni Stinson	S. C. Weever	Chalybeat Springs, Ky.	791	
1840	Enon	E. C. McCoy	Wm. Depriest	Grayville, Ill., Harmony, Grass Creek, Caldwell, Sharon, Owens	890	

IN THE UNITED STATES.   283

Year	Place			Churches	No.	Notes
1841	Mt. Gilead		Jacob Speer	Wm. Reavis, jr	ville, Bethlehem, Mt. Olive and Zion	681	
1842	Black River		do do	A. H. Polk	Un. As'n formed this y'r	869	
1843	Union		Robert Lee	do do	Union, Ill. and Salem	938	
1844	Owensville		B. T. Dunn	W. W. Williard	Columbia	848	
1845	Mt. Gilead		J. B. Stinson	do do	Skillet Fork, Wt co. Ill	800	
1846	Owensville		T. J. Montgom'y	A. H. Polk	Cumberland As'n form'd this year	834	
1847	Enon		Jacob Speer	do do		758	
1848	Zion, v. c.		G. P. Cavanah	do do	Honey Creek & Sharon	777	
1849	Columbia		Wm. Reavis	do do		715	
1850	Mt. Pleasant		Jacob Speer	Wm. Reavis	Bethany & Mt. Zion	618	John B. Stinson
1851	Mt. Gilead		G. P. Cavanah	do do	Wabash	702	Jesse Lane, sr., Gregg's Hymn Book appeared.
1852	Black River		Jacob Speer	T. M. Strain	Richland, Otter Creek	910	
1853	Owensville		Jas. Blackburn	G. P. Cavanah	and Ky. Creek	1051	
1854	Union		Jacob Speer	T. M. strain	Baron, Providence, Bethabra, Hickory Hill, Arrington Prairie, Union Ill.	971	
1855	Columbia		do do	do do	Barren Fork	1108	
1856	Enon		Benoni Stinson	A. H. Polk	Bethlehem	1109	Thomas Fuller
1857	Owensville		Jacob Speer	T. M. Strain	New Liberty	1157	
1858	Mt. Pleasant		J. W. Camp	Henry Ayers	Patoka	1575	J. W. Camp
1859	Mt. Gilead		Jacob Speer	Newton Skelton	Cynthiana	1383	Cavanah,s Hymn Book appeared
1860	Columbia		G. P. Cavanah	A. H. Polk	Union Chapel, Mt. Pleasant, Clear Creek, Johnson Prairie, Ill.	1110	
1861	Owensville		T. M. Strain	Wm. Land	Princeton and Pleasant Grove	1133	
1862	Ft. Branch		Jacob Speer	J. M. Foster	Bethel Chapel	1118	
1863	Johnson Prairie	T. M. Strain	A. H. Polk	Willow Branch and New Salem, Ill	1213	

EARLY HISTORY

Year	Church	Name		Union, Bethel & Palest'n	No.	Name
1864	Oakland City	A. H. Polk	Newton Skelton	Union, Bethel &Palest'n	1200	G. P. Cavalah..
1865	Barren Chapel	do do	do	Wabash, Ill., Hazzleton, Franklin Chapel	1128	
1866	Mt, Pleasant	Alvah Parker	do		1310	
1867	Enon	T. M. Strain	do	Bethlehem, Mt. Marja and Independence.	1412	
1868	Columbia	A. H. Polk	do	Mt. Olive, Beech Grove, Antioch, Ill	1553	
1899	Mt. Olive	Jacob Speer	T. M. Strain	Mt. Pisgath	1785	Solomon Reavis, sr., & Ruth A. ʌtinson,
1870	Mt. Pleasant	J. G. Ensle	do do	Bethesda & Springfield	1433	Benoni Stinson, Alvah Parker and Jas. Blackburn.
1871	Owensville	Jacob Speer	W. Blackburn		1448	
1872	Columbia	T. M. Strain	Newton Skelton	Welborn Chapel	1662	
1873	Ft. Branch	F. M. Kerr	D.B. Montgom'y	Mt. Vernon	1670	
1874	Bethesda	J. G. Lane	W. Blackburn	Oak Grove, Ill. & New Liberty, g c	1714	
1875	Oakland City	Jacob Speer	D.B. Montgom'y		1679	
1876	Mt. Olive	W. Blackburn	do	Mt. Zion	1670	J. G Ensle
1877	Bethlehem	Wm. Clark	do		1357	R. B. Burlison
1878	Mt. Pleasant	Jacob Speer	do		1408	
1879	Columbia	Wm. Sturgeon	do		1483	
1880	Owensville	T. M. Strain	do		1333	
1881	Mt. Zion	Jacob Speer	do	Foresythe Chapel	1393	

Below we give the names and Post Office address of ministers.

NAMES AND POST OFFICE ADDRESS OF MINISTERS.

Jacob Speer, Wm. Clark and D. B. Montgomery, Owensville, Indiana.

A. H. Polk and Felix Polk, Princeton, Indiana.

T. M. Strain, H. C. Clinton and Francis Wood, Ft. Branch, Indiana.

H. C. Cockrum, Oakland City, Indiana.

Wm. Sturgeon, Cynthiana, Indiana.

G. W. Moore, Evansville, Indiana.

Wilson Blackburn, W. J. Blackburn, Wm. Tennison, A. Burlison and J. A. Baily, Mt. Vernon, Indiana.

Josephus Latham, Francisco, Indiana.

UNION ASSOCIATION, KENTUCKY.

In 1840, Liberty Association, while in session with Enon Church, had twenty churches represented and 890 members. This was a fine showing for our people who for a few years before this had been well nigh swallowed up by the surrounding opposition.

The meeting of this Association was a large and an enthusiastic one. The great feature of this meeting, as regards its business transactions, was the matter of dividing Liberty Association into two bodies.

I have already stated that the General Baptist ministers had unfurled the banner of the Cross on the soil of Kentucky and Illinois. Elder Stinson having been kept in the field as a missionary, a good part of the time, had succeeded in extending the borders of the denomination, not only in Indiana, but in other adjoining States. Therefore:

"According to an appointment of the Liberty Association of General Baptists, a committee, consisting of Elders Benoni Stinson, John B. Stinson and Jacob Speer, convened at Caldwell Church, in Caldwell county, Kentucky, in October, 1840, and constituted Union Association of General Baptists, composed of the following churches and messengers:

Liberty, Harbin Baldwin and John T. Watson, with fifty-three members.

Chalybeate, Jacob Holeman, Wiley Jenkens, Squire Holeman and Philip Massey, with thirty-four members.

Caldwell, John Crider, John Holeman, Jesse Nichols, James S. Jones and Wm. Dremnon, with thirty-three members.

Union, James M. Hunt, with four members.

Grassy Lick, with twenty-two members.

Liberty, of Caldwell county, with eight members.

Sharon, with nine members.

Total membership, one hundred and sixty-three.

After the organization was completed, Elder Benoni Stinson delivered a discourse from 1st Tim., 4th chapter, 9th and 10th verses.

Elder Jacob Holeman, (father of Dr. Jeff. Holeman) was the first Moderator of this Association and Jesse Nichols, Clerk.

This body agreed to hold four quarterly meetings during the year, and adopted the Constitution, By-Laws and Articles of Faith of the Liberty Association of General Baptists.

This circumstance marked a new era in the history of the Liberal Baptist movement and had a telling influence on the success of the cause. It was a matter of much joy to our friends generally, and none seemed to enjoy it like Elder Benoni Stinson. He had been, under God's providence, not only foremost, but the very founder of this movement in the West. He regarded this success with feelings of great satisfaction, and gave most of the credit to the brethren and elders, who had been co-workers with him. Above all he was always in the habit of giving God the glory for all the success by which the cause so dear to him was made to prosper. I never knew a man who was more humble under great spiritual prosperity, and he always seemed to esteem the humblest of his brethren better than himself.

This new Association, planted on the soil of Kentucky, near where he had spent his youthful days, was very gratifying, not only to Elder Stinson and his brethren in the liberal movement, but it was hailed by the liberal people of other denominations, as well. A deep interest was manifested by the brethren in Kentucky. The ministers there were zealous and effective workers. It is true that they suffered persecution there, from merciless attacks made upon them by the old school Baptists, as were the brethren in Indiana, when Liberty Association was first formed. I say here, once for all, that I do not attribute any bad motive to those stern old brethren of predestinarian sentiments for doing as they did, for like Paul, on a certain occasion, they doubtless thought they were doing God's service, and like him, they may have lived in all good conscience before God, up to the day of their death. It is but human to err. We should not, therefore, judge brethren with harsh judgement. The name of this new Association was Union, and that body of people deserve the name. A nucleus was now formed in Kentucky, around which liberal Baptists could cluster, and this was another step in advance as the sequel will show. Among the old ministers of this Association, I remember well the names of George W. McAndrews, E. Hancock, Jacob Holeman, E. C. McCoy and W. W. Jenkens. I believe those good men have all died many years ago but they left behind them a glorious record.

I was not very well acquainted with Elders McCoy and Jenkens. They had the reputation of being very zealous and effective workers in the cause of Christ, but with Elders McAndrew, Hancock and Holeman, I was well acquainted, and of them I will here speak a few words in detail.

ELDER GEORGE W. MCANDREW.

Elder McAndrew was a man above mediocrity, as to intellect. He possessed a good English education and was a man of close application and some culture. He was an earnest and eloquent preacher and was very popular. His sermons disclosed not only much breadth of thought, but they were full of pathos and directness. He labored both in Indiana and Kentucky, with success, having the entire confidence of the brethren wherever he went. His social qualities were of a high order and his company was sought for by christians of all denominations. His affections were so strong that when he met the brethren at one of the annual meetings or Associations, he was filled with joy, and when he parted with them he often shed tears. To him the love and unity which bound christians together was a living principle. He could sing, with all his heart,

> "Blest be the tie that binds
>   Our hearts in christian love;
> The fellowship of kindred minds
>   Is like to that above."

But like some other bright and shining lights, Elder McAndrew died before he reached what is called the meridian of life. He was mourned by a large circle of friends both in Kentucky and Indiana, for he lived a while in both States. He died, trusting in, and calling upon, the name of the Lord.

ELDER ESMA HANCOCK.

Elder Hancock was a man of but little education, but he was possessed of an excellent memory and good common sense, and when he began to preach he applied himself closely to the study of theology so that he acquired information very rapidly and by that dilligence and perseverance which always tell on a good man in a good cause, he advanced to the front rank among the ministers of our denomination, and so zealous was he to propogate the doctrines of our church that his voice was heard on the Trade Water and on the Cumberland river, and in many other portions of Kentucky, where he wielded much influence for good. He was stricken down in the midst of his usefulness, but the time, place and circumstances of his death are unknown to me.

ELDER JACOB HOLEMAN.

Elder Holeman was a man of fine ability as a preacher and possessed great power in exhortation. He, too, was a very social and loving man, and was very useful to the church. His education was very limited, having been an old backwoodsman on the "dark and bloody ground" of Kentucky, but he had talents which eminently fitted him to win souls to Christ, and it was his meat and drink to do his Master's will. The good influences set to work by him are still going on and his memory is still cherished by all who knew him. He died at a good old age, full of honors, with bright hopes of a blissful immortality. He was the father of Elder Miles Holeman, of Clayville, Kentucky, who was a United Baptist minister and very useful, but died quite young. Dr. Jeff. Holeman, now of Evansville, Indiana, is a son of his, also. It was with such men as these that the doctrines of a general atonement and open communion were defended in Kentucky. Men of any less integrity, fortitude and perseverance would have yielded to the opposition with which they had to contend.

The second meeting was held with Chalybeate Church, commencing on the 8th of October, 1841. Members 258, a gain of 95.

The third meeting was held with Liberty Church, Caldwell county, Kentucky, on Friday, before the third Sabbath in October, 1842. Six new churches, Pleasant Hope, Shady Grove, Zion, Mt. Lebanon, Salem and New Hope were received. Members 237, a loss of 21.

G. P. Cavanah was a delegate from Shady Grove Church. He was not then a minister.

This Association insisted that a minister must belong to some church, one of which he was pastor, and further insisted that churches remunerate their pastors for services, which indicates that the churches were a little lax in this particular.

The fourth meeting was held with Mt. Lebanon Church, in Henderson county, Kentucky, in October, 1843. Three new churches, Mt. Enon, Mt.

Zion and Friendship, were received. Members 311, a gain of 74.

We find the following in reference to membership in the church:

"Resolved, That fellowship and Baptism are both necessary to church membership."

They also refused to advise the Presbytery to licence promising gifts unless they come recommended from the church to which they belonged.

The fifth meeting was held with Pleasant Hope church, Davis county, Kentucky, in October, 1844. Three new churches, Free Communion, Freedom and Mt. Gilead, were received. Members 406, a gain of 175.

Elder Jacob Holeman was appointed missionary, to labor in the bounds of this Association, until the next meeting.

This Association agreed to the proposition of Liberty Association to hold a General Association every two years. If this general gathering could have been sustained our numbers would have been much larger to day than they are.

The sixth meeting was held with Free Communion Church, Crittenden county, in October, 1844. One new church, Pleasant Grove, was received. Members 395, a loss of 11.

The seventh meeting was held with Pleasant Grove

Church, Muhlenberg county, Kentucky, in 1846. Members 362, a loss of 33. Two new churches, Ballard and Lewis Creek, were received.

At this meeting the fifth article of the Confession of Faith was made to conform with the fifth article of Liberty Association, which had been changed in 1865 to read: "That he that endureth to the end the same shall be saved."

Also, the eleventh article was amended by adding in brackets, (infants and idiots excepted.)

We concluded that our brethren in Kentucky were persecuted for their liberal views as were our fathers in Indiana. We hear them at this Association saying that, "for the comfort and satisfaction of the people of God, we consider it necessary to give the number of General Baptists in the world." They then enumerate Liberty Association, Indiana, 975; North Carolina, 845; Eastern States, 30,000; Wales 19,000; England, 27,000. They included all of which they then knew, that held to the doctrines of the General Baptists. They further say:

"We do not boast of numbers, but would rather rejoice that we remain identified in bearing testimony with those of the same faith and order, who lived at the time of, and ever since the days of the Apostles."

The eighth meeting was held with Zion Church, Muhlenberg county, Kentucky, in August, 1847. Members 164.

We must bear in mind that at the seventh meeting this Union Association was divided, by mutual consent, begining at Henderson and running thence to Madisonville, including Mt. Lebanon Church, thence to Princeton, Kentucky. All on the west of this line was constituted into Cumberland Association of General Baptists. This will account for the decrease in membership.

We now find this Associating starting out to battle for General Baptist principles, with just one member more than she had at her organization, seven years previous.

The ninth meeting was held with Salem Church, Muhlenberg county, Kentucky, in August, 1848. Members 228, a gain of 54. One new Church, G. R. Union, was received.

At this meeting Liberty and Cumberland Association were invited to act in concert with Union Association, in preparing a circular letter on the subject of free communion, and also of condensing the minutes of said three Associations.

The tenth meeting was held with Mt. Gilead Church, in Hopkins county, Kentucky, in August, 1849. Members 267, a gain of 39.

We find the following in reference to ministers taking a letter from the church to which they belong:

"Resolved, That in the opinion of this Association that any minister drawing a letter of dismission from our watch care should not be permitted to preach or administer any of the ordinances, until his credentials be renewed by our Presbytery."

This is certainly a good resolution and ought to be strictly adhered to. This, doubtles, was done in order to keep some men from bringing reproach upon the principles for which they were contending. Any man who withdraws from the fellowship of any church ought not to carry credentials from said church.

At this meeting the churches were advised to liberate promising young gifts who wished to exercise their gifts in exhortation or preaching, for a limited time, or until some future meeting of the Associational Presbytery, where they could be fully examined concerning their ministerial gifts.

The eleventh meeting was held with Liberty Church, in Henderson county, August, 1850. Members 310, a gain of 43.

Soon after the organization of this Association, it held quarterly meetings. Soon after, it discontinued them and adopted semi-annual meetings.

At this, the eleventh meeting, it was divided into three districts, but still remained in the same annual Association.

The twelfth meeting was held with Pleasant Hope

Church, Daviess county, Kentucky, August 1851. American Union Church was received. Members 373, a gain of 63.

At this meeting a Missionary Society was formed under the name of "The Home Mission of the Kentucky Union Association of General Baptists."

The Association at this session took a firm stand in opposition to intemperance.

The 13th meeting was held with Green River Union Church, (this is the same church that has been refered to under the name of G. R. Union) in November, 1852. Sharon Church was received. Members 272, a loss of 101.

It appears that this Association had been infested with some imposters under the guise of the ministry, as they resolved not to invite strange preachers into their pulpits unless they come well recommended from the church to which they belonged.

They also placed themselves on record as being open or free communion, or, in other words, they were willing to receive to the Lord's Supper all that Christ received.

The fourteenth meeting was held with Free Union Church, McLean county, Kentucky, October, 1853. Members 301, a gain of 29.

The fifteenth meeting was held with Sharon Church, Henderson county, Kentucky, October,

1854, but we have not seen any minute of this meeting.

The sixteenth meeting was held October, 1855. Members 252.

At this meeting it was earnestly urged upon the various churches to secure the regular services of some pastor and to liberally remunerate them for their labors.

The seventeenth meeting was held with Pleasant Hope Church, McLean county, Kentucky, October, 1855. We have not the statistics or proceedings of this meeting.

The eighteeth meeting was held with Liberty Church, in Henderson county, Kentucky, October, 1857. Members 280.

Elder W. W. Lock, J. D. Gregory and John Onyet appeared with a letter of correspondence from the Ohio Association of General Baptists in Illinois and Kentucky. The Ohio Association also sent delegates to Liberty Association this year.

This is the first mention we hear of this Association, but it appears from her minutes that she was organized in 1855, or two years previous to this date, and fifteen years after Union Association, and nine years after the organization of Cumberland Association. We will give the history of Ohio Association in its proper place.

The nineteenth meeting was held with Mt. Gilead Church, Hopkins county, Kentucky, October, 1858. Green River and Paradise Churches were received. Members 304.

This meeting appointed delegates to meet in convention with the other Associations at Corydon, Kentucky, in order to draw up a constitution for a General Association.

It appears that the Associations were so scattered and weak that the General Association did not prove a success.

The twentieth meeting was held with Green River Church, Muhlenberg county, Kentucky, in October, 1869. This minute is, also, missing.

The twenty-first session was held with Mt. Lebanon Church, Webster county, Kentucky, in October, 1860. Shady Grove Church, Webster county Kentucky, received. Total members 324, a gain in two years, of 20.

This Association received a correspondent from United Association of General Baptists in Indiana. It also opened a correspondence with the Cumberland Association of Free-Will Baptists, in Tennessee. Also with the Mt. Moria Association of Free-Will Baptists in Alabama.

The twenty-second meeting was held with Pleasant Hope Church, in 1851. Representatives only from Green River Union, American Union and Pleasant Hope Churches, were in attendance.

They adjourned until October, 1862, to meet with Pleasant Hope Church, McLean county, Kentucky, and had no minutes printed.

The twenty-third session met with Pleasant Hope Church, in October, 1862.

Representatives from American Union, Elder Lud Brackett; Green River Union, Elder Jacob H. Igleheart; Pleasant Hope, Ben. Johnson and George L. Davis.

The Association organized and adjourned, but did not have any minutes printed this year.

"There was no public attendance at either of the Associations in 1861 and 1862, on account of the war troubles in this part of Kentucky.

GEO. L. DAVIS.

The twenty-fourth meeting was held with Mt. Lebanon Church, Webster county Kentucky, in October, 1863. Five churches were represented: Mt. Lebanon, Mt. Gilead, Pleasant Hope, Free Union and Shady Grove. Total membership 145.

At this meeting new life began to spring up. Quite an extended correspondence was received, and again we see this devoted people, who have labored under many difficulties, start almost anew on their mission of labor and love. I believe their number is less this year than at any time in their history, excepting 1861-62, when no statistics were given.

The twenty-fifth meeting was held with Shady Grove Church, Webster county, Kentucky, in October, 1864. Members 307, a gain of 162.

At this session we see this Association full of energy and zeal, renewed most of their former correspondence and organized an Associational Presbytery to examine any candidate for the ministry that should be sent up from the churches with a recommendation for licencing or ordination. Elders I. H. Henry and R. Head were appointed to write an essay on the qualifications and duties of Deacons.

In their letter of correspondence, we find this expression:

"We would gladly say that the Lord has revived his work in some of our churches. Our prospects for the future are growing brighter"

We here insert a short biographical sketch of Elder I. H. Henry, who figured very conspicuously among the people many years after this.

ELDER ISAAC H. HENRY.

Among the able and most useful ministers of the General Baptist denomination in Kentucky, so far as my knowledge extends, Elder Isaac H. Henry is, perhaps, the most prominent of any now living. He was born in Hopkins county, Kentucky, October 22, 1828, and professed faith in Christ in his thirteenth, and united with the church in his fifteenth year, thus learning to love and obey his Saviour in childhood. In love and favor with his neighbors, he established for himself a character which won for him the esteem of all who knew him and gave promise of future usefulness. He never obtained much education, but his great desire to inform himself, to the end that he might be useful in the cause of the Master, prompted him to read and study very much, and while many other young men were giving themselves up to pleasure, going to places of amusement, he was poring over his books and studying the Scriptures. Although his talent for preaching began to develope itself at an early age, he was diffident, and being of a modest and retiring disposition, he did not enter into the full work of the ministry until the 6th day of November,

1859, when he was ordained by Elders John Onyet, L. C. Onyet, C. Mason, Wm. Milligan, John D. Gregory and A. A. Stoval. Not being fully satisfied with his attainments he went to Owensville, Indiana, in the spring of 1860, and studied under Elder Geo. P. Cavanah, for four months, during which time he also attended the Owensville Academy, which was managed by Professor Jacob F. Bird, who was a very efficient teacher. During his stay, and studies here, he made such advancement in both theology and the sciences, that he went home, to Kentucky, and entered upon his work in the gospel field, with renewed energy and was very successful in the cause which has always been dear to him.

Elder Henry has preached extensively in Kentucky and often visits Illinois and Indiana. He is very much wedded to his high calling and his services are frequently required as pastor, so that when well, he puts in his time in preaching, some place, nearly every Sabbath. Bro. Henry does not aspire to be a great man, but he is a plain, matter-of-fact man, and wishes, above all things, to be useful rather than showy. His words are few and well chosen. He has a natural dignity which appears to fit him quite well. He is very social among his friends and is not only a good disciplinarian but he makes an excellent presiding officer. His manner, in the pulpit, is plain and frank and his sermons are delivered with much force and earnestness and his logic is very good. His character has always been good and no charge has ever been preferred against him in the church.

Elder Henry is distinguished for his devotion to the cause of temperance and urges his views in this behalf with much success, being himself temperate in all things.

He is also much devoted to the Liberal Baptist cause. It has long been his ardent desire to see all other Liberal and the General Baptists brought into nearer relation with each other, and some plan adopted by which a co-operation could be inaugurated by the General Association, or a General Convention, which would, in some way in the not very distant future result in a consolidation of all the free communion and free salvation Baptists in the United States into one body.

In conclusion, I will say, that he is a good writer, as his correspondence, in the columns of the General Baptist Herald, will attest. I could say much more of his abundant labors in the Master's cause, but I have filled the space allotted for this sketch."

The above was written in 1878. Elder Henry has been in very poor health nearly ever since, but we are glad to learn that he is now somewhat improved and preaching to the churches in different parts of Kentucky.

The twenty-sixth meeting was held with Green River Union Church, in Ohio county, Kentucky, in October, 1865. Chalybeate Springs received. Members 311, a gain of four.

"At this meeting Elder A. Pearce preached to a large congregation. The Lord's Supper was administered. All christians or lovers of Christ were invited, who were in good standing in their churches. "But let a man examine himself and so let him eat of that bread and drink of that cup, for he that eateth and drinketh unworthily, eateth and drinketh damnation to himself, not discerning the Lord's body. 1st. Cor., 11th chap., 28th and 29th verses." "Who art thou that judgest an other man's servant to his own master, he standeth or falleth? Rom. 14th chap., 4th verse.

This we find in the minute, which very clearly set forth their practice on the communion question.

Elder I. H. Henry was appointed General Home Missionary and ordered to visit every church in the Association and report at the next session.

The twenty-seventh meeting was held with Pleasant

Hope Church, McLean county, Kentucky, in October 1866. Four new churches, Bethlehem, Coperas Springs Mulberry Hill and Liberty. Members 584, a gain of 273.

This was a year of success and encouragement to this body.

Elders Benoni Stinson and A. H. Polk preached on Sabbath and Sabbath night. These sermons were so highly appreciated that a request was made by this Association for these sermons to be published. If they were I have never seen them.

Elder I. H. Henry reported his missionary labors and said he had labored in five protracted meetings and traveled fifty days, witnessed fifty-one conversions, baptised thirty-three, received $134 85 and pledges for $168.

The twenty-eighth session was held with Mt. Lebanon Church, Webster county, Kentucky, October, 1867. Mt. Pleasant and Pleasant Grove churches received. Members 612, a gain of 28.

Elder I. H. Henry was Missionary this year and worked 186 days, received $370.

We find that at this meeting some overtures were made in order to unite this Association with the Little Bethel Association of United Baptists. We presume the desired union was not effected.

The twenty-ninth meeting was held with Liberty

Church, Warren county, Kentucky, in October, 1868. New Harmony Church received. Members 982, a gain of 70.

At this meeting the Missionary Board was divided into two divisions. The one north of Green River consisted of Bros. Ben. Dexter, Charles Morgan and J. R. Dexter. The Board south of Green River consisted of Bros. W. A. Marks, Patrick Hall and H. H. Wise.

It seems that this plan did not prove successful as only the Board north of the river reported. These two Boards were relieved and a new Board appointed, consisting of Elder R. M. Smith and Bros. E. C. Atherton and G. L. Davis.

Elders I. H. Henry, R. M. Smith and Bro. G. L. Davis were appointed to correspond with the Free-Will Baptists of the East, in reference to a union between the two bodies.

The history of Liberty Association, in Indiana explains this whole matter, therefore we will not speak further of this union in connection with the other Association except when we come to the Associations in Southern Illinois.

The thirtieth meeting was held with New Harmony Church, Todd county, Kentucky, in October, 1869. Green's Chapel, New Hope, Hopewell and Indian Camp Union churches received. Members 933, a gain of 251.

It appears that the Cumberland Association of General Baptists was, at this time, in rather a weak condition, as she expressed a wish to become consolidated with Union and Union agreed to this provided the churches of Cumberland come as other new churches. This was not accepted however.

The thirty-first meeting was held with Mt. Gilead Church, Webster county, Kentucky, in October, 1870. Mud River Union and Macedonia churches received. Members 1137, a gain of 294.

This year the Association reports twenty-one ordained ministers and four licentiate.

We note the death of Elders L. Bracket, Isma Hancock and E. C. Atherton.

The thirty-second meeting was held with Mt. Union Church, Allen county, Kentucky, in October, 1871. Received, Little Rock and Sebree churches. Members 1534, a gain of 437.

ELDER JACOB H. IGLEHEART

"Departed this life, August 19th, 1871, aged sixty four years. He spent the greater part of his life in the church and was a faithful minister of the gospel among us for over thirty years. He was a faithful christian, a kind husband, a loving father and a good citizen. He died, as he had lived, in the Lord. We sympathize with a bereaved church, wife and children. Although to mourn when the good are taken away, is natural, we mourn not as those who have no hope, for he fell with his armor on, and his end was peace."

The thirty-third meeting was held with Shady Crove Church, Webster county, Kentucky, in October, 1872. Received, Corinth, New Friendship, Scuffletown, Cedar Grove and Union churches. Members 1590, a gain of 56.

The thirty-fourth meeting was held with Hopewell Church, Ohio county, Kentucky, in October, 1873. Received Walker's chapel and Walnut Grove. Members 1636, a gain of 45.

Elders I. H. Henry, J. N. Joiner, M. Z. Holland, M. B. Covington and Dr. Holmes were appointed a soliciting committee to build up a permanent Home Mission fund.

The thirty-fifth meeting was held with Macedonia Church, Simpson county, Kentucky, in October, 1874. Received, Clayville church. Members 1677.

The Association advised the churches to have, at least, one sermon preached during the following year, on the subject of baptism and the support of the gospel.

The thirty-sixth meeting was held with Union Hill Church, Henderson county, Kentucky, in October, 1875. Received, Free Union and White Oak Springs churches. Members 1155.

We see a very great loss and conclude that it must have been on account of the distance of many of the churches from Henderson county, in which the Association was this year convened. Therefore, the Association was this year divided and the new Association took the name of Mt. Union, which was finally organized in 1876.

We note the death of Elder J. N. Joiner.

Union Association, at this time, was in correspondence with nearly all the General Baptist Associations in the United States.

The thirty-seventh meeting was held with Clayville Church, Webster county, Kentucky, in Octo- 1876. Received, West Salem and Star Hope churches. Members 1063.

We find in the minute of this meeting, a constitution of a Finance Committee, the true principles of which are set forth in the third section of article 2nd. Speaking in reference to this committee, it says:

"They may receive gifts, donations and bequests for the use and benefit of the General Baptist denomination, in any sum or amount, and invest said sums in any way they may think best for said de nomination and may use any profits arising from such sums, for any missionary or religious enterprise, but shall forever hold the principal inviolate."

If all of our Associations had established something of this kind in their first organization all the Associations combined could have done a great general Home Mission work, which is greatly needed at the present time.

At this meeting Union Association declared herself in favor of a closer union among all liberal Baptists and favored a State Association in Kentucky, to hasten forward such a union in that State.

The thirty-eighth meeting was held with Pleasant Hope Church, McLean county, Kentucky, in October, 1877. Received Pleasant View and Oak Grove churches. Members 1101, a gain of 38.

We find all of the enterprises of this Association, in this year, in excellent working order, and the brethren full of hope and energy.

The thirty-ninth meeting was held with Star Hope Church, Webster county, Kentucky, in October, 1878. Members 809.

The fortieth meeting was held with Green's Chapel Church, Muhlenberg county, Kentucky, in October, 1879. Members 1105.

The forty-first meeting was held with Copperas Springs Church, Webster county Kentucky, in October, 1880. Received Enon Church. Members 1130 and 14 ministers.

It is not because we did find these brethren zealously engaged at the three or four last meetings, we did not say more about them. No, to the contrary, they are doing their work well. We did not find any new plans introduced in those meetings, because they have learned, by long experience, what is best for them and the cause of Christ, and this they are doing well. When I say that they are flourishing and prosperous, this is saying a great deal, yet it is true.

We have drawn these short sketches from the minutes of the Union Association, which Bro. Geo. L. Davis, of Calhoun, Kentucky, has very kindly furnished us. I find that Bro. Davis has been clerk of this Association for twenty-one years, and has done his duty well.

On the next pages will be found a table which exhibits the date, place, Moderator, Clerk and members, date of new churches and death of ministers. I have avoided, as much as possible, mentioning such things as were actually necessary to mention in Libty Association and some that must be mentioned in connection with General Association.

The following are the names of the ordained ministers belonging to this Association, in 1881:

I. H. Henry, James Cowen, M. Fraser, N. T.

Duncan, R. Head. H. E. Todd, Joseph Lee, J. H. Uttley, H. A. Gregg, M. B. Covington, H. L. Echols, A. Pearce, Wm. King, B. Johnson, J. H. Kirtly, B. Brackett, J. H. Dame, D. Craig, B. T. Igleheart, F. Crabtree and J. N. Carner.

The table below exhibits the date, Moderator, Clerk, new churches received, total members, and death of ministers of Union Association.

Date.	Churches.	Moderator.	Clerk.	New Churches.	Members.	Remarks.
1840	Caldwell	Jacob Holeman	Jesse Nichols	Liberty, Chalybeate Sp's, Caldwell, Union, Grassy Lick, Liberty, Caldwell co., Sharon	163	
1841	Chalybeate	E. C. McCoy	do do	Pleasant, Hope, Shady Grove, Zion, Mt. Lebanon, Salem, New Hope.	258	
1842	Liberty	S. W. McAnd'ws	H. Baldwin	Mt. Enon, Friendship	311	
1843	Mt. Lebanon	E. C. McCoy	S. W. King	Free Communion, Freedom, Mt. Gilead	406	
1844	Pleasant Hope	do do	G. F. Wallace	Pleasant Grove	395	
1845	Freedom	W. W. Jenkens	E. S. Baldwin	Ballard, Lewis Creek	362	
1846	Pleasant Grove	E. C. McCoy	P. F. Ogelby		164	
1847	Zion	do do	B. B. Landermon	Green River Union	228	
1848	Salem	do do	do do		267	
1849	Mt Gilead	do do	G. B. Cavanah		310	
1850	Liberty	C. M. Frasier	Jas. Ellis	American Union	573	
1851	Pleasant Hope	do do	do do	Sharon	272	
1852	Green R. Union	L. Brackett	do do		306	
1853	Free Union	A. Pearce....8	L. P. Whitny			The minute of this mt'g is missing
1854	Sharon					
1855		L. P. Whitney	W. W. Karney		252	
1856	Pleasant Hope	L. Brackett	G. L. Davis			Minutes missing
1857	Liberty				280	
1858	Mt. Gilead	J. H. Igleheart	W. W. Rarney	Green River, Paradise	304	Minutes missing
1859	Green River					

IN THE UNITED STATES.   315

Year	Church					Notes
1860	Mt. Lebanon	do	do	W. G. Sammons	Shady Grove		324	No minutes printed
1861	Pleasant Hope	J. H. Igleheart	G. L. Davis			No minutes printed
1862	Pleasant Hope	L. Brockett	do			145	
1863	Mt. Lebanon	J. H. Igleheart	do			367	
1864	Shady Grove	do	do			311	
1865	Green R. Union	L. H. Henry	do		Chalybeate Springs	584	
1866	Pleasant Hope	M. Frasier	J. T. Frasier		Bethlehem, Coper'as Springs, Mulberry Hill, Liberty		
1867	Mt. Lebanon	A. Pierce	G. L. Davis		Pleasant Hope, Pleasant Grove	642	
1868	Liberty	L. H. Henry	do		New Harmony	682	
1869	New Harmony	J. H. Igleheart	do		Green's Chapel, New Hope, Hopewell, Indian Camp, Unity	933	
1870	Mt. Gilead	M. Frasier	do		Mud River Union, Macedonia	1197	
1871	Mt. Union	L. H. Henry	do		Little Rock, Sebree	1534	Jacob H. Igleheart died
1872	Shady Grove	do	do		Corinth, New Friends'p, Sculfletown, Cedar G'v.	1590	
1873	Hopewell	M. B. Covington	do		Union	1653	
1874	Macedona	L. H. Henry	do		Walker's Chapel, Walnut Grove	1677	
1875	Union Hill	do	do		Clayville	1165	
					Free Union, White Oak Springs		
1876	Clayville	do	do		West Salem, Star Hope	1063	
1877	Pleasant Hope	do	do		Pleasant View, Oak Gr'e	1101	Mt. Union As'n organz'd
1878	Star Hope	do	do			809	
1879	Green's Chapel	M. Frasier	do		Enon	1105	
1880	Coperas Springs	A. Pierce	do			1130	
1881	Mt. Lebanon	do	do	H. L. Echols	Good Hope	1172	

CUMBERLAND ASSOCIATION.

At the seventh meeting of Union Association, as has been stated, by mutual consent, was divided and begining at Henderson and running to Madisonville, then to Princeton, Kentucky. All the General Baptist churches west of this line were organized into a new Association on Friday before the second Sabbath in October, 1846. Elders Benoni Stinson, John B. Stinson and Jacob Speer assisted in organizing this new body. This also took place at the same church where Union Association had been organized in 1840, by the same committee as above mentioned.

This body appears to have been quite successful at first and spread very rapidly, so much so that in a few years it had planted several more churches in Kentucky, and several in Illinois, so by November, 1854, six churches in Illinois were organized into Ohio Association.

After this it does not appear to have prospered so much and probably was much reduced by the troubles incident to the late war, as were many other General Baptist Associations. In 1869 she made overtures to Union Association for a consolidation of the two bodies. This was not effected. However, some of her churches joined the Union Association and some went to the Ohio Association, in Illinois. This left Cumberland so weak as to nearly disorganize her forces. I am informed that within the last few years she has rallied and gone to work in earnest and now numbers about five hundred members.

I have no means of telling what ministers went into the organization, nor who their ministers are now. I have made repeated efforts to reach some correspondent in this body, but have so far been unsuccessful. What I have written has been gathered from the minutes of Liberty and Union Associations and from parties who had known something of these people at different times since their Association was organized.

SOUTHERN ILLINOIS ASSOCIATON.

This branch of the liberal Baptist family had its origin in the year 1850, under very peculiar and unavoidable circumstances, and was formerly confined to, or began in the counties of Randolph, Jackson and Perry, in the southern portion of the State, the founder of which was the Rev. Henry Smith Gordon, a native of Pennsylvania. He emigrated with his fathers family, to Missouri, when but a child and located near St. Louis, where he grew to manhood, married and removed to Randolph county, Illinois. He was born in the year 1816, and at the age of about twenty united with the Missionary Baptist Church, at Georgetown, Illinois.

Shortly after, he was called to the ministry, with which church he lived and preached, acting as missionary, organizer and pastor, for about ten years, during which time he attended Shertliff College, at Alton Illinois, where he received the greater part of his education. After his return from college he continued to preach, and on April 28th, 1850, he organized a church at Looney Springs, in Jackson county, Illinois, with nine members, as follows: John McLaughlin, John Burlison, Mary Henry, Sarah White, Serena Bradly, Mary White, Nancy Petty, Jane Burlison and Susan Harrison, all of whom endorsed the doctrines of the Baptist church. With but one exception, they desired that their christian neighbors and friends should enjoy, with them, the privileges of the Lord's Supper, which they believed was not under the control of priest or preacher, and it became a subject of much interest and argument among the members. Finally the subject was refered to Brother Gordon, who informed them that it was contrary to the rules of the Baptist church. However, the agitation was continued with such earnest importunities that eventually, in his own words: "I yielded to their entreaties and gave my consent, although I had never publicly advocated free communion in my life," for the justice of their claim was so apparent and their cause so scriptural that "I yielded my acquired denominational prejudices and invited all believers to a seat at the Lord's Table," which offence, in the eyes of close Baptists, was so heritical that he was called to account for this departure from Baptist usages, for which offence he was excluded for—in the language of the moderator—"damnable heresy."

That this history may be complete and set forth all the facts connected with the case, I will insert here, the trial and exclusion of Rev. H. S. Gordon, from the Georgetown Missionary Baptist church, as prepared and published by the committee who were appointed for that purpose:

We, the committee, appointed by the newly organized Free Communion Baptist Church, at Georgetown, Randolph county, Illinois, to prepare and publish an account of the trial and exclusion of Rev. H. S. Gordon from the old Baptist church of that place, make this report:

At the monthly meeting of the old Baptist Church held December 17th, 1850, the Moderator, T. Rawson, inquired if some of their members had not violated Baptist usuages in communing with the Looney Springs Church, at its last meeting. Whereupon Bro. Gordon made this explanation:

The Looney Springs Church which I constituted last April, is in a prosperous condition, and now numbers between fifty and sixty members. The last meeting was a sacramental occasion; the membership was invited to seats; visiting members of the same faith and order were next invited, whereupon a number of the members of Georgetown Church came forward.

Now, said Bro. Cordon, I have extended the invitation as far as our denomination permits, but does this church wish to extend it further? I submit the matter to you. All who wish to extend it to all believers in Christ, please rise up. The church unanimously rose up. All christians were then invited, and several came. After which the church resolved to investigate the matter at its next meeting, and Revs. Peck, Boykin, Peters, Lemon, Arnett, Philips and Hale were invited as a council of ministers, to be present at the next monthly meeting, January 18th, 1851. Peter Hagler, acting as Moderater, the subject was taken up for investigation, but instead of investigating it the church was formed into a regular court to try the said H. S. Gordon and others, for being public offenders.

T. Rawson then proceeded to read several letters received; one from D. L. Philips, also some articles from the Western watchman; one written by Peck, one by Boykin, and others, in answer to the invitation sent them by the church.

The defendent, Gorden, then asked if these letters were to be received in evidence in the case, and he was informed by the moderator they would.

The defendants then urged that they should be tried by the Bible and not by usages; saying, if our conduct has been contrary to the Bible we will acknowledge and forsake it; but try us by the Bible! the Bible!! the Bible!!! alone, and not by usage. They urged in vain. The Bible was not to be the rule in this case.

Every church has a right to make its own laws, said Arnett.

Bro. Gordon then insisted upon the impropriety of making usages the rule of our conduct and mentioned several historical instances as illustrative of what usages had been, and often they had been wrong. He had not proceeded far before some of the brethren became exceedingly restless and began to mutter and talk. At length their indignation rose so high that they could not restrain their feelings any longer, and springing from their seats, brethren, in a tone of perfect rage, cried out, put him out! turn him out! he is not of us! turn him out! we are not going to be abused in our own house, this way! put him out! and the defendant was not allowed to proceed further.

Bro Arnett was then called on to give his opinion in the matter. He arose and gave a very sympathetic exhortation to those who had violated Baptist usages, but charged all the sin on Bro. Gordon and exhorted him to be an example to the flock, and to adhere to those customs of the church that had been long in use, telling him that Methodists, Presbyterians, &c., would not come if he did invite them; that they were all close communionists, anyhow, and that he would lose his reputation if he entertained such notions; that the ministers of the South District Association always thought a great deal of him, but now they would abandon him, and that his course would hurt his brethren's feelings; that he, himself, had always been a good friend of his, and had taken him in one cold night and treated him kindly, and concluded by urging him to acknowledge his faults. To all of which Gordon made a short reply.

Elder Hale then arose to speak in behalf of those charged, but was refused to be heard in their favor. He insisted he had a right to speak, for the church had invited him there, but the Moderator decided against him and the defendant was not allowed any counsel whatever.

After much wrangling, a motion was made to adjourn, but the defendants objected, unless the church would agree to meet again. We do not want the matter to stop in this manner, said they.

The Moderator then said: The defendadts have made this difficulty. Now if they will just let us alone——

At this juncture Bro. Gordon arose and asked the congregation who made this difficulty? and if there was a single person in the house who had ever heard him preach or teach the doctrine of free communion. No one said they had.

Well if we have never preached or talked about it, why does the Moderator ask us to let them alone?

Now, said he, I do, for the first time, publicly avow it. I do believe all christians should commune together.

He then asked time to give some scriptural reasons why he believed so.

Ten minutes was then allowed him, when he stated some eight or ten objections to restricted communion.

On motion and second, it was decided that these persons had violated Baptist usage, but unanimously agreed that the sisters be excused on the score of ignorance, but Bro. Gordon knew better; therefore, he should make acknowledgement.

He replied that he was not convinced that he had done wrong, therefore he could make no acknowledgments until he was convinced of his error from the Bible.

More than that, no acknowledgments could be satisfactory to the church, because a very respectable majority of it thought he had done right.

After much confusion, and evidently angry feelings among the accusers, themselves, they finally succeeded in forming the following:

Resolved, That Rev. H. S. Gordon be excluded from the fellowship of this church, but those good sisters, who had been exhonerated from all charges, on account of ignorance, was not allowed to vote, and the resolution was carried by a small majority, and H. S. Gordon stood excluded.

In view of the above facts, the unreasonablness of the charge, and the base injustice done Bro. Gordon, the greater part of the old church became dissatisfied and notice was given that on the following Saturday a meeting would be held at the residence of Deacon J. P. Short, for the reason that the old church house was refused them, to consider the propriety of organizing a new church.

The time came and Rev. R. A. Bradley was chosen Moderator and John McLaughlin Clerk.

The meeting was then addressed by Rev. H. S.

Gordon, Dr. Job Lawrence, Rev. John Mathews and Mr. Lofton, Esq., and resulted in the organization of a church with twenty-five members, all former members of the old church.

Bro. Gordon was chosen pastor, and continued to serve the church regularly, for about fifteen years.

During the following summer about twenty-five more were added to their number.

The old church having refused the use of their house for our meetings, and treated the committee who asked for the same, so contemptuously, that the new organization proceeded at once to the erection of a new house of worship in sight of the old one, and their zeal for the cause of truth and religious and Bible liberty, as contrasted with adopted rules and usages, was so prompting and inspiring, that in three months time the new building, which was both neat and commodious, was completed and occupied by the young church, which for some years was known as the Free Communion Baptist Church.

Bro. Gordon's ability and his peculiar adaptation to the work into which he was so unexpectedly called to take up and advocate, and in fact to become the leader of a more advanced and liberal view of christianity at a time in the history of the Baptist church when it was anything but popular, enabled him to reach the people with what would seem to be almost supernatural power. In his efforts to propogate what he conceived to be the teachings of the Bible his church grew rapidly and and surely.

In the mean time Looney Springs Church grew in numerical strength and popularity and R. A. Bradley and John McLaughlin were ordained to the ministry.

About this time Bro. Gordon organized the Pipestone Church, in Perry county. Also, the Pleasant Ridge Church, in the southern part of Randolph county.

There now being four churches holding to the same views on the communion question, it was deemed expedient to organize an Association. Consequently, in the following year, October, 1851, there was formed the Southern Illinois Association of Free Communion Baptists, with the following churches and delegates:

Georgetown Church, Rev. H. S. Gordon, J. T. Short and F. Garner.

Looney Springs, Revs. R. A. and Wm. Bradly, and D. Underwood.

Pleasant Ridge Church, Robert Moore and Joseph Robinson.

Pipestone Church, E. T. Reese and J. A. Bradley.

This Association was organized at Georgetown, Randolph county, Illinois.

There were, at this time, only four ministers, Revs.

H. S. Gordon, R. A. Bradly, Isaac Hale and John McLaughlin. The latter died shortly after he was called to the ministry. Soon after, however, Wm. Bradley was ordained, and from that time to the present, has been one of the most untiring and indefatigable workers and the success of the denomination is owing largely to his zeal and earnest persistancy.

For the next three or four years the new churches battled hard against the many influences with which every reform has to contend. At the same time, not knowing that there was any Baptist churches in the country holding similar views on the great question that had been the cause of our origin, and for a long time we were called Free-Willers, by way of "nick name," because of the liberal views entertained on the communion question, as, also, on the atonement as opposed to Calvinism.

The new churches grew rapidly and the cause gained much favor, generally, under the preaching of our pioneer ministers, and as its power and influence for good spreatl and widened and had began to attract the attention of the public, it was for the first time providentially apprised of the existence of a body of people in Indiana, called General Baptists, holding the same doctrinal views.

In the fall of 1854, Rev. H. S. Gordon, Rev. Wm. Bradley and Deacon J. P. Short, equipped with wagon and team, blankets and some provisions, started out on what, in that day, was deemed a long and tedious journey, to attend a meeting of the Liberty Association of General Baptists, in order to form acquaintance with them, learn from whence they came, who and what they were, their doctrines, &c. Said visit resulted in a fraternal and reciprocal correspondence, which was continued for many years. Finding that we were all espoused to the same cause and agreed in doctrine and church government, and in order to give strength, through union of effort, in the year 1856 we adopted the name of General Baptists, which name we bore for about twenty years.

In the meantime the work had spread rapidly in every direction until its churches had been dotted over five or six counties in the southern part of the State.

About this time, through the preaching of Rev. Wm. Carlyle, Robt. Lee and Silas Parker, the work spread eastward and now embraced about seven counties. The good work was prosecuted vigorously by those earnest, self-sacrificing men and success seemed to follow, and God's blessing attend them wherever they went to preach the word. Many souls were converted and made happy, and God's kingdom wonderfully built up. Although opposition was to be overcome and our close Baptist brethren never lost an opportunity to hinder the advancement of the work, declaring and contending that our ministers were not duly and regularly qualified to administer the ordinances of the church or solemnize marriage, and in short were not in the "regular apostolical succession." But conscientious convictions impelled them forward with irristible force, until prejudices began to give way, and christian toleration and liberty, untrammelled by usage, beheld the light of a brighter day, and General Baptist became largely, in many parts of the country, the prevailing denomination and their ministerial strength had been wonderfully increased by the addition of quite a number of newly ordained ministers; among whom we call to mind, J. M. Madglin, Willis Charles, W. P. Hale, J. Teffertillar, J. C. Gilliland, Jas. McIntosh W. L. Smart, A. Pearson, G. A. Gordon and others and the work continued to enlarge and increase.

Perhaps in the year 1865 or 1866, we held our Association with Mt. Olivet Church, in Hamilton, Hamilton county. Among other visiting brethren present at that meeting was Rev. J. S. Brown, from Lebanon, Illinois, formerly a minister in the Close Baptist church, who had withdrawn from them on account of the communion question, and had associated with him, Rev. Harry Thompson, M. A. Shepard, and others, and had organized a number of churches on the free communion principle, throughout St. Clair and Washington counties, and feeling that in union there is strength, he asked for his churches admission, which request was granted, and they were received and henceforth formed a part of the Southern Illinois Association.

Our work had now spread over eight or nine counties, and a desire to still further enlarge their denominational work, usefulness and strength, by united effort.

The Association sent Revs. Wm. Bradley, G. A. Gordon and J. Gilliland, as delegates to a convention which was called to meet in Indiana, to discuss and advise as to the propriety, and lay plans looking to the union of all General Baptists in the United States, which resulted, finally, in the organization of a General Association, and in the year 1871 the Southern Illinois Association became a member of that body, and by united effort their influence for good began to be realized and their position respected everywhere and God graciously blessed the work and extended his kingdom.

In the year 1869 the Association having grown so large that it was inconvenient for the churches to be represented by their delegates at the annual Associations it was agreed to divide the territory and form a new Association. In view of this fact it was arranged that all the churches east of the Illinois Cen tral Railroad should be organized into, and known as, the Mt. Olivet Association. All west to retain the old name.

As time passed on a more intimate acquaintance with the Free-Will Baptists was cultivated. Delegates from that body from different parts of the United States corresponded with, and visited us, from time to time, which on our part was reciprocated, and as we learned more and more of them, of their doctrines, plans and facilities for doing aggressive and successful work in the way of education, publication and missionary enterprises, and believing that greater good could be accomplished by union of effort of all liberal Baptists, holding substantially the same religious views, there was called a meeting of the Association to consider the advisability of consolidation with the Free-Will Baptists. Consequently, in October, 1875 there was organized the Central Illinois Yearly Meeting of Free-Will Baptists, composed of all the churches belonging to the Association, which had been divided into two quarterly meetings heretofore. Also, a number of churches in Johnson and Williamson counties, known as General Free-Will Baptists, built up under the labors of Rev. W. H. Blankenship and others, they having passed through many of the hardships incident to every departure from established rules and usages. These three Quarterly Meetings now constituted the new Yearly Meeting. Since that time we have been known and recognized as Free-Will Baptists. Our borders have been extended rapidly and three other Quarterly Meetings have been added to our number, making now six Quarterly Meetings in all.

1st, Looney Springs; 2d, Lebanon; 3d, Makanda; 4th, Wayne County; 5th, Franklin; 6th St. Francis Quarterly Meeting, in Missouri; thus occupying a much larger field than ever before, by nearly one-half.

Its borders embraced now, the counties of Randolph, Perry, Jackson, Union, Williamson, Johnson, Hamilton, Franklin, Jefferson, Wayne, Edwards, Washington, St. Clair, and two counties in Missouri, having an aggregate membership of 2224 at our last annual report in 1881, with fifty churches and forty-two ordained ministers.

Among the number of ministers who have done much for the success of our beloved cause and have sacrificed both time and money, and given the best energies of their lives, we might mention Revs. H. S. Gordon, Wm. Bradley, Wm. Carlyle, W. H. Blankenship, Harry Thompson, J. C. Gilliland, G. A. Gordon, M. A. Shepard, T. O. McMinn, J. C. Cully, David Ashby, J. S. Gullege, W. H. Copas, and many others; then there is a host of brethren, some of whom are resting from their labors and now sleep with the fathers who have been, and are faithful, devoted and self-sacrificing servants of the Master, and strong pillars in the church of Christ.

Through the many changes, trials and perplexities of these anxious years the founder of the liberal Baptists of Southern Illinois, has struggled, contending firmly for the faith once delivered to the saints, and has lived to see liberal Baptist doctrines and sentiments so thoroughly inculcated in the minds of the people, and so universally endorsed and admired and so kindly received and practiced, that no grander appreciation of his labors could be bestowed, nor to his ability a more flattering tribute paid, than the endorsement by so many hundreds of the cause he early espoused, nor a stronger assurance of Heavens approval, than to know that under God's blessing, success has attended him and his early co-laborers, of whom only two or three are now living, and to all of whom belong the privilege of bearing many of the scars and reproaches that always attend every departure from the old beaten way.

I add the names and Post Office address of the ministers of our Yearly Meeting, at present:

H. S. Gordon, Percy, Randolph county Ill.

Wm. Bradley, Murphysborough, Jackson county, Illinois.

G. A. Gordon, Campbell Hill, Jackson county, Illinois.

W. R. Wilson, Rockwood, Randolph county, Illinois.

W. A Bishop, Carbondale, Jackson county Illinois.

J. H. Cully, Carbondale, Jackson county, Illinois.

J. W. Freeman, Carbondale, Jackson county, Illinois.

J. Mullenax, Carbondale Jackson county, Illinois.

C. Phelps, Pomona, Jackson county, Illinois.

A. S. Tripp, Pomona, Jackson county, Illinois.

Ab. Pearson, Chester, Randolph county, Illinois.

J. C. Gilliland, DeSoto, Jackson county, Illinois.

J. D. Tindale, Rockwood, Randolph county, Illinois.

H. S. Nations, Pine Hill, Missouri.

———— Hartell, Pine Hill, Missouri.

M. E. Stephens, Makanda, Jackson county Illinois.

Y. B. Sutter, Tamaroa, Perry county. Illinois.

M. A. Shepard, Lebanon, St. Clair, county, Illinois.

H. Thompson, Lebanon, St. Clair county, Illinois.

S. E. Rogers, Ashly, Washington county, Illinois.

J. H. Smith, Ashley, Washington, county, Illinois.

B. F. Keller, Laur, Illinois.

L. S. Brayfield, Franklin county, Illinois.

W. D. Cockram, Franklin county, Illinois.

Isham Belbry, Franklin county, Illinois.

P. O. Franklin, Franklin county, Illinois.

N. C. Curry, Franklin county, Illinois.

T. O. McMinn, Carterville, Williamson county, Illinois.

W. L. Smart, South America, Illinois.

J. Gullege, Marion, Williamson, county, Illinois.

J. F. Kirk, Cottage Home, Williamson county, Illinois.

I. W. Isaacs, Thompsonville, Franklin county Illinois.

J. W. Phelps, Tamaroa, Perry county, Illinois.

N. M. Roberts, Thompsonville, Franklin county, Illinois.

W. L. Miller, Makanda, Jackson county, Illinois.

W. C. Travelstead, Jackson county, Illinois.

W. E. Clark, Liberlyville, Missouri.

W. H. Copas, Liberlyville, Missouri.

J. Wood, DeLassus, Missouri.

W. Mitchell, St. Joe, Missouri.

John Rhodes, Bone Gap, Illinois.

Rev. Moon, Bone Gap, Illinois.

G. A. GORDON,

March 15th, 1882. Campbell Hill, Ill.

OHIO ASSOCIATION.

On Saturday, November 25th, 1854, Smyrna, Union, Philadelphia, Freedom, Friendship and Pleasant Hill churches from Cumberland Association of General Baptists, together with three new churches, to-wit: Sneads Chapel, Mt. Pleasant and New Liberty, numbering 414 members were by Elders Peter F. Ogilly, sr., Wm. W. Locke and John D. Gregory, organized in to an Association at Union Church, Hardin county, Illinois. This body of people adopted the Constitution, Rules of Decorum and Confession of Faith of the Cumberland Association of General Baptists and took the name of Ohio Association.

This Association has held annual meetings regularly ever since its organization. The Ministers who were most active in the early history of this Association, were those above named together with John Onyett, Charles Onyett, W. W. Hurt, Caswell Mason, Asa Lanear, Moze Lanear, Wm. Milligan, E. Oxford and J. R. Oxford. All but the three last named have finished their course on earth and gone to their reward. The names mentioned, both living and dead are and were men of irreproachable character and some of them were men of considerable Ministerial ability.

"The Ministers who are now and have been doing active service for some time in this Association, are John Thornton, J. B. Tucker, J. T. Ledbetter, B. L. Ledbetter, W. E. Gray, T. D. Gossage, Calvin Jackson, F. M. Randolph and Dr. M. E. Barker.

Elder Thornton has been a *very active* Minister for the last twelve years."

The Association has several licentiates as follows: J. Jack, A. Briggs, G. Vaughn, J. Blair, A. Dutton, J. Shadawin, J. Plemmons and J. Burns, who is probably ordained.

This Association now numbers about seven hundred members and is in a better working condition than it has been in some years previous. We would have been glad to have inserted short biographical sketches of those old veterans in the Ministry and those deceased Ministers. To obtain what we have of these, has been the most difficult part of our work. We have never met but two of these Ministers and our acquaintance was very short, having only met them at General Associations. We have requested Elder Wm. Millikan to send us short biographies of those old Ministers which we will insert if they reach us in time. Brother J. A. Oxford, of Sparks Hill, Illinois, has kindly assisted in obtaining material for this sketch.

ELDER WILLIAM MILLIKAN

Was born April 6th, 1814, in Jefferson county, Tennessee. His parents were members of a close communion Baptist church, and his father a Minister, who died during the late war. Brother Millikan professed religion at an early age, and united with a close Baptist church, and remained with that people until he became acquainted with the General Baptists, whose doctrines and usages were congenial with his understanding of the scripture. Among these people he became a Minister and was ordained May 2d, 1857, and continued to work among them with much zeal, earnestness and success for a number of years, but from a want of financial support he has been compelled to leave considerable of the Ministry and resort to secular employment to sustain his family. He has been a member of the church forty-two years and called to pass through many sore afflictions or trying persecutions, yet no charge of immorality or dishonesty has ever been brought against him. He has been a member of the Ohio Association in Illinois ever since its organization.

He has been married twice, first to Miss Barbara L. Cole in 1847. After her decease he was married to Mrs. Josephine Dale in 1878. He is now, April, 1882, in very feeble health, yet he can say in the language of the Apostle: "Though the outward man perish yet the inner man is renewed day by day." Brother Milikan feels that his labors have not been sufficiently rewarded by his brethren. But he is resigned and submissive and expresses a strong hope of meeting many of them beyond the grave. He urges the necessity of our young men qualifying themselves for the Ministry and insists on the churches giving them a support.

UNITED ASSOCIATION.

In the beginning of the history of this body of people it is necessary to give a brief sketch of the life of Elder Samuel T. Thompson, who "was born in Louisa county, Virginia, on the 15th day of June, 1816". His education was quite limited. He came to Pike county and in 1838 professed religion June 1843, and united with the Flat Creek church of United Baptists, and was baptized by Elder John Almon February 1843. He was licensed to preach the Gospel in the fall of 1843, and was ordained in the fall of 1844 by Elder John Almon, Frances Slator and Deacon Wm. McComic from a close study of the scripture. Elder Thompson soon became convinced that close communions, which was practiced by the United Baptists, was an error, therefore he, in company with seventeen members and one licensed preacher, Thomas Jones, withdrew from the United Baptists in 1851 and constituted a church on the articles of Faith of the Liberty Association of General Baptists, which they gave the name of Flat Creek Church of free Communion United Baptists, with Elder Thompson as their Pastor, and they continued to plant churches successfully until in 1859 when they numbered 8 churches. When Elder T. M. Strain and G. P. Cavanah, from Old Liberty Association of General Baptists, visited them and they agreed to unite with some churches in Warrick county, which belonged to Old Liberty Association of General Baptists.

Accordingly in September 1860 Elder S. T. Thompson with the following churches and their representatives met with Little Bethany Church, Warrick county, Indiana, and organized United Association of General Baptists. The original churches were Flat Creek, Bethel, Mt. Olive, Little Bethany, Mt. Zion, Enon and Ridge. These are the churches that

Elder Thompson planted before Elder Strain and Cavanah visited them and the following are the churches that were granted letters from, Old Liberty Association in order to join United, which were admitted at this first meeting in 1860, Richland, Bethabara, Mt. Gilead, Otter Creek, Sharon, Mt. Olive, Bethany and Union. This gave United Association 15 churches and 845 members to start with. At the second meeting held with Mt. Zion church, Pike county, Indiana, we find the following list of Ministers, most of whom the writer has met, but many of them are now 1881, deceased. Ordained Ministers.

S. T. Thompson, Ransom Voils, H. B. Borders, Jacob Cokes, John Stephenson, John Lacer, J. G. Lane, James Thomas, Levi Voils, Wm. Carter, H. H. Griggs, T. A. Price, Solomon Rhodes, Wm. Sturgeon, James Houghland, H. Borders, J. Powel, J. R. Lacer, Jacob Houghland, David Perkins J. J. Collins and O. C. Bright,

This Association was a working body and great prosperity followed their labor.

In ten years after their organization, or in 1870, they numbered thirty-eight churches and 2017 communicants. At this date it was found expedient to letter off Mt. Olive, Pilgrim, Ephisus, Pleasant Grove, Union, Hosmer, Nashville, St. Joseph, Wood, Flat Creek, Pleasant Ridge, Mt. Tabor,

Enon and Mt. Pisgah churches to form a new Association which was constituted on Friday, before the fourth Sabbath in September, 1870, and took the name of Flat Creek, an account of which will follow soon. At their annual meeting in 1871, they numbered twenty-three churches and 1320 members. In tracing their history through the next ten years, or up to 1881, we find them engaged in supporting all the enterprises of our denomination, and their labors have been blest with a continual, steady growth, and they now number twenty-six churches and 1745 members. This Association has never had to contend with any serious difficulties and may be considered one of the most prosperous Associations in the General Baptist connection.

They now number twenty-five ordained ministers and three licentiates. The following are the names of the ordained ministers:

S. L. Purdue, Robt. Bullock, J. M. Bullock, E. S. Bates, Isaac Barrett, G. Campbell, L. Spradley, James Hart, John Stephenson, C. C. Boyer, J. Hinder, F. M. Boardman, A. Price, I. S. Hay, L. Houchins, David Perkins, James Wiggs, G. W. Hogars, W. T. Topper, O. C. Bright, M. B. West, W. Chesser, Levi Voils, H. Brown, W. L. Stephens.

The licentiates are, H. Hart, J. E. Perkins and J. Burton.

This closes the history of this interesting body of people, with the exception of some biographical sketches of deceased ministers, which will now follow.

Elder David Perkins, who was a member of old Liberty Association and has been a member of the United Association for many years, has preserved a complete file of minutes of this Association and it is from these that we have been enabled to write the preceeding account, with the exception of that part which relate particularly to Elder S. T. Thompson, which we obtained from an article written by Elder F. M. Kerr, who was a son-in-law of Elder Thomson. We have not given the increase and decrease of this Association, as we have of old Liberty, Union and some others, nor do we consider it necessary to follow all the Associations through their trials and persecutions, as we have old Liberty and Union in particular, for what has been said of these two may, with a very little variableness, be said of all of General Baptist Associations in the west. The ministers in this Association are generally uneducated, but they are zealous workers for the cause of Christ.

Below we give the names of Moderators and Clerks. The figures opposite their names indicate the number of times each one served.

MODERATOR.

Elder S. T. Thompson,	- - - -	3
do	Thos. A. Price, - - - -	1
do	Solomon Rhodes, - - -	2
do	David Perkins, - - -	5
do	J. G. Lane - - - -	3
do	John Stephens - - -	1
do	Levi Voils, - - - -	3
do	A. C. West, - - - -	1
do	I. S. Hay, - - - -	3

CLERK.

Temple Woolsey, - - - - -	2
J. Green, - - - - -	1
S. W. Parker, - - - -	8
J. M. Fuller, - - - - -	2
Elder W. T. Hopkins, - - -	1
T. J. Downs, - - - -	2
Henry Kelly, - - - - -	2
Joshua McKenney, - - - -	1
Elder J. G. Lane, - - - -	1
T. J. Hargan, - - - -	1
Rice Wilson - - - -	1

ELDER SOLOMON RHODES.

"Elder Rhodes was born in the State of Kentucky, July 11th, 1811, and came to Warrick county, Indiana, when quite a small boy. He professed faith in Christ, August, 1847 and united with M. E. church, but soon became dissatisfied with some of its doctrines and usages. He cast his lot with the Mt. Gilead church of General Baptists, in the fall of 1847, whose doctrines were perfectly congenial with his religious sentiments. He was licensed by a presbytery consisting of Elders Thomas Fuller and Alvah Parker, in December, of the same year.

In September, 1848, a presbytery, consisting of several ministers, among whom were Elders T. M. Strain, Jesse Lane, sr., and Alvah Parker, ordained Elder Rhodes to the full work of the ministry, and he entered at once upon a life of activity and usefulness in the Master's cause.

Elder Rhodes was not so brilliant and fluent as some other men, but he was noted for his untiring energy and zeal. His heart was always in the work and he was loved and honored by all who knew him.

But few, if any, ever accomplished more good in the United Association of General Baptists than Elder Rhodes.

He was an excellent exhorter. His main power was in revival meetings. Some conversions nearly always followed his meetings, thus building up the churches both in membership and spirituality. In proof of which we cite you to Bethany, his old home church, which numbers 225 members. Elder Rhodes was an uncompromising Baptist, advocating their principles wherever he went, traveling from one neighborhood to another, sparing neither time nor means for their success.

After a life of thirty-three years as a faithful and truly devoted christian, he fell asleep in Jesus, in the full triumph of a living faith, January 1st, 1880, being seventy-nine years old."

This sketch was furnished us by Bro. S. W. Parker, a son of Elder Alvah Parker, who now lives near Boonville, Warrick county, Indiana.

LIBERTY ASSOCIATION, MISSOURI

This Association was organized in 1862, either in Bolinger or Cape Girardeau county, by Elders Wm. Darnell and Uriah Stratton. When the first churches were planted I am not able to say, but it is very evident, that these men were very successful, for soon many new churches were planted and an Association gathered, which increased so rapidly, that many of its churches were lettered off to form the New Liberty Association in 1869, and it is still a large and growing body, and now, 1881, numbers 30 churches and 860 members and I find in their minutes of this year the names of 17 Ministers, which are as follows:

James F. Young, J. M. Bolin, W. P. Stoval, W. L. Gower, T. B. Helm, H. H. Stratton, T. H. Newel, J. Nelson, N. Stratton, J. M. F. Young, M. E. Helton, T. J. Strafford, J. W. Bolin, J. A. Parish, W. R, Darnell, J. M. Green, U. Stratton. They keep a general Missionary in the field all the year and are doing a great work.

Elder Silas Parker, who formerly belonged to the Mt. Olivet Association of General Baptists in Southern Illinois, was their Missionary last year and at their last Annual Association held in October, 1881, reported as follows:

"In connection with other brethern I held protracted meetings, one at Asherville, five conversions, one at New Lisbon, fourteen conversions. Brother Helen, the Pastor, baptized ten persons. I have constituted three churches, traveled 1200 miles, preached 150 times, gave 50 exhortations, witnessed 50 conversions, baptized 38 persons." At their last session "a general increase was reported, six new churches were received". This is all the imformation I have obtained of this Association.

If the sale of this book justifies and a demand is made for another edition, it would be well for the different Associations to appoint some one of their number to furnish material for the history of each Association with the meager information from some of the Associations, most all of the interesting incidents are left out. Elder G. A Gordon has furnished a good model in the history of the Southern Illinois Association.

If any party or parties are interested enough to send me additional accounts of interest, I will carefully put them away, even if I never use them, they can be found in the future. We have but little idea of the vast amount of trouble there is in securing those things, until we begin to look for them.

THE CENTRAL ILLINOIS ASSOCIATION.

Some time during the late war, probably in 1862 or 1863 some Free-Will-Baptists from the Cumberland Association of Middle Tennessee, and some General Baptists from Kentucky moved to Franklin county in Southern Illinois, they found there some General Baptists. These people frequently met each other and on comparing their church government and articles of Faith, there was no difference between them.

Therefore they began to preach together and organized several churches, the oldest of which were Friendship, New Hope, Springdale, Union, Free-Will and Freedom. They then met in Franklin county, Illinois, and organized the Central Illinois Association of General Free-Will Baptists on the articles of Faith of Liberty Association of General Baptists. This Association continued to prosper until 1874 it numbered 547 members, about this time or perhaps a few years before. This Association became nearly, if not altogether disorganized. The trouble that caused the division among these people was the question of raising the salary of Ministers. Four churches went to the Free-Will Baptists north, four to the Southern Illinois Association of General Baptists, and in 1879 four remained undecided, not knowing what to do.

UNION GROVE ASSOCIATION.

This Association has churches in the counties of Wayne, Clay, Marion, Jefferson and White in Illinois.

As has been stated in the history of Liberty Indiana, churches were planted in Illinois. The first of these was organized by Elder Benoni Stinson in the fall of 1853. At that meeting Elder Stinson, assisted by Elder Samuel Branch of the Free-Will Baptist, ordained James W. Gwin and Thompson Fares to the full work of the Ministry.

This church united with Liberty Association in Indiana. Elder Gwin continued to preach with great success and organized another church on the 26th day of March, 1859. Elder Gwin and Elder Branch ordained Hesekiah H. Brown and Wm. M. Montgall. These Ministers preached to these two churches and at other points, until in the fall of 1863 they numbered four churches, and asked permission of Liberty Association to be constituted an Association in Illinois. Accordingly Elder Benoni Stinson met with these brethern and their four churches in 1863 and organized Union Grove Association of General Baptists. Since then these people have worked faithful, and now, 1881, number 17 churches, 16 ordained Ministers and 593 members. Elder Gwin who was in the organization of the first church in this Association, is the same man that Elder Poyner mentions in connection with the history of the Social Band Association of General Free Will Baptists in Missouri and Arkansas.

Elder H. H. Brown is now quite old and we believe he lives in or near Johnsonville, Wayne county, Illinois. Elder Wm. M. Montgall was born in Orange county, Ind., in 1830, moved to Illinois about 1842, and united with Arington Prairie Church in 1856 and was soon licensed to preach. Elder Montgall was a true and faithful Minister and success followed his labor. He was respected by all as a worthy Minister. He was to the Union Grove Association what Elder G. P. Cavanah was to Liberty. The Association feels that in his death they sustained almost an irreparable loss, and like Elder Cavanah, he lingered for about two years with that dread disease, consumption, and in 1869 peacefully fell asleep in the full confidence of a grand and glorious immortality with Christ and his redeemed. Let those people continue to pray that his mantle may fall on some of their young men. Elder W. D. Wendle of Xenia, Clay county, Illinois, has kindly furnished us

352   EARLY HISTORY

with material for this Association. We here append the names of all their Ministers:

Elders H. A. Madon, W. D. Wendle, J. W. Wood, T. M. Richardson, J. F. Clevenger, A. Tyler, S. C. Sherwood, G. W. Pennington, H. H. Brown, M. C. Tubs, A. D. Shearhorn, A. Perry, J. P. Turner, R. Keirsey, R. T. Forth, J. H. Windle, E. Brown, M. R. Durell.

MISSOURI ASSOCIATION.

In order to properly instruct the reader, we will give a brief sketch of the life of Elder Thomas Norris. Norris was born in Gates county, North Carolina, February 6th, 1810. His parents died when he was a child, and he was raised without any book education. Was married to Pennina Piland; moved to Kentucky in 1834; professed religion and united with the Mt. Lebanon Church of General Baptists of Union Association of Kentucky, August 11th, 1842, and was baptized by Elder J. M. Hunt. He at once began to try to read his Bilble and Hymn book and to work for the cause of Christ. He was licensed to preach at Liberty Church, Henderson county, Kentucky, April 18th, 1844, by the following presbytery:

Elders Jacob Holman, W. W. Jenkins, Charles W. Brown, Benoni Stinson, and was ordained at Mt. Lebanon Church of General Baptists, Henderson county, Kentucky, December 28th, 1846, by the following presbytery; Elders James M. Hunt, M. Fraser, M. L. Hunt, and moved in company with Samuel Piland to Ozark county, Missouri, in the Fall of 1846. On Saturday before the first Sabbath in January, 1847, Brother Norris and wife and Samuel Piland and wife held a council and agreed to form themselves into a church, and for their government adopted the Constitution, Rules of Decorum and Articles of Faith of the Union Association of General Baptists of Kentucky. This church was called Mt. Lebanon and is the beginning of the General Baptists in this part of Missouri. Elder Norris was now in a strange country, uneducated and poor in this worlds goods, having to labor hard for the support of his family and surrounded by other denominations, it was thought that his Ministerial labors would prove a failure. But he was zealous, faithful and devoted to the cause of his Master, regularly attending his Saturday and Sabbath appointments, sometimes walking from five to twenty miles to meet his congregations. God blessed his labors and in a few years Mt. Lebanon Church was the largest in that entire community, and soon other churches were organized and some young Ministers raised up in the country. In his travels he met other Liberal Baptists and uniting their labors with his, the Free Communion Baptists were taking the lead in this country, when the late civil war broke out.

In time of the war Elder Norris preached as much as the times and circumstances would admit, but during the war the most of the churches were disorganized, Mt. Lebanon however still maintained her organization. At the close of the war Elder Norris found himself alone again, so far as General Baptists were concerned. In time of the war he was on the side of the Union; soon after the war he organized Liberty and Spring Creek Churches and revivals followed at each of these churches. In 1866 their numbers had so increased that they discussed the propriety of concentrating their forces into an Association. Therefore delegates from Mt. Lebanon, Liberty, Spring Creek and Union churches met with Mt. Lebanon Church in Ozark county, Missouri, on the 1st day of December, 1866, and organized Missouri Association of General Baptists by electing Elder Thomas Norris, Moderator, and Wm. Norris, Clerk. There were at the meeting reported 182 members. They also adopted the Constitution, Rules of Decorum and Article of Faith of the Union Association of General Baptists in Kentucky.

About this time, or 1867, at their second meeting they ordained to the full work of the ministry, J. M. Lewis, R. M. Miller and W. T. Miller. Up to this time Elder Norris had pastored all the churches. Elders J. M. Lewis and R. M. Miller soon made valuable ministers, but alas! in a few years R. M. Miller was called from the walks of men, in the very prime of life, but J. M. Lewis is now, 1881, an able minister, and nearly ever since 1867 some new minister has been added and some of them are doing valuable work for Christ.

Elder A. Cobb, a Free-Will Baptist, went into the organization of the Missouri Association, but soon went back to the Free-Will Baptists, but now he belongs to the Little Vine Association of General Baptists.

Elder Norris is now, May 7th, 1881, still living and is seventy-one years old, but is able to preach regularly to two churches, and in his declining years has the satisfaction of seeing the Associations blest with a goodly number of able and useful ministers.

The material for this account was furnished us by the Hon. Wm. H. Norris, who was then, 1881, a member of the Missouri State Legislature. He was clerk of the convention that met to organize the Association in 1869, and is a member of Missouri Association at present.

The minutes of 1881 do not give the names of ordained ministers, separately.

The table below exhibits the date, Moderator, Clerk, new Churches received, total members, and the death of Ministers of Missouri Association.

Date.	Churches.	Moderator.	Clerk.	New Churches.	Members.	Death of Ministers.
1866	Mt. Lebanon	Elder T Norris	W. Norris		182	
1867	Mt. Lebanon	do	J. C. Miller	Two	294	
1868	Union	do	J. Hailey		171	One
1899	Spring Creek	do	do do			No Statistics obtainable
1870	Mt. Lebanon	do	do do		395	
1871	Liberty	do	do do	Three	393	
1872	Kirk Woods	do	do do	Two		
1873	Bethlehem	do	J. C. Miller		584	No Statistics obtainable
1874	Spring Creek	do	Wm. H. Norris	Three	514	
1875	Mt. Lebanon	do	do do		652	
1876	Pleasant Grove	do	J. Hailey	Six	674	One
1877	Little Vine	Eld. J. M. Lewis	do	Two		At this date there was a resolution adopted granting those churches that wished to form a new Association east of the Big Fork of White River and Little Vine Association was soon organized
1878	Liberty	Eld. T. Norris	J. Hailey		647	
1879	Mt. Hope	Eld. J. M. Lewis	do	One	657	
1880	Spring Hill	do	do	Three	748	
1881	Mt. Lebanon	do	S. E. Norris	Prospect, Antioch, New Prospect	849	

The above table shows the statistics, in part, of the Missouri Association.

FLAT CREEK ASSOCIATION.

As has been stated above, the Flat Creek Association was constituted in 1870. The original churches of the United Association, with some others, constituted this body of General Baptists. Elder S. T. Thompson, or "Father Thompson," as he was commonly called, may very properly be considered the founder of this people, as he organized most of the churches that first constituted it, with several others that were left in the United Association.

Notwithstanding, Elder Thompson did much for these people in preaching and planting churches, he in reviewing his ministerial life regretted very much that in the only part of his life he had taught the churches not to remunerate the faithful pastor for his labor.

A few years before he died, however, he felt that this teaching was wrong and endeavored, as much as possible, to correct his error, and taught that they that preach the gospel shall live off the gospel. This has been a grave mistake with too many General Baptists, not early in United and Flat Creek Associations, but in all of the General Baptist Associations. Therefore, we find many of our ministers are compelled to follow some secular employment in order to sustain their families. The Flat Creek Association does not seem to have prospered as much as some other General Baptist Associations. They probably have more to contend with and their forces are more scattered.

Bro. J. O. M. Selby sends me the names of some of the deceased ministers who first belonged to this body.

Elder William Woods died some time prior to 1873. Elder Thomas died in 1876; Elder P. Boling, in 1876; the date of Elder Simeon Wood's death is not known; Wm. T. Hopkins died November 5th, 1877. We have endeavored to obtain a few lines setting fourth the peculiar characteristics of these brethren, but have not succeeded.

The Flat Greek Association, with a full representation, numbers about 500 members. It has, at this time, 1881, the following ordained ministers:

Wm. M. Chesser, J. J. Laswell, J. W. Shouse, J. G. Jackman, I. Smith, R. M. Lucas, A. C. West, D. F. Philips, J. N. Baggarly, J. Evans, Wm. F. Robertson and F. E. King.

The licentiates are: I. Pearson, and T. K. Nelson.

If the hands of those brethren could be loosed so that they could devote all their time and energy to serving the church, this field would yield an aburdance of fruit. This, we hope, may be so, in the very near future.

This completes the history of the General Baptists in Indiana. We are well aware that this work is very incomplete but we hope that what we put on record may aid some one in the future to do a better work.

MT. OLIVET ASSOCIATION.

In March, 1855, Elder Wm. Carlisle, an ordained minister, who was a member of Mt. Pleasant Church of General Baptists, in Posey county, Indiana, which belonged to Liberty Association, organized Zion Church of General Baptists in Hamilton county, Illinois. Elder Carlisle was living in Hamilton county at this time, and on learning of some Free Cummunion Baptists in Jackson and Randolph counties, Illinois, he and R. C. Culty and I. H. Burlison were appointed by Zion Church to meet with those Free Communion Baptists, at their next meeting or Association, which convened on Friday, before the third Sabbath in October, 1855.

This Association consisted of Georgetown, Looney Springs and Pipe Stone Churches, and Elders

Wm. Bradley, R. A. Bradley, H. S. Gordon and Isaac Hale.

Elder H. S. Gordon and R. A. Bradley had, in 1854, come as delegates to Liberty Association and desired a union with the General Baptists and the Liberty Association had reciprocated this greeting by appointing Elders Benoni Stinson, Alvah Parker and J. W. Gwinn, to meet with those brethren and confer with them in regard to the proposed union. The union was effected and Zion Church united with this Association, which from this date, took the name o- the General Baptist Association of Southern Illinois. The Lord blest and prospered these people and they gained strength, until in 1868, they numbered twenty-three churches and as many ministers. About this time the question of a union between the General Baptists and the Free-Will Baptists north and east was agitated all through the General Baptists denomination east of the Mississippi River. This whole matter is fully detailed in the history of Liberty Association and the reasons assigned for so much trouble.

This Association however was divided in sentiment on the Union question, the western part, which was the strongest, favoring it, the eastern and weaker part, opposing it. This state of things continued until 1869, when by mutual consent the east part of the

Association was lettered off to organize a new Association, and Elders Wm. Bradley and J. C. Gilliland were appointed to assist in this work. Accordingly the churches which received letters of dismission met with Shadsville church in White county, Illinois, on Friday before the 4th Sabbath in September 1870, and organized Mt. Olivet Association of General Baptists.

Among the Ministers that went into the organization of the Association were Elders Wm. Carlisle, E. A. Philips, Willis Charles and W. P. Hale. Several new churches have been added to this Association from time to time, but some of her churches have gone to the Free-Will Baptists and some have been desolved. She has now 8 or 9 churches with a membership of over 400.

The ordained Ministers are Willis Charles, W. P. Hale, N. M. Wibbe, Peter Prince, D. W. Ashby, Wm. Carlisle, J. E. Cox, Editor of the Golden Rule.

Licentiates: W. J. Gualtney, John Horgett.

It will be observed that in point of Ministerial ability Mt. Olivet Association compares very favorably with any Association in the denomination and many have been added to her numbers since her last session in 1881, and it is believed that a brighter day is dawning for this devoted band of christian workers.

BETHANY ASSOCIATION, MISSOURI.

Of this Association we know but very little. It has never been represented in the General Association. We have never seen or held correspondence with any one belonging to the Bethany Association. It was reported to the General Association in 1874 and again in 1880, and supposed to number about 500 members. We do not know in what part of Missouri it is located, but it appears to be remote from any of the other General Baptist Associations. As we never have seen any account of any correspondence between it and any of the sister Associations in Missouri, Elder T. J. Davis informed us however, that there really was such an Association in existance, but he had learned that about 1880 it was in rather a disorganized state and feared that it would become extinct.

AN ASSOCIATION IN ARKANSAS.

This Association is partly located in White county, Arkansas, although we have not succeeded in obtaining the P. O. Address of any of them, still we know that there is such an Association, and it is represented as being very large and influential, having fine churches and able Ministers, in all the larger towns. We yet expect to hear more from it soon. I have also heard of another General Baptist Association in Arkansas, called the Strawberry Association, but do not know its location.

There is also a small group of General Baptists near Carter's Store in Washing county, Arkansas, with one licensed Minister and they doubtless have formed a church before this time, and is probably the commencement of a new Association. We have been in correspondence with Mr. Harvey Lee, besides we are personally acquainted with several of those who are with him, some of the Kirkpatricks and Richards. This closes the history of the General Baptists now known to us. We have some knowledge of the following Associations of Free-Will Baptists Associations, who only differ from us in name. And the indications now are, that in a few years these two bodies will unite as one people under the name of General Free-Will Baptists, to this we give our hearty Amen. In Missouri we find the Big Creek, Pleasant Hill, South West Associations, Crane Creek, State Line General Free-Will Baptists and North Missouri Free Communion Baptists. Besides these six in Missouri, we find in Arkansas the Polk Bayou, Mt. Zion, Liberty and the Vernon Association in Alabama, Cumberland in Tennessee and several others of which we know nothing, except of their existance. The seperate Baptists who are located in Kentucky, Indiana, Illinois, Missouri and Iowa number eleven Associations and differ from us only in name, and they are in very friendly correspondence with us and have several times discussed the propriety of adopting the name General Baptists.

THE SOCIAL BAND ASSOCIATION OF GENERAL FREE-WILL BAPTISTS IN MISSOURI AND ARKANSAS.

This Association is located in Ripley county, Missouri and Randolphs county, Arkansas, and probably there are churches in some other adjoining counties.

In the year of 1870 Elder David Leroy Poyner, an ordained Minister, belonging to the Central Illinois Association of General Free-Will Baptists moved with his family to Ripley county, Missouri. He and one son and one daughter had their letters from the General Free Will Baptists of Southern Illinois. These were all the Free Communion Baptists in that section of the country. He found there a few Methodists and Campbellites (as they are called there) and some United or close cummunion Baptists, and about twenty-five miles from his house lived Elder Gwin, formerly a member of the Liberty Association of General Baptists in Indiana, and who went into the organization of Union Grove Association in Illinois. Brother Poyner had with him a few copies of the Minutes of the Association, to which he belonged in Illinois.

These he distributed among the people and began to to preach what he understood to be doctrines taught by Christ and his Apostles. The peculiar characteristics of which was a general atonement and open communion.

Notwithstanding brother Poyner felt that he was weak, he remembered that his Lord had said, that "out of weakness will I bring strength", therefore he resolved to go like David met Goliah "in the name and strength of Isreal's God", so he organized a church on saturday before the second Sabbath in August 1871, at Sugar Tree Grove Church in Ripley county, Missouri, on ten members, then one at Brier Creek, with eleven members, then one at Macedonia in Randolph county, Arkansas, with seven members, and one at New Hope in same state and county on twenty members. By this time, 1875, four young men to-wit: S. Davis, E. Davis, A. Barrett and L.

J. Thorneburg, had been duly licensed and ordained. Then the four churches with their delegates met in convention with Brier Creek Church and organized the Social Band Association of General Free-Will Baptists.

We have now, 1881, writes Elder Poyner, closed our seventh annual meeting, peace and harmony has prevailed. We have gained steadily but slowly, we now have ten churches with over 400 members, eight ordained ministers. The four above mentioned and myself with M. R. Langley, C. B. Dilda and F. M. Bates.

Our licentiates are: U. C. Davis, J. F. Murphy and D. N. King.

Brother Poyner further says, we believe that the gospel is free and should be preached to the poor without money and without price and that it is the duty of the church to look after the need of both ministers and members.

This account which is so full of interest, has been furnished us by Elder Payner, who in the hands of God was the worthy founder of this Association. Elder Poyner was born July the second, 1823, in Caswell county, North Carolina, professed religion in 1845 and united with the General Free-Will Baptists in Illinois 1867, licenced and ordained in the same year and is now 58 years old and it is hoped that his already useful life may be spared yet many years. The Liberal Baptists are doing a wonderful work in Missouri and Arkansas, and from what we can learn, there is reason to believe, that all those Baptists under the name of General and Free-Will Baptists will unite and take the name of General Free-Will Baptists. This would certainly be a proud move for liberal principles in the south-west. There is the Liberty, New Liberty, Missouri, Bethany and Little Vine, St. Clair Associations of General Baptists in Missouri and Arkansas, and of the Free-Will Baptists in the same state. There is Big Creek, Pleasant Hill and Crane Creek in Missouri and the Mt. Zion, Polk Bayou and Liberty in Arkansas, and the Social Band which carries both names and lies partly in both states. Here we see thirteen Associations of which we have some knowledge lying adjacent to each other and many more of which we have no particular account and there is no difference between them, only the name and the name of General Free-Will Baptists would accommodate all, let the Union be affected.

MT. UNION ASSOCIATION, KENTUCKY.

There were no General Baptists in Allen county, Kentucky, until 1863, when Elder M. G. Bonner moved to this county and commenced preaching the General Baptist doctrine, and in that Fall he assisted in holding two or three revival meetings. At one of those meetings the writer found peace with Christ. Elder M. J. Bonner, assisted by Elder D. G. Crane, organized two churches that Fall, one at Mulberry Hill school house, Allen county, and one at Liberty Church, Warren county. The former was constituted February 8th, 1863, with thirteen members. The latter about the same time with a small number. We toiled on with but a few members attending our regular meetings, some become discouraged, for we had to bear persecution from other churches, and the frowns of the world, for we were out, as it were, in the wilderness by ourselves. Thus we went on until 1866, when we appointed delegates with a petitionary letter to attend the Union Association of General Baptists, which met at Pleasant Hope Church, McLean county, Kentucky, which was about seventy miles from us; we went on horseback.

Our petition was granted and our two little churches became members of that body.

At this meeting the writer had the pleasure of hearing Elder Benoni Stinson preach on Sabbath to a large congregation and at night listened to Elder A. H. Polk, both from Liberty Association in Indiana.

We met with a good many General Baptists at that meeting. Our two little churches at that time numbered forty-nine and fifty-four members. In 1870 Mulberry Hill, now known as Mt. Union Church, built a good house and numbered ninety-three members. Another church was organized at Franklin, Simpson county, Kentucky.

In 1876 we petitioned the Union Association for letters of dismission in order to be organized into a new Association on account of the great distance between us. The Union Association met this year at Clayville, Webster county, Kentucky, a distance of one hundred and twenty-five miles from us. Our request was granted and Elders I. H. Henry and M. P. Covington appointed to organize the Association which they did on Friday before the second Sabbath in December, 1876, at New Harmony Church, Todd county, Kentucky, with six churches and five hundred and seventy-seven members. Mt.

Union Association has been organized five years and now, 1881, numbers nineteen churches, nineteen ministers and 1115 members. We often became discouraged in this world, but if God is for us who can be against us. The above has almost entirely been taken from an article written by Elder E. L. Kelsey, who is a member of the Mt. Union Association. This article appeared in Vol. 2d, No. 44 of the Golden Rule, June 9th, 1881. This Association first planted churches in Allen and Warren counties, now they are in four others in Kentucky, to-wit:

Simpson, Butler, Todd and Grayson, and Mason and Sumner in Tennessee. At their last Association held August, 1881, they reported nineteen churches and twenty-four Ministers. The rapid growth of this Association has thrown the churches at such a distance from each other, that they considered it expedient to divide the Association, which will probably take place in 1882. The Ministers now belong to this Association are Wm. L. Harris, W. B. Lightfoot, M. Y. H. Holland, J. A. Justice, L. W. Spann, B. C. Goodrum, A. Cay, S. Cay, Wm. Smith, W. L. Emery, D. Anderson, Jno. M. Burden, N. W. Nash, Wm. George. W. Pearce, J. M. Bonner, W. D. Meados, E. B. Stinson, James Burden, M. A. Taylor, G. N. Covington, Jas. M. Frazier, J. P. Stinson, Bird Weaver.

LITTLE VINE ASSOCIATION.

Little Vine Association of General Baptists is located in the counties of Howell and Oregon in Missouri, and Fulton county in Arkansas, and is the direct offspring of the Missouri Association of General Baptists and was organized June 29th, 1878, on the following churches: Little Vine, Little Zion, Old Union, Violia and South Fork. The Ministers were Peter McCracken, J. B. Mahand, W. J. F. Hopkins, A. Colb, T. H. Welch. Ministers since the organization, G. W. McDannel, H. H. Shubart, J. W. Harris, W. R. Hines.

Churches received since the organization, Good Prospect, Pleasant Hill No. 1, Pleasant Hill No. 2, Trace Creek, Union Grove and Vienna. It is now 1881, three years since the little Association was constituted on five churches, five Ministers and 180 members. It now has eleven churches, nine Ministers and 350 members, and is full of faith and energy, and working zealously for the cause of Christ. This may appear like a very short sketch of this Association, still it is a good one. This was furnished me by Elder Peter McCracken. Our Western brethren write like practical busniess men; they say a great deal with a very few words. They are modest men and avoid everything that appears superfluous.

NEW LIBERTY ASSOCIATION, MISSOURI.

In the year 1869 the Beachwell church in this Association, was organized. There lived in the neighberhood of Valley Ridge, Dunklin county, Missouri, a young man by the name of T. J. Davis, commonly called Tom Davis, who was born June 23rd, 1840, in Meahley county, in the state of Tennessee, who with many others had been converted a short time previous to the above date, or on July 27th 1867. I believe at a revival conducted by the Methodists, Mr. Davis was raised by regular Baptist parents, but he could not unite with that church on account of the doctrines of predestination held by that denomination. He could not unite with the United or Missionary Baptists, on account of their close communion sentiments. He could not unite with the Methodists because they did not hold and practice that immersion, was the only proper mode of Baptism. He could not unite with the Campbellites, for he did not believe that men and women are converted or regenerated in the act of immersion. Therefore it seemed like a foregone conclusion that he was lost so far as church relations was concerned. However about that time he had some business at the county seat of Stoddard county, which was about twenty-five miles from his home. After he attended to this he started to return home and was soon overtaken by a sprightly little man who seemed full of life and conversation, soon a conversation like the following ensued.

The little man asked Mr. Davis if he was religious. Mr. Davis answered in the affirmative. Have you any churches where you live. Yes sir. What kind of churches. Almost all kinds, Regular Baptists, United Baptists and Methodists &c., &c. Have you any General Baptists. No sir. I never heard of the General Baptists, what do they believe. Well sir, they believe that in the atonement of Christ salvation was made possible for all men. They believe in the Trinity and believe in Baptism by immersion. They believe that Jesus Christ is the door into his church and that all of the Lords people are one in Christ and as such have a right to commune together at the Lords table. Here is one of our minutes sir, I belong to the Liberty Association of General Baptists in Missouri.

We have a church about twenty-five miles from your house and our monthly meeting comes on Saturday before the——Sabbath, come and hear us and understand us more perfectly. This was the doctrine that was congenial with the understanding that Mr. Davis had of the scriptures. And he exacted a promise from the little man to visit his neighborhood and organize a church, if a sufficient number could be found who wished to be constituted into a General Baptist Church, and they separated. Mr. Davis went to his home and carefully compared the articles of Faith with the scriptures, and at a meeting held in his neighborhood soon after, he announced that on a certain Sabbath, he would have a meeting at a certain place which he then mentioned. It was noised abroad that Tom Davis was going to preach at the said time and place and it is reported that persons came from several miles in every direction to hear him.

It appears that Tom had quite a reputation among the unconverted and was a noted character for miles around. However when a very large and respectable congregation had assembled, all expecting to hear Tom Davis deliver his first discourse. He arose and said: It appears that the people are expecting to hear me preach to-day. I did not say that I would preach but only announced that I would have meeting here to-day and quite a meeting we have, and I simply wish to tell these people that I have found a denomination who hold and practice the very doctrines which I have believed ever since my conversion and that is the General Baptists". He then opened the minute that the little General Baptist Preacher had given him and read the articles of Faith and commented on them one by one, until he had finished the whole 13 articles, which was the confession of Faith of the Liberty Association of General Baptists in the state of Missouri. Now, said Tom, "if there is any one else here who believes as I do and desire to go into the organization of a General Baptist Church, let them come forward and give me their names and I will send and get a General Baptist Preacher to come and organize us into a church. To the astonishment of almost all present, 19 persons came forward and cast in their lot with Tom, who made their number 20. A short time after this the little preacher Elonzo Fowler fullfilled his promise and organized this little band into a church on the first Sabbath in September 1869. This church took the name of Beachwell. On the same day Tom Davis was licensed or liberated by this church to exercise his gifts in public. He was also chosen as its Pastor and has continued such ever since and this church now, June 1882 numbers about 200 mem bers. This church united with the Liberty Association in Missouri and become the nucleus around which gathered several other lively churches which together with some others belonging to the Liberty Association, were on November 11th 1869, set off into a new Association, which took the name of the New Liberty Association of General Baptists. The delegation, when they had come together to organize, formed themselves into "a circle which is typical of gods eternal love", and joining hands sang and prayed, then extended to each other the right hand of fellowship; then they chose J. F. Patterson as Moderator and C. B. Hyson, Clerk.

This Association was organized on 887 members and now numbers 1083. The number of churches that went into the organization was 17, nine of which were in Stoddard, five in Dunklin and one in Butler county, Missouri, and two in Clay county in Arkansas. They now have 21 chusches. I find in their last minute the following list of ordained ministers:

T. J. Davis, W. E. Almon, L. McFarland, H. H. Noble, J. H. Payne, T. J. Stafford, W. E. Bray, W. D. Ferris and R. M. Hatley.

Licentiates: S. J. Bird, J. W. Boyd, Samuel Dumeree, J. W. Kinney, John Bridges, W. M. Froners and J. W. Miller.

Elder Davis is an uneducated man but he is well

read and an able defender of General Baptist principles. He is probably five feet ten inches high, with square shoulders, light hair, fair skin, with hazle eyes. He is modest and unassuming, not courting controversy with any one. Nevertheless, when the principles which he holds as dear to him as life are trampled upon he rallies at once, and the man who is so unfortunate as to come in contact with him seldom gets away without feeling the worse for the contest.

He is a great power in Southeast Missouri. It is reported of him that so intent was he on preparing himself for the sacred office of the ministry that he has frequently been known to work hard all day, then take his chair by the fireside and there, almost forgetful of self, would pour over his books until the crowing of the chickens warned him of the approach of day.

We have never met Elder Davis but once, which was at the General Association in 1880, and he then spoke in highly commendable terms of all his brethren in the ministry and seemed to consider them all as better qualified ministers than himself.

Part of this sketch, especially the dates were obtained from Elder Davis, part from their minutes and part from other parties.

GENERAL ASSOCIATION OF GENERAL BAPTISTS.

We have seen that the Liberty Church, in Vanderburgh county, Indiana, about one mile and a half below Evansville, was organized in 1823, with thirty three members. In 1824 Liberty Association was organized with four churches and two hundred and one members. These people continued to plant churches in Indiana, Kentucky and Illinois, until 1840 when they numbered 890 members, when by mutual consent the Association directed, and Union Association, in Kentucky was organized. We desire, now, to exhibit the increase for each ten years.

In 1845 these two Associations agreed to hold a General Association every two years. This, however, was not sustained. In 1846 the Union Association divided and Cumberland Association constituted.

In 1850 these three bodies probably numbered 1200 members, a gain, in ten years, or from 1840 of about 310.

In 1854 Ohio Association, in Illinois, was constituted from churches belonging to Cumberland Association.

The Southern Illinois Association of Free Communion Baptists was organized in 1853 and took the name of the Southern Illinois Association of General Baptists in 1854 or 1855, I am not certain which.

The United Association, located principally in Warrick and Pike counties, was constituted in 1860. At this time the General Baptists must have numbered 2500, a gain of 1300 in ten years, or more than 100 per cent.

In 1862 Liberty Association, Missouri, was organized.

Then follows Union Grove, Illinois, in 1864; Central Illinois General Free-Will Baptists, probably in 1863 or 1864; Missouri, in Missouri, in 1867; Flat Creek, in Indiana, in 1870; Mt. Olivet, Illinois, in 1870.

From 1860 to 1870 we find a gain of six Associations, or 100 per cent. in the number of Associations, and about 8,000 members, a gain of 5,500, which is over 200 per cent.

By referring to the history of Liberty Association in Indiana, you will see that a convention of liberal Baptists in the United States, had met in 1867, at Fort Branch, Gibson county, Indiana, and pursuant to adjournment, met with Columbia Church, in the same county, in 1868, and laid the foundation for an organic union, which, however, was shortly afterward destroyed. However, a like convention met in 1867 with old Liberty Church, in Vanderburgh county which failed to reconcile the troubles referred to this meeting. If I am not mistaken, it was Rev. Ransom Dunn, Professor of Biblical Theology, in Hillsdale College, Michigan. That suggested that the General Baptists organize themselves into a General Association which would the better prepare them for considering the question of uniting with other liberal Baptists, therefore this convention adjourned to meet with Harmony Church, Gallitia county, Illinois, on Wednesday, November 2d, 1870. The convention met accordingly, with representatives from Liberty, Indiana, and Ohio and Mt. Olivet, Illinois. After organizing temporarily, Elder John Onyet was chosen Moderator and Elder G. W. Moore, Secretary. A constitution and by-laws were adopted, together with the articles of faith of Liberty Association, in Indiana. As an introduction to the constitution setting forth the design of the General Association, we find the following:

"The constitution of the General Association of General Baptists of the United States of America, which is designed to comprise all the annual Associations in the General Baptist denomination in the United States and to complete the organization of the connectton, to consolidate the body by harmonizing its different parts, keeping a common interest in view and producing a unity of sentiment and discipline, to concentrate its strength in the common cause of the Redeemer, and by a fraternal interchange of views among its members to promote a growth of grace and a knowledge of gospel truth."

This very clearly sets forth the original design of the General Association. The Clerk was authorized to have printed 500 copies of the Minutes and distribute them among the various Associations. Elder J. G. Ensle was much interested in this move, and it was through his influence that Liberty Association was represented at this organization, proffering to pay the expense of our delegates if the Association neglected it.

Major J. B. Cox, of Vanderburgh county, Indiana, accompanied Elder Moore and was of much service in the organization and has since remained a faithful supporter of the General Association.

The second meeting of this body convened with Liberty Church, Vanderburgh county, Indiana, November 3rd, 1871. Liberty, United and Flat Creek, Union, Kentucky; southern Illinois; Ohio; Mt. Olivet, Illinois and Missouri were represented.

At this session the Constitution and By-laws were revised and remain as they are at present.

See Constitution and By-laws:

CONSTITUTION OF THE GENERAL ASSOCIATION.

ARTICLE 1.—The name of this Association shall be the General Association of General Baptists.

ART. 2.—The objects of this Association are to bring into more intimate and fraternal relations and effective co-operation various bodies of Liberal Baptists.

ART. 3.—The General Association shall be composed of the representatives of Baptist bodies as harmonize generally with the doctrine and usages of the Association now constituting the body, who may be admitted from time to time, on their own application.

ART. 4.—The officers of the General Association shall be a Moderator and Clerk.

ART. 5.—The Moderator shall be elected at each regular session in such manner as the body may choose, and shall perform the duties usually performed by presiding officers, serving until his successor is elected. A stated Clerk shall be elected from time to time, who shall continue in office until superceded by a new election.

ART. 6.—In the letters from the several bodies shall be expressed their respective churches in fellowship, those received and those dismissed since the last meeting of this Association, and time and places of holding their respective annual meetings, together with a statistical report of their numerical strength.

ART. 7.—No body shall be entitled to less than one member, and one for every two hundred members, and one for each fractional over one hundred members.

ART. 8.—This Constitution may be altered or amended by a majority vote of any regular meeting, if the proposed amendment shall have been presented at the last preceding regular meeting and approved by that body, and published in the Minutes, with notice that it will be acted upon at the next meeting.

ART. 9.—Each session of the General Association shall determine the time and place of holding the next session.

BY-LAWS.

ARTICLE 1.—Each session of the General Association shall be called to order by the Moderator, when present, and in his absence, by the member having seniority of years.

ART. 2.—Each session and adjourned sitting shall be opened and closed with prayer.

ART. 3.—Ten members shall constitute a quorum, provided not less than three Associations are represented, but a smaller number may adjourn from time to time.

ART. 4.—After the opening of each session a committee shall be chosen to examine credentials. After the report of this committee, and enrollment of members present, the Association shall proceed to the election of a Moderator.

ART. 5.—At each session such standing committees may be appointed as the Association may deem proper.

ART. 6.—It shall be the duty of the Clerk to furnish each session of the Association with a book of records, containing the doings of its previous meetings.

ART. 7.—Anyone wishing to retire while the Association is in session, shall first obtain leave of the presiding officer. No member shall absent himself from the Association during its session without first obtaining permission from the Association.

ART. 8.—No person shall be allowed to speak more than ten minutes at any one time, nor more than twice on any subject, without leave of the Association.

Art. 9.—It shall be the duty of the Association to appoint a committee of three, to be called the Central Board, whose duty it shall be to inaugurate and execute a general system of domestic Missions; they shall appoint such sub-committees, and employ such agents and missionaries as they may deem proper; they shall hold their position until superceeded by a new appointment; may fill all vacancies that occur in their own body, and shall make to this Association, at each regular session, a detailed report of their doings.

Art. 10.—No debate shall be allowed on any motion except the same be in writing, and seconded by a member of the Association.

Elder I. H. Henry,	Ch'm Com.
Elder G. A. Gordon,	Cl'k Com.
Elder A. H. Polk,	" "
Elder F. M. Kerr,	" "
Elder W. L. Smart.	" "

A Central Board on Home Missions was appointed, consisting of Elders A. H. Polk, I. H. Henry, and J. C. Gilliland, and a general correspondence opened up with all Liberal Baptists.

At the third meeting the committee on credentials reported the following list of delegates: Liberty Association, Indiana, Elder A. H. Polk, G. W. Moore, T. M. Strain, F. M. Herr, Jacob Speer, Wilson Blackburn, Wm. Clark and Bro. Daniel Miller. Union Association, Elders Y. H. Henry, Miles Frasier, Absolom Pierce, M. J. H. Holland, L. W. Powell, E. T. Arnold, E. L. Kelsey. Mt. Olivet Association, Elders Wm. Carlisle, Silas Parker, J. W. McIntosh. United Association, Elder J. G. Lane, Solomon Rhodes, Joshua McKenney, David Perkins, James Hart, R. Bullock and Bro. S. W. Parker. Ohio Association, Elders F. Holland, John Onyet, W. L. Smart, E. Oxford, J. Jack. Southern Illinois Association, Wm. Bradley, M. A. Shepard, G. A. Gordon, Jno. Griffin. Southern Kentucky Separate Baptists, Elder L. W. Whiles. Cumberland Association Free-Will Baptists, Tennessee, Elders Robert George, J. W. Gower, S. H. Lancoster, W. H. Head, G. R. Head. Shelby Association Separate Baptists in Central Illinois, Elder Joseph Perryman and Bro. C. H. Roney. Ohio State Association of Free Communion Baptists, Rev. S. D. Bates.

In point of business talent and Ministerial qualifications, this was one of the ablest representations that the General Association has ever had. Elders Joseph Perryman, S. Rhodes, John Onyet and Bro. Daniel Miller have been dead several years. Elders

J. G. Lane and J. W. McIntosh went to the M. E. Church, and subsequently Elder Lane went to the Missionary Baptists. Elder Kerr's credentials were revoked on account his efforts to pervert the ordinance of the church. The rest of these delegates so far as I know, are still faithful to the doctrine of the Liberal Baptists.

Some confusion was brought about at this meeting on the subject of a union among Liberal Baptists, which has been fully detailed in the history of Liberty Association, Indiana, which was the cause of a majority of these men never meeting with the General Association again. At the fourth meeting held at Eldorado, Illinois, the union question or change of name was again considered in a rather confused and boisterous manner, and renewed again at the fifth meeting, held with Liberty Church, Vanderburgh county, Indiana, and again at the sixth meeting at Oakland City, Gibson county, Indiana, where a better feeling existed among the brethren, and more christian courtesy has prevailed in the discussion of the union question ever since. It is hoped that good will come out of those discussions in the future, but it is very evident that they proved very disastrous to the General Baptists interest during the four or five years of so much ungarded and vehement controversy. However it has brought about a better acquaintance among Liberal Baptists everywhere. We have learned the location and history of many of which we knew nothing before the organization of the General Association.

At the meeting held at Oakland City, there was some important work done in regard to our educational interest, but as I intend to devote a separate chapter to each of the subjects of Home Missions Publication and Education, I will pass this by for the present.

At the seventh meeting held at Sebree City, Webster county, Kentucky, 1876, it was proposed to change the name of the General Association of General Baptists, to the name of "Baptists General Association."

At the eighth meeting held with Mt. Gilead church Warrick county, Indiana, in 1877, the committee on policy or the General Association, reported unfavorable to the change of name and suggested that the General Association confirm strictly to the doctrines of General Baptists for that they considered essential to the existence of the denomination.

At the ninth meeting held at Liberty church, Vanderburgh county, Indiana, 1878, the Association resolved that the great work of the General Association for the following ten years was the building up and maintaining three grand institutions, to-wit: The

Publication, Home Mission and Educational interest. These resolutions have been adhered to ever since. The success attending these enterprises is shown in the chapters relating to these subjects.

The tenth meeting held at Boonville, Warrick county, Indiana, 1879, was probably one of the most gloomy and discouraging in the history of this body. Only four Associations represented by delegates and four by letter and only eleven representatives. Dr. Holman, who had anticipated a large delegation, was so disappointed and overwhelmed with grief, that he suggested, that the General Association be disorganised. The writer believed that he could see indications of success in the future, and one indication was that the very best of feeling prevailed throughout the entire session. At this meeting a course of study was recommended to those preparing for the ministry, which is as follows: First years course.

The eight common school english branches with the addition of natural Philosophy and Rhetoric junior year.

1.—Mental Phylosophy by Haven.
2.—Moral Phylosophy by Wayland.
3.—Evidences of Christianity by Hopkins.
4.—Church history by Gregory Butler and Hass.
5.—Homilitics by Shed.
6.—Canon of the old and new Testament by Stewart.
7.—Pastorial Theology by Shed and Pond.

THIRD YEAR:

1.—Systematic Theology by Butler.
2.—Dictionary of religious knowledge by Layman Abbot.
3.—Commentary by Foucet, Jamison and Brown, (one work.)
4.—History of the Bible by Kitto.
5.—Logic by Javons.
6.—Analogy by Butler.

There was and perhaps may still be some misunderstanding about this course. The General Association did not desire to force this course upon any ordained or licenced Minister, but only wished to urge the necessity of all of our Ministers studying the course. It will do all of us good to read this whole course.

Then it was designed to be a guide for all of our Ministers in search of such books. If the writer had known of such a course of study at the time he was licenced, it would have saved him many years of close application to other matter that did not materially assist in his Theological studies. It is hoped that all of our Ministers and especially the young will appreciate this course and be benefitted by it.

The eleventh meeting held with old Liberty church

in Vanderburgh county, Indiana, 1880, was a pleasant and profitable one, eight Association was represented by delegates. Elder Billy Harris gave an encouraging report from Kentucky, Elder T. J. Davis brought refreshing news from Missouri and brought information of the existence of several Associations heretofore unknown to us.

From 1870 to 1880 we hear of Bethany, Missouri, and an Association in Arkansas, date of organization not known. Social Band General Free-Will Baptists in 1875 in Missouri and Arkansas. Mt. Union Kentucky, in 1876 and Little Vine in Missouri and Arkansas in 1878, New Liberty in Missouri in 1880.

The General Association at this meeting numbered 12,367 members, a gain in ten years of 4367 members, a net gain of over 54 per cent. The minutes of this meeting show that the General Baptists are better organized than at any time since those early General Baptists in the New England States were merged into the close communion Baptists denomination.

The twelfth session was also held with Liberty church in November, 1881, and was one of the most interesting sessions of this body. There is a great work to be done in the next ten years, but we can not write for the future, still it is only reasonable to suppose that if the General Baptists work energetically and harmoniously, that in 1890 their numbers may be swelled to 30 or 40 thousand.

Home Missions see essay in minutes by D. B. Montgomery.

The following table shows the time, place, Moderator and Clerk of each Association:

DATE	CHURCHES	COUNTY	STATE	MODERATOR	CLERK
1870	Harmony	Gallitfn	Illinois	John Onyet	G. W. Moore
1871	Liberty	Vanderburgh	Indiana	J. G. Ensle	do do
1872	Mt. Pleasant	Posey	do	I. H. Henry	do do
1873	Eldorado	Saline	Illinois	do do	D. B. Montgomerd
1874	Liberty	Vanderburgh	Indiana	John Onyet	do do
1875	Oakland City	Gibson	do		Lee Tomlin
1876	Sebree City	Webster	Kentucky	I. H. Henry	J. G. Lane
1877	Mt. Gilead	Warrick	Indiana	J. G. Lane	A. H. Polk
1878	Liberty	Vanderburgh	do	Jeff. Holman	G. W. Moore
1879	Boonville	Warrick	do	Jacob Speer	D. B. Montgomery
1880	Liberty	Vanderburgh	do	W. P. Hale	do do
1881	Liberty	Vanderburgh	do	do do	do do

A DENOMINATIONAL PAPER.

We have made mention of most of these enterprises in the history of the Annual Associations. We will connect them as closely as we can. In the year 1843 Liberty Association appointed a committee to take under consideration the advisability of publishing a denominational paper. You will remember that at this time we only had Liberty and Union Associations and a little more than 1,000 members. This was just twenty years after the first church was organized. The committee, after duly considering this question, reported unfavorable to the enterprise. However, two years after, in 1845, Elders Benoni Stinson and Wm. Reavis, jr., engaged, as individuals, in the publication of the Original General Baptist Herald, as a semi-monthly. This paper was received with joy by the General Baptists and a committee appointed to take it under the direction of the denomination and to make its appearance as a weekly. After struggling hard to sustain it for some months, it was finally suspended.

We hear no more of a General Baptist paper for

394　EARLY HISTORY

fifteen years, or 1850, when the General Baptist Banner was started, an account of which may be found in the history of the thirty-seventh meeting of Liberty Association. It, however, met with the same fate as the Original Herald.

About twelve years after this, or July, 1872, Bro. Joshua McKenney, of Richland City, in Spencer county, Indiana, began the publication of the second General Baptist Herald, with Elder J. G. Lane as associate editor. He continued to publish the paper at Richland for several months, when it was moved to Calhoun, Kentucky, and finally to Evansville, Indiana. Financial embarrassments caused Bro. McKenney to solicit the General Association to take charge of the Herald. Accordingly, in 1873, at the General Association, at Eldorado, Illinois, Elders J. G. Ensle, D. B. Montgomery, Bros. R. B. Richards and Maj. J. B. Cox, were appointed to look after the interest of the Herald.

It was found that a joint stock company was the only way to save the paper. As well as the writer remembers the following are the persons that made up the stock company and gave of their means to purchase and continue the paper: Elders J. G. Ensle, D. B. Montgomery, and Brothers, J. B. Cox, Daniel Miller, Henry Angel, Wm. Raglan, G. B. Young, Minor Young, Henry C. Daugherty, Wm.

Fairchilds and Henry Clark. This company took charge of the paper about the first of January, 1874, with Henry Angel, President, J. B. Cox, Secretary and Treasurer, and Elders J. G. Ensle and D. B. Montgomery, editors. These two continued to edit the paper together until about June, 1875, when, on account of business at home, Elder Ensle resigned and D. B. Montgomery edited the paper until January, 1876, when the stock company suspended and sold the press and subscription to Col. John Cockrum, of Oakland City, Indiana. The company then deducted five hundred dollars from the amount of sale, on condition that the unexpired time of subscribers be filled out by the new company.

Under the management of Col. Cockrum, Elder J. G. Lane was made editor, except the few copies edited by Prof. Crawford. However, the first managers of this stock company were Col. J. W. Cockrum, President; Rev. J. G. Lane, Secretary; Moses Smith, Esq., Treasurer; Prof. S. P. Crawford, Editor and General Agent. Of Prof. Crawford, the General Baptists knew but little, before he became editor. He only edited a few copies and resigned and went East. We know nothing of him since.

Elder Lane continued to edit the paper until after the death of Col. J. W. Cockrum, after which a new board of managers was elected, consisting of the -following brethren, at Boonville, Indiana:

T. J. Hargan, President; Rice Wilson, Secretary and Treasurer; Branock Wilkerson, B. Fuller, Wm. Fisher, T. J. Downs, Col. W. Cockrum, of Oakland City, Indiana, Elder Willis Charles, of Mt. Vernon, Indiana, J. O. M. Selby, of Petersburg, Ind.

This board elected T. J. Hargan editor, who continued to edit the paper at Boonville, Indiana, until the General Baptist Herald was suspended. It has not made its appearance since.

THE GOLDEN RULE.

The prospectus of this paper appeared some time in May, 1879. The first number appeared on June 5th, of the same year, which gave a guarantee that the paper would continue for six months, then for twelve months. The paper has been sent regularly ever since, with a few exceptions. This paper has been much appreciated by our people, that is, by those who have taken it. The General Baptists proper ought to take twelve hundred papers. This would be a very low estimate, not quite one paper to every twelve members. Then the other liberal Baptist in the West ought to take at least eight hundred papers, this, at two dollars per copy, would give our people an interesting paper.

All of these papers have done good and the Golden Rule justily deserves the credit of being the best paper ever published by the General Baptists. From the consideration that the editor started under many embarrassments without means and a very limited acquaintance with the denomination, still he went to work with his own hands and brains and after a short time brought his brother J. P. Cox to be a partner. They not only gave us a good paper but have rallied many of the old supporters as well as quite a number of new ones, both for subscription and correspondents. The Golden Rule has probably done more to strengthen and organize the General Baptists, than all of the other papers, and has certainly brought about a much better acquaintance among the Liberal Baptists in the south and west. It is with pain and grief that the readers of this little paper learn that Elder J. E. Cox has decided to suspend the Golden Rule November 1st, 1882, simply because the subscription is not sufficient to justify a continuation of its publication. What will become of our publishing interest in the future, remains yet to be developed.

The Golden Rule was first published at Evansville, Indiana, then moved to Mt. Vernon, Indiana, then to Evansville again, then to Enfield, Illinois, where it is at this time, January, 1882.

The Christian Union was a General Baptist paper, published at Dexter City, Missouri by Elder C. B.

Hysom, the first number of which made its appearance April, 1880. This was a valuable little paper, something near the size of the Golden Rule and was well calculated to do much good, especially for our brethren in the west. But alas, it finally suspended and turned over its subscriptions to the Golden Rule which filled out the unexpired time of subscription. The Golden Rule suspended June 1st, and the Open Door appeared June 15th, 1882.

GENERAL BAPTIST HYMN BOOKS.

The first General Baptist Hymn Book was published by Elder H. A. Gregg in 1851. Elder Gregg is now very old and is well known by all the Associations in Indiana, Illinois and Kentucky. He now belongs to Union Association and was a delegate to to the General Association in 1881. This book was well received. It contained a good selection of hymns with many original ones, by Elder Gregg. We now find many of the old members preferring it to any other hymn book. I do not know how many editions were published, perhaps not more than one. The Cavanah book in 1858, another hymn book was compiled by Elder G. P. Cavanah, known as the

General Baptist Hymn book. This book was very popular, probably not so much on account of the merits of the book, as the high esteem for its compiler. Though the book in itself was a good one. There has been several editions of this book. After Elder Cavanah's death the sterotype plates fell into the hands of the Evansville Journal Company, which supplied them for many years, or until about 1880. I need not speak further of Elder Cavanah at this time as his biography describes his standing among General Baptists as well as other denominations.

THE MANUEL OF PRAISE.

The Journal Company ceased publishing the Cavanah book in 1879. Therefore at the General Association in 1880, Elder J. E. Cox, Editor of the Golden Rule, presented the Manual of Praise, which was referred to the committee consisting of

Elder Willis Charles of Mt. Olivet Association.

Elder J. P. Joice of Ohio Association.

Elder Wilson Blackburn of Liberty Association, Indiana.

Elder A. C. West of Flat Creek Association.

Elder David Perkins of United Association.

Elder T. J. Davis of New Liberty Association, Missouri.

Elder Billy Harris of Mt. Union Association.

Elder H. A. Gregg, author of the first Hymn Book, and Elder Dr. Jeff Holman of Union Association.

The committee reported as follows:

"We, the committee on Hymn books", having examined the "Manuel of Praise", find it in every respect suitable for a standard Hymn book for General Baptists and recommend its adoption by the Association.

The different enterprises on Hymn books proved successful, except that none of them was very renumerative to the publishers. Each one met the demand of the church at the time of publication.

GENERAL BAPTISTS HISTORY.

Where is the history of the General Baptists, is a question frequently asked. The answer to this question is that Mr. Adam Taylor wrote of the Ancient General Baptists in Europe and England, and Mr. Richard Wright in 1827 wrote a history of General Baptists in the United States. However both of these histories have been out of print for many years.

Many other histories, such as Ivimey, Crosby, Orchard, Crampp, Benedict, Backus, Wood and many others have written concerning General Baptists.

With these facts before us it is astonishing that some modern historians know so little of the history of General Baptists. However the history of the General Baptists in the western part of the United States has never yet appeared before the public in book form.

At the eighteenth meeting of Liberty Association in Indiana in 1841, that body resolved to take up a subscription for the purpose of publishing a General Baptist history. This enterprise did not succeed. In our opinion nothing could have aided our people so much at that time as the contemplated history, but at that time our people were few in number and poor in this worlds goods. Therefore the book was not published.

THE LIFE OF ELDER BENONI STINSON.

Sometime in the year of 1874, Capt. Wm. Reaves of Evansville, Indiana, whose early life had been among the General Baptists as one of their ablest Ministers. Commenced to write the ''life of Benoni

Stinson, together with a short history of the General Baptist denomination, as organized by Elder Stinson and others, to which was added short biographical sketches of several other prominent Elders and Laymen, both in the General and Regular Baptist denomination". We have quoted quite freely from this work and many of our biographical sketches were written Elder by Reavis. The first part of this work was published in a pamphlet of 27 pages in 1876 and subsequently much of it appeared in the General Baptist Herald, and was highly appreciated by its readers. It is much regretted that this work was not published in book form as it would have proved of inestimable value as a future reference.

DR. JEFF. HOLMANS HISTORY.

In 1876 while Dr. Holman lived at Clayville, Kentucky, the General Baptists were being sorely pressed by the Close Communion Baptists. Brother Jeff. Holman who is a son of Elder Jacob Holman and now an ex-representative of the Kentucky Legislature, was very popular among General Baptists, as well as highly esteemed among all religious bodies as a member of Clayville Church. Dr. Holman felt that grievous burdens were being heaped upon the General Baptists. Therefore he felt called upon to rise and defend their doctrines.

In order to do this he delivered a lecture on church history, which was a valuable treat to his own denomination and highly commended by those who differed with him as being an excellent epitome of General Baptists history. A considerable part of this lecture appears in an introduction to my book. The merits of this lecture justly gives it a place among the standard works of General Baptists Literature. We have made these statements in regard to the writings of these brethren, in order to show what has been done in the way of writing a history of the General Baptists.

HOME MISSIONS.

The General Baptists have always been a missionary people, and through their self-sacrificing ministry a great deal of missionary work has been accomplished at a very early period Liberty Association began to organize for mission work. As early as 1831 at their eighth meeting they sent Elder Benoni Stinson out as general missionary, who at their next meeting made an encouraging report. Subsequently Elders Jacob Speer, Wm. Reavis and others followed in this work. The same kind of work has been done in all of the General Baptist Associations, sometimes adopting one plan and sometimes another. As has been detailed in the history of Liberty Association, Indiana, some other Associations have endeavored to build up permanent funds. The General Association is much interested at this time in a concentrated effort of all General Baptists. Grand opportunities are now opening up for our people. May God help them to consecrate of their means and plant churches in many of the waste places within their borders. It seems to us that the entire south west is rapidly taking hold of Liberal Baptists principles, General atonement and open communion must be the watch-word and, success will follow.

EDUCATIONAL INTEREST.

We now come to treat of our educational interest. Upon this enterprise it seems to us that all of our institutions hinge, and upon this our future success depends. We have seen that our first effort in this direction was in 1837, when we endeavored to establish an Academy at Evansville, and subsequently another proposition of the same kind in 1857.

In 1867 Col. J. W. Cockrum and others built Oakland Institute at Oakland City, Gibson county, Indiana, which was intended to become a General Baptist College, and a considerable stock was taken for that purpose, but not enough to purchase it, so it remained in possession of the stockholders of whom Col. Cockrum and wife were the largest.

Finally in 1875, while the General Association was in session at Oakland City, Col. Cockrum decided to donate his interest to the General Baptist denomination, and Col. Wm. Cockrum agreed to donate ten acres of Land for College ground. These donations were made on condition that the General Baptists endow the institution. Thus encouraged our people went to work in earnest and the endowment was increasing rapidly, when it was announced that Col. J. W. Cockrum and wife were dead. The papers were already made out, ready for signature just as soon as Col. Cockrum could secure a few small shares of stock in the possession of other parties. Alas, he was taken suddenly ill, became delirous and remained so until death relieved him.

This disorganized the whole plan and the property fell back to Col. Cockrum's heirs. This would have been a great achievement for General Baptists, could it have been carried out.

The school at that time was self-sustaining. Prof. Lee Tomlin had built up a reputation for this school and students gathered here from many counties. Thus enthused, our people would soon have run the endowment up sufficiently to have carried on a school equal to the demands of the General Baptists at that time.

Notwithstanding this loss and the preceding failures, our people still wished for a college. Therefore at the General Association in 1878, while in session with old Liberty Church, Vanderburgh county, Indiana, a committee was appointed on the subject of education, which reported, "that we recognize the great deficiency in education among our people and especially among our ministry. Therefore resolved, that we recommend that a theological school be established as soon as possible, at some place that may be selected by this body, and further recommend that seven Trustees be appointed by this body, whose duty it shall be to consider the practicability and all necessary arrangements for the accomplishment of this object, whereupon Elders G. W. Moore, D. B. Montgomery, Willis Charles, Drs. T. J. Hargon and Jeff. Holman, Bro. J. O. M. Selby and May J. B. Cox were appointed as such Trustees.

In 1879 the General Association met at Boonville, Indiana. At the reqeust of Elder G. W. Moore El.

der I. H. Henry was made Chairman of the Board of Trustees and Elder Moore relieved and Elder Wilson Blackburn added. Elder Henry on account of poor health sent a letter to the Board of Trustees, thanking the General Association for the confidence reposed in him but declined to serve and suggested that some younger man take his place. Therefore Elder Willis Charles was elected Chairman of the Board and remains there at present.

In 1880 this Board reported to the General Association held with old Liberty Church, that they had organized a Board of Trustees under the laws of the State of Indiana, and adopted a constitution and by-laws, see constitution and by-laws, and had secured a deed to property in the City of Evansville, Indiana, valued at $15,000 and had secured endowments to the amount of $6,000.

The Trustees continued to increase the endowment taking subscriptions to become binding when $50,000 shall have been subscribed. At the General Association in 1881, the Trustees reported additional endowments to the amount of $9,000 making in all $30,000.

If the Citizens of Evansville give the proper encouragement, the College will be located at Evansville. The Trustees expect to open school by September, 1882, and the prospects are favorable for a good attendance.

The Officers at present are:

Elder G. H. Ball, D. D. President of College.

Elder Willis Charles, President of Board.

G. B. Young, Treasurer.

Other Trustees: J. B. Cox, D. B. Montgomery, Jeff. Holman, Syd. Ball. J. O. M. Selby, Brannoch Wilkerson.